Essays on the World Economy
and its Financial System

Essays on the World Economy and its Financial System

Edited by
BRIGITTE GRANVILLE

THE ROYAL INSTITUTE OF
INTERNATIONAL AFFAIRS
International Economics Programme

Published for the Tokyo Club:
The Brookings Institution (USA)
IFO-Institut für Wirtschaftsforschung (Germany)
Institut Français des Relations Internationales (France)
The Royal Institute of International Affairs (UK)
Nomura Research Institute, Ltd (Japan)

First published in Great Britain in 2000 by
Royal Institute of International Affairs, 10 St James's Square, London SW1Y 4LE
(Charity Registration No. 208 223)

Distributed worldwide by
The Brookings Institution, 1775 Massachusetts Avenue NW,
Washington, DC 20036-2188, USA

British Library Cataloguing in Publication Data
A CIP catalogue record for this book is available from the British Library.

ISBN   1 86203 104 5

Typeset in Garamond by Koinonia
Printed and bound in Great Britain by the Chameleon Press Limited
Cover design by Matthew Link

CONTENTS

FOREWORD

The Asian currency crisis which erupted in July 1997 and its repercussions around the world have made us all too aware of the fragility of the global financial system. The establishment of a workable international financial architecture is a major challenge for the global community. The Tokyo Club Foundation for Global Studies asked its T5 member institutions to research this important issue. As President of the Tokyo Club, I am extremely pleased to see these research results appear in this fine book published by the Royal Institute of International Affairs (RIIA).

The Tokyo Club was established in 1987 under the initiative and funding of Nomura Securities Co. Ltd. in order to channel the expertise of major think tanks to enhance the operation of the global economy. The Club organizes the T5 network, a cooperative research grouping of leading think tanks in G5 countries, and the AT10 network, a similar grouping of ten prominent think tanks in East Asia. The RIIA has been an active member of the T5 since its inception. Through these two groupings, representing advanced economies across the world and developing economies in East Asia, the Tokyo Club is uniquely positioned to deal with a far-reaching issue such as the international financial architecture. We asked two researchers from the AT10 to participate in this T5 research project in order to broaden its scope as well as to balance the discussion.

I should like to thank the RIIA for the fine work of editing and publishing this book. The Tokyo Club continues to strive to make an intellectual contribution to the smooth running of the global economy by commissioning research in global as well as East Asian economic issues. This is only possible with the support of member institutions, friends, and the interested public, for which we are always grateful.

Shozo Hashimoto
President
Tokyo Club Foundation for Global Studies

CONTRIBUTORS

Dr Barry Bosworth has been a Senior Fellow in the Economic Studies Program at the Brookings Institution in Washington, DC since 1979 and served as Research Associate from 1971 to 1977. He was Director of the President's Council on Wage and Price Stability, 1977–9; Visiting Lecturer at the University of California, Berkeley, 1974–5; and Assistant Professor, Harvard University, 1969–71. He received his PhD from the University of Michigan in 1969. His research has concentrated on issues of capital formation and saving behaviour. His current projects include a study of the US social security system, with Gary Burtless, and an examination of capital flows to developing countries, with Susan M. Collins. Recent publications include *Prospects for Saving and Investment in Industrial Countries; Saving and Investment in a Global Economy; Economic Growth in Asia: Accumulation Versus Assimilation* (with Susan Collins); and *Aging Societies: A Global Perspective* (with Gary Burtless).

Professor Ralph C. Bryant has been a Senior Fellow in the Economic Studies programme of the Brookings Institution since 1976, and is the Edward M. Bernstein Scholar at the Institution. His primary fields of expertise are international economics, monetary economics, and macroeconomic policy. He was Director of the Division of International Finance at the Federal Reserve Board and the international economist for the Federal Reserve's Federal Open Market Committee. He has frequently participated in advisory groups and served as consultant to organizations such as the Federal Reserve, the US Treasury, the Congressional Budget Office, the World Bank, the IMF, the OECD, and the National Science Foundation. Educated at Yale and Oxford, with a PhD in Economics from Yale, he has been a visiting fellow, scholar and lecturer at a number of institutions worldwide. He belongs to many professional associations, including the American Economic Association, the Econometric Society, the Royal Economic Society, and the Council on Foreign Relations. He has published widely and is currently working on a study of capital flows and international financial architecture, *Turbulent Waters: Cross-Border Finance and International Governance;* and on *The Government's Budget and Economic Prosperity,* an analysis of the long-run consequences of budget deficits and accumulating government debt. He is also a co-organizer of a new Brookings project, Global Dimensions of Demographic Change. His most recent published book is *The International Coordination of National Stabilization Policies* (Brookings, 1995).

Professor Edward K.Y Chen, educated at Hong Kong University (BA, MSocSc) and Oxford University (DPhil), is currently President of Lingnan University in Hong Kong. He was Director of Centre of Asian Studies at the University of Hong Kong from 1979 to 1995. He has held visiting appointments at Yale, Oxford and Stockholm Universities and at the University of California. His research interests focus on Asian economic development problems, with particular reference to foreign investment and technological change. Professor Chen was a member of the Legislative Council of Hong Kong, 1991–2, a member of the Executive Council of Hong Kong, 1992–7, and Chairman of the Consumer Council, 1991–7.

Olivier Davanne is Scientific Adviser to the Conseil d'Analyse Economique (CAE), an independent advisory panel created by the French Prime Minister in July 1997. He is also an Associate Professor at the University Paris-Dauphine. Before joining the CAE, he held various senior positions in both the private and the public sector. From June 1997 to June 1998 he was Senior Economic Adviser to the French minister in charge of labour and social affairs policies. From 1993 to 1997 he was senior economist and then co-director of European economic research at the American investment bank Goldman Sachs. From 1983 to 1993, he held various positions in the French ministry of Finance. He was Senior Economic Advisor to then head of the Treasury, M. Trichet, in 1991, and Senior Economic Adviser to the French Finance Minister, M. Sapin, in 1992–3.

Dr Rolf Dumke has been Head of Department, World Economy and European Integration, at the Ifo Institute for Economic Research, Munich, since 1994. From 1989 to 1994 he was Professor of Economic and Social History at the University of the Armed Forces, Munich. He has a BA in Economics from Yale University and a PhD from the University of Wisconsin, Madison. Recent publications include *Currency Management Costs* (with A. Juchems, A. Herrmann and H. Sherman, Kogan Page, 1998, for the European Commission's 'Single Market Review' series); 'Comparative Economic Growth in Transition Countries and Emerging Market Economies' (in German), a project for the German Ministry of Finance (to be published by Weltforum Verlag, 2000); *A Re-evaluation of the German Social Market Economy* (forthcoming); *Democracy and Growth* (with Thorvaldur Gylfason, MIT Press, forthcoming).

John Forsyth was educated at the University of Cambridge, reading history as an undergraduate and economics as a postgraduate. He joined Morgan Grenfell in 1968 and became their Chief Economist in 1973. From 1978 to 1988 he was a Director of Morgan Grenfell & Co. Ltd with responsibility for trading and capital market operations. From 1988 to 1991 he was a Group Director. Since 1992 he has taught at the Centre of International Studies, Cambridge University's postgraduate school of international relations, where he is responsible for the economics course. His main research interest is in the relationship between the development of economic and political systems. He is a member of the International Economics Advisory Board of the Royal Institute of International Affairs.

Dr Brigitte Granville is Head of the International Economics Programme at the Royal Institute of International Affairs. Prior to this she was chief macro economist and Vice President of JP Morgan for Russia. Her extensive experience in the field of international economics includes acting as economic adviser to the government of the Russian Federation, economist to the European Commission Delegation to Moscow, associate professor at the New Economic School in Moscow and consultant to the World Bank. She is the author of a wide range of books and articles, and lectures throughout the world. She gained her PhD at the European University Institute in Florence.

Denis Hew is a senior analyst in the Bureau of International Economic Studies at the Institute of Strategic and International Studies (ISIS) Malaysia. His main research area is in international finance and capital markets. He holds a PhD in Finance from the University of Manchester, UK.

Hidehiro Iwaki has been Head of the Socioeconomic Research Unit at the Nomura Research Institute since 1999, and has previously held posts there as economist and senior economist. From 1996 to 1998 he was Principal Economist at the OECD. In 1991 he was a Guest Scholar at the Brookings Institution. In 1999–2000 he was a member of the Economic Council in the Economic Planning Agency, Government of Japan. He has an MBA in Business Economics from the University of Chicago, and a BA in Economics from the University of Tokyo.

Pierre Jacquet is Deputy Director of the French Institute of International Relations (IFRI) in Paris and chief editor of IFRI's quarterly review *Politique Etrangère*. He teaches economics at Ecole Polytechnique. He is also Professor of International Economics and Head of the Department of Economics and Social Sciences at the Ecole nationale des ponts et chaussées. His fields of interest include globalization, international monetary and financial issues, the coordination of economic policies, trade policies and negotiations, and European integration. His recent publications include 'Making EMU a success' (with Rudi Dornbusch), in *International Affairs*, Vol. 76, No. 1, 2000; 'The case for joint management of exchange rate flexibility', Working Paper of the Institute for International Economics (with C. Fred Bergsten and O. Davanne), July 1999; 'EMU: a worthwhile gamble', *International Affairs*, 1998; and (with Wendy Dobson), *Financial Liberalization at the WTO*, Institute for International Economics, 1998. He is a member of the Conseil d'Analyse Economique, an independent advisory panel created by the French Prime Minister in 1997. He also belongs to the Société d'Economie Politique and to the Cercle des Economistes, a club of 25 economists who contribute a daily editorial on a French radio channel, Radio Classique. He is a guest professor in corporate programmes at the French business school INSEAD.

Dr C. H. Kwan is a senior economist at the Nomura Research Institute in Japan and a visiting fellow at the Center for Northeast Asian Policy Studies at the Brookings Institution. He has served on various policy committees of the Japanese government, including the Economic Council (advising the Prime Minister) and the Council on Foreign Exchange and Other Transactions (advising the Minister of Finance). Dr Kwan specializes in the Asian economy and Japan–Asia economic relations, with emphasis on exchange rate issues. He is the author of *Economic Interdependence in the Asia-Pacific Region: Towards a Yen Bloc* (Routledge, 1994).

Gomathy Nambiar is a senior analyst in the Bureau of International Economic Studies at the Institute of Strategic and International Studies (ISIS) Malaysia. Her main research area is in macroeconomic and development policy analysis. She holds two Master's degrees – in Development Economics (Williams College, US) and Demography (University of Pennsylvania, US).

Dr Heidemarie C. Sherman has been Senior Economist, International Economics Division, at the Ifo Institute for Economic Research, Munich since 1980. She gained her PhD from Wayne State University, Detroit in 1970. She previously taught at the University of New Hampshire (1970–79). She was seconded as Chief Economist, Group Planning, to Shell International Petroleum Company, London (1993–5). Publications include: (as co-author and co-editor) *Monetary Implications of the 1992 Process* (Pinter, 1990); 'The Economics of German Unification' in Heitger and Waverman (eds), *German Unification and the International Economy* (Routledge 1993); (with Fred Kaen) 'The Behaviour and Thinking of the Bundesbank' in Cobham (ed.), *European Monetary Upheavals* (Manchester University Press, 1994); (with Fred Kaen) 'German Banking and

German Corporate Governance', *Tokyo Club Papers* No. 7, 1994; (as co-author) *Currency Management Costs* (Vol. 6 of The Single Market Review, Subseries III: Dismantling of Barriers, EU GD XV, Kogan Page), 1996; (with Fred Kaen and Hassan Tehranian) 'The effects of Bundesbank discount and Lombard rate changes on German bank stocks', *Journal of Multinational Financial Management*, 1997; (with Robert Koll) 'Implications of Financial Integration and Monetary Union on EU Financial Centres', EC Commission, 1997; (with Fred Kaen) 'The Listing of German Firms on the New York Stock Exchange: A Corporate Governance Perspective', *Tokyo Club Papers*, 1998.

Zainal Aznam Yusof is the Deputy Director-General of the Institute of Strategic and International Studies (ISIS) Malaysia. He holds a BSc (Econ.) from Queen's University, Belfast, an MA (Development Economics) from the University of Leicester and a DPhil (Economics) from Oxford University. He was attached to Economic Planning Unit of the Prime Minister's Department from 1969 to 1988. During the 1987–8 academic year, he was a Visiting (Fulbright) Scholar at the Harvard Institute for International Development (HIID), Harvard University. He served as a Deputy Executive Director of Malaysian Institute of Economic Research (MIER) from 1988 to 1990. Prior to that, he was the South East Asia Regional Economist at Kleinwort Benson Research (Malaysia) Sdn Bhd. From 1990 to 1994 he was the Adviser in Economics at the Bank Negara Malaysia. He was appointed a member of the Working Committee of the National Economic Action Council (NEAC) in January 1998, and of the Securities Commission in March 1999.

INTRODUCTION

Brigitte Granville

In the wake of the financial turmoil of 1997–8, the object of this book is to understand some of the sources of instability in the international monetary system. Were these sources of instability due to poor macroeconomic management by the countries directly affected or to the defects of the so-called international financial architecture, or to both?

This book brings together views from various countries and perspectives, and by doing so aims to reach a better understanding of the vulnerabilities of the present international monetary structure. Its aim is therefore rather modest; it avoids offering a big 'plan', a temptation best described by Barry Eichengreen (1999) when he writes with humour that:

> George Soros proposes an international debt insurance corporation, Henry Kaufman an international credit-rating agency, Jeffrey Garten an international central bank, Jeffrey Sachs an international bankruptcy court, Stanley Fisher an international lender of last resort. I am reminded of the cover of *The Economist* magazine last fall, when the crisis was at its peak. It showed a little man – presumably a professor – on the steps of a public building, holding up a sign. 'The end of the world is near,' it read. 'I have a plan.'

Scammell (1977, p. 17) remarked that:

> To speak of an 'international monetary system' is illusory. It implies a mechanism of interrelated parts, functioning for some clearly defined end, according to known laws. It implies knowledge, certainty and predictability. All these attributes the international monetary system possesses but in a varying degree. To describe it as a system is an over-simplification, permissible only in the interests of economic analysis. When moving from the precise formulations and general prescriptions of economic theory to the real world of policy it is necessary to remember that we leave the realm of system and precision for a world of approximation which operates not by law but by tendency.[2]

Scammell concluded that the 'international monetary system' can be simply described as the relationships among currencies, with all that those relationships imply for the conduct of national affairs, and these relationships may not have been organized with deliberation.

This broad definition still holds. What has changed in the last fifteen years is that markets for all sorts of securities have grown rapidly, encouraged by financial liberalization, both at the level of foreign exchange controls, which led to capital crossing borders, and at the level of domestic financial markets, which led to increased competition and innovation within the financial system. In turn, derivative products and repurchase agreements (repos) have encouraged flows of capital across borders by allowing market participants to manage risks and enhance reward. The decline in world interest rates in the early 1990s contributed to the redirection of global investment flows (mainly the savings of rich countries) towards high-yield assets in emerging markets.

On the other hand, the economic and financial systems of emerging markets proved poorly equipped to accommodate such huge inflows of capital. A large part of these inflows was directed to the rapidly growing so-called 'tiger' economies of East Asia. These economies found themselves faced with the 'open economy trilemma':[1] that is, countries cannot simultaneously maintain independent monetary policies, fixed exchange rates, and an open capital account. Financial instability 'occurs when shocks to the financial system interfere with information flow so that the financial system can no longer do its job of channelling funds to those with productive investment opportunities'.[2]

Financial intermediation relied almost exclusively on banks, and when these banks collapsed under the combined weight of bad loans and foreign-currency-denominated debt, no alternative source of intermediation was to be found. The central banks of emerging countries were faced with the dilemma of having to rescue their banking systems while also maintaining the exchange rate parity of their domestic currencies. Their room for manoeuvre was extremely limited. On the one hand, if the central bank had loosened monetary policy to make credit available, this would have risked uncontrolled devaluation, which in turn would (and did) destroy many large banks funding themselves through short-term borrowings in foreign currencies. On the other hand, the central bank could tighten monetary policy to preserve the exchange rate parity but in doing so further drained from the economy much-needed liquidity. In the face of both a currency crisis and a banking crisis, this dilemma is not easy to solve. Things are made worse by the lack of 'credibility of the central bank as an inflation-fighter',[3] which means that when the central bank acts as a lender of last resort,

---

[1] See Obstfeld and Taylor (1998).
[2] Mishkin (1999), p. 6.
[3] Ibid., p. 15.

this immediately triggers inflationary expectations, in turn leading to higher interest rates.

The increasing importance in international finance of securities markets, and especially bond finance, has sharpened the debate on the merits of extending capital market integration to equities. Rogoff (1999) has reached the conclusion that substantial gains can be achieved from global equity markets. But unfortunately the bias in international finance is towards debt finance, and especially towards intermediation by banks through the syndicated loan market. Banks are highly leveraged institutions and have throughout their history periodically fallen into crisis. Countries with more diverse financial sectors – comprising commercial banks lending to the bond issues of public capital markets and a healthy supply of equity finance – are much more likely to weather financial storms. Such diversity also reduces the cost of capital. Diverse capital markets, aside from acting as backup to the credit process in times of stress, compete with the banking system to lower costs for all borrowers in more normal circumstances.

The counter-argument to the diversification of sources of funding is that the financial systems of most continental European countries escaped much of the 1998 financial turmoil and in general are less prone to banking crises. Until recently the financial sectors of continental Europe were dominated by universal banks, and capital markets are still less developed than in the US or in the UK. These continental European banking sectors retained substantial state shareholdings, while such institutions rarely exhibit the dynamism and innovation that many private-sector banks have employed for their own prosperity and that of their economies. But even in continental Europe, development of the capital market could be highly beneficial. Although the academic debate is far from closed, it seems that having well-developed capital markets would be likely to help mitigate the effects of international financial instability, as more firms would have alternative sources of funds and thus a better chance of shelter from investor risk-aversion.

The condition of the advanced industrial economies is of major consequence for the so-called emerging markets both in terms of experience and more fundamentally given the range and scale of investment resources such as pension funds generated by these economies. The economic assessment of these countries is therefore fundamental in attempting to understand the shape of the present international monetary system and also the potential for reform or improvement.

The first part of this book therefore reflects on *The Economies of Three Major Western Players*. While Barry Bosworth focuses on the growth success of the US economy, John Forsyth compares the growth differential between the US and the euro zone and notes that in the latter the debate is concentrated on high unemployment and pension reform. Hidehiro Iwaki analyses an analogous situation in Japan. In other words, both Europe and Japan seem to be lagging behind the US, mainly owing to a reluctance to fully accept and accommodate the reality of global financial flows, and the market forces underlying those flows.

What is especially interesting in Chapter 2 is that Bosworth attempts to assess whether the expansion of the US economy is thanks to 'good luck or good policies'. Very little seems to have been due to good policy, and much more attributable to good luck. While domestic demand has been a major source of strength, the sustainability of the expansion owes much more to the passivity of inflation in the face of large and unexpected reductions in unemployment. In turn inflation performance, more than the strength of domestic demand, was the key to sustained expansion in the 1990s, and its reversal is the major potential threat to the continuation of growth.

In seeking to explain the achievement of the US economy in combining sustained high growth rates with inflation kept under control, Bosworth distinguishes three factors. The first is the greater efficiency of labour markets. This efficiency has been achieved by institutional change, such as the reduction in trade union power, and by the effect of workers sensing the competitive implications of globalization, and moderating their demands accordingly. The second factor is the favourable external conjuncture reflected in the depressed prices of commodity and other inputs for much of the past decade. The third factor is the controversial issue of productivity gains driven by the new economy. Bosworth here joins Robert Gordon in saying that 'while the gains in productivity have contributed to the low rate of aggregate inflation, computers do not seem to have done much to raise the productivity of the computer-using industries.' But whatever the reasons, the restrained behaviour of inflation stands out as the most striking feature of the expansion. While a full explanation of this economic success is still lacking, the accommodating stance of US monetary policy throughout the period has made an important contribution. Even if today's apparent prospect of ever growing budget surpluses is not realized, there will still have been a remarkable reduction in the stock of US public debt.

Bosworth's assessment of the US economy is especially useful when compared with John Forsyth's analysis of the European economy. Indeed, there, the low growth performance of the European economy is attributed to overprotective social safety nets and pay-as-you-go pension systems putting into question the Maastricht criteria for debt sustainability. Also in contrast to the US experience, Europe's relative success in reducing inflation and failure to sustain growth is attributed to the Maastricht rules biased towards price stability and against growth. Moreover, the persistence of unemployment rates in the range of 10–12 per cent and the low participation rates in many European countries do suggest that the inflexibility of European labour markets provides a partial explanation of Europe's low growth rate relative to that of the US. In addition, the Maastricht criteria for both debt and deficit levels are seriously questioned given the level of unfunded pension liabilities. In other words, if the success of the US is mainly due to good luck Forsyth's chapter shows that the poor growth performance in Europe can be fully attributed to bad policy and highlights the need for more market reform, especially in the social sphere.

This verdict is very much shared by Hidehiro Iwaki in his reflection on the Japanese economy (Chapter 3). For Iwaki, Japan has not adapted structurally to the globalization of world markets, while economic activity should be seen as 'free unless specifically restricted'. Here too the importance of reforming the public pension system is stressed; and unless market reforms are undertaken, Japan will remain on a path of slow growth.

It was stated earlier that this book is not concerned with proposing revolutionary plans, but this is not to say that the authors refrain from advancing policy responses to identified vulnerabilities. In the second part of the book, *Assessment of and Responses to Financial Turmoil*, Edward Chen, in Chapter 4, analyses the Asian crisis and answers criticisms such as the importance of cronyism and the exclusive reliance on banks as financial intermediaries. One of the lessons is that financial liberalization in developing countries should include the development of efficient capital markets to finance corporate expansion. Chen also raises the issue of institutional reforms and financial liberalization, arguing that the latter should be 'tuned' to local institutions and culture. At the same time local institutions and culture should be changed slowly so that they can work more harmoniously with the new institutions. Some of Chen's proposals, derived from the lessons of the financial crisis, include the need for improved cooperation between the Bank for International Settlements (BIS), the World Bank and the IMF. The G-7 forum too, Chen thinks, should be modified to include China, South Korea and Brazil, with Hong Kong, Singapore and Russia as observers.

The issue of capital controls is also introduced and taken further in Chapter 5 by Zainal Aznam Yusof, Denis Hew and Gomathy Nambiar, who consider the case of Malaysia. For these authors, the main point of the Malaysian experiment with selective capital controls since September 1998 has been to create a breathing space; it was not seen as an end in itself or as an alternative to reforms. The issue of capital controls links directly to the question of exchange rate arrangements and the sustainability of fixed exchange rates in a world of increased capital mobility. As pointed out by Scammell (1997, p. 71):

All systems of exchange rates have one implicit conceptual feature in common: the belief that the international monetary system is one which is held in equilibrium by a series of equilibrium rates of exchange. For the gold standard theorist the equilibrium rate was, hopefully, that at which the external value of the currency was pegged by its mint parity.

For the supporter of flexible exchange rates, irrespective of the degree of flexibility, the equilibrium rate was the sought-for level towards which the actual rate should always be tending.

The current 'conventional wisdom' is that, given capital mobility, there is a straight choice between flexible and very hard peg exchange arrangements. Flexibility is in general loosely defined, making one wonder what really differentiates flexible from intermediate exchange rate arrangements. Currency boards (CBA) are said to be more credible than fixed exchange rates but here again the theoretical framework for such an assertion is weak and seems to rest purely on the fact that to abandon a currency board is costly, while the same holds for fixed exchange rate regimes. The credibility of such a system is said to be achieved because the monetary authorities' loss of freedom to print money is set by law, and therefore the political cost of altering such exchange rate regimes is high. But as with other fixed exchange rate regimes, if the fiscal position is unbalanced and the banking sector poorly regulated, there is little chance for such a system to survive a speculative attack. It is revealing, for instance, that Estonia is planning to abandon its currency board. Indeed:

> Due to increasing capital inflows (parallel to an increasing trade deficit) and an economy near overheating, the real exchange rate has experienced that familiar peg phenomenon, a substantial real appreciation. The lack of a more sophisticated set of macro economic policy tools, which would enable the monetary authority to cool down the economy and achieve a sustainable external balance places doubts on the long-term prospects of the CBA.[4]

The truth is that very little progress has been made theoretically on the question of exchange rate arrangements given capital mobility. In Part III, *In Search of an Exchange Rate Regime*, Olivier Davanne and Pierre Jacquet, in Chapter 6, review the choice of exchange rate policy options and find it too limited. They therefore set themselves the task of developing what they call a fourth option, a system of 'adjustable reference parities' that is clearly a member of the fixed but adjustable family of exchange rate regimes but that offers greater flexibility. Such an approach provides a more flexible alternative for countries wishing to anchor their domestic policies on an exchange rate target. The authors' concern then turns to the central question of how to practise floating rates and to the issue of how to improve international exchange rate monitoring as a first step towards a practice of regular coordination of economic policies.

For C. H. Kwan too, in Chapter 7, the present polar approach to exchange rate arrangement is not satisfying. Indeed 'although it has become fashionable

---

[4] Eden et al. (1999), p. 38.

to eliminate intermediate regimes as viable options in favour of either free float-ing or firm fixing, neither of these polar regimes seems to be appropriate for Asia's developing countries at this stage.' Kwan recognizes clearly the difficulty with intermediate exchange rates arrangements where the central bank (CB) has two targets: the monetary base and the band of the crawling peg. Capital flows create conflict between these two targets. An open capital market immediately con-fronts the monetary authorities with a decision over controlling interest rates or the exchange rate. While the convention is that a peg (crawling or galloping) has become 'understood as a band in which the margins on either side of the central parity are less than or equal to 2.25 per cent',[5] the trilemma cannot be solved, or even eased, by the actual width of the band on either side of the central parity. The experiences of Portugal and Spain in 1995 illustrate this point very well:

> The ERM2 mechanism, which will link the euro to non-euro EU currencies, is intended to be more flexible than the ERM of the early 1990s, since bands are considerably wider. However, it needs to be recog-nised that in March 1995, strong pressures within the wider bands also developed, leading to the devaluation of the peseta and escudo. In practice, well before exchange rates reach the 15 percent limit of fluctu-ations, strong expectations of a realignment develop, forcing changes in a crisis atmosphere.[6]

This leads to the present consensus of preferring more flexible exchange rate arrangements. But the definition of 'flexibility' is extremely loose. The reality is rather different since a large range of alternative exchange rate arrangements exists – from very hard currency pegs to managed floats and many variations in between. Obstfeld (1998, p. 8) comes closer to giving a definition:

> The choice between fixed and floating exchange rates should not be viewed as dichotomous. In reality, the degree of exchange rate flexibility lies on a continuum, with exchange-rate target zones, crawling pegs, crawling zones, and managed floats of various other kinds residing between the extremes of floating and irrevocably fixed. Indeed, the notion of a 'free' float is an abstraction with little empirical content, as few governments are willing to set monetary policy without some consideration of its exchange rate effects.

This notion also tends to ignore the fact that:

> not stressed by the traditional literature on the choice of exchange-rate regime is the authorities' objective function, in particular the trade-off

---

[5] Mussa et al. (2000), p. 48.
[6] Masson (1999), p.17.

between a desire to control inflation (that is, to provide a nominal anchor) and a wish to limit fluctuations in competitiveness or to minimise output losses.[7]

But when both interest rate and exchange rate are targeted, tensions always arise. One answer discussed in the literature is to adopt alternative ways to anchor inflationary expectations. However, the necessary framework (such as modelling the transmission mechanism of monetary policy, estimating the impact of exchange rate volatility on inflation and inflationary expectations, and calculating the output gap) is often lacking in emerging markets. Kwan rightly points out that 'it is also unclear why targeting inflation is superior to targeting the exchange rate in terms of credibility and macroeconomic stability'. He also points to some inconsistency in advising a move to polar exchange rates. For instance, it is stressed in the literature that managed floating only works when certain institutional and political prerequisites are in place. But

such prerequisites would be demanding: they would include establishing credibility in monetary policy without using the exchange rate as a nominal anchor, developing liquid and efficient forward and futures currency markets so that corporations can hedge their foreign exchange positions at low costs, and preventing bureaucrats and politicians from abusing their power to influence the exchange rate in order to favour privileged sectors (p. 145).

Kwan therefore reaches the conclusion that 'if the institutional and political prerequisites for adopting a floating exchange rate regime are lacking and costly to realize, it may be worthwhile for Asia's developing countries to reconsider the alternative of trying to achieve the prerequisites of the intermediate regimes instead.' His preferred approach is to improve the intermediate regimes with explicit exchange rate targets so as to make them less vulnerable to currency speculation. In his view, therefore, the solution is to strengthen the institutional framework at both the national and the international level.

The question of optimal exchange rate arrangements is even more acute for the central and east European (CEE) candidates for EU accession. Assessing this issue is the difficult task which Rolf Dumke and Heidemarie Sherman assigned themselves in Chapter 8. The central question is: what are the best exchange rate options for these countries on their way to Economic and Monetary Union (EMU)?

For instance, if one considers exchange rate arrangements for countries at the beginning of the transition process, fixed exchange rates played a special role in anchoring the price level and relative prices. With time, under pressure of

[7] Eichengreen et al. (1999), pp. 5–6.

capital flows, fixed exchange rates came under strain, and this led to the recommendation that countries should adopt crawling pegs. But during the financial crises of the 1990s, 'crawling peg' regimes were swept away, leading to today's consensus that, given capital mobility, the choice is between flexible and very hard peg exchange rate arrangements.

As the transition process progresses, the rationale for the exchange rate acting as an anchor for price levels loses its special importance and the exchange rate becomes only one part of the overall economic strategy. The CEE countries aspire to be part of the EU, with its economic and monetary union. None of them currently meet all the Maastricht qualification criteria (on inflation, government deficit, public debt, long-term interest rates and exchange rate stability), but these criteria are used as benchmarks in shaping their economic policy.

The question is not whether the CEE countries should join EMU but whether there are risks involved with their exchange rate strategy given the capital account liberalization required under Maastricht. The choice they face is threefold: currency boards, a band around an adjustable parity (i.e. ERM2) or flexible exchange rates. The authors assess each of these options and join Jeffrey Frankel (1999) in his assertion that 'no single currency regime is right for all countries or at all times'.

In the fourth part of this book the discussion moves to the question of *Managing Risks in an Integrating World Financial System*. In Chapter 9 (by Brigitte Granville) the focus is on Russia. The multiple decisions of the government and the Central Bank of Russia (CBR) on 17 August 1998, which led both to the devaluation of the rouble and to default on the internal debt, had unforeseen dramatic repercussions on the global financial market. The Russian default not only intensified a broad repricing of risks in emerging economies, but also challenged the view that the international community, working through the international financial institutions, was able and willing to bail out countries in difficulty. This episode marked a turning point in the debate on changes to the global financial 'architecture'. The 1998 Russian debt crisis episode has shown that the assumption 'too big to fail' could not hold any longer and that therefore any risk management strategy needed also to reassess the process of debt restructuring. The Russian crisis will prove to have had a long-term beneficial impact in introducing uncertainty. This very uncertainty provides the necessary discipline.

Chapter 10, by Ralph Bryant, concludes this book. Bryant first resets the context of the debate on international financial architecture by reminding the reader that 'the world polity and economy ... are at messy, intermediate stages of evolution'. Reform of the international financial architecture is therefore about the evolution of international collective governance. By collective governance, Bryant means above all better information as the antidote to financial instability. Higher standards of financial reporting and economic data collection and presentation will help prevent the asset price volatility associated with initial and subsequent repricings. In 'emerging market' countries, the agenda of micro and institutional reform also has a role to play here, especially in fields such as contract enforcement by an impartial judicial system. But Bryant also argues more ambitiously in favour of extending judicial contract enforcement mechanisms to the international plane. In his view this is a necessary extension of the more conventional goal of achieving improved global standards of national and enterprise accounting. The approach adopted by Bryant in addressing these issues is what he labels pragmatic incrementalism – that is, a middle-of-the-road position which neither regards markets as omnipotent in coping with any difficulties that materialize nor espouses the other extreme of rebuilding national borders and enhancing the powers of international financial institutions. This pragmatic approach is extremely valuable in the current debate. It assesses realistically the various dilemmas of the international monetary system and outlines realistic steps to improve the functioning of this system by reviewing the various attempts at improving standards and prudential oversight for an integrating world financial system.

Nevertheless, as rightly emphasized by Bryant, sound standards and effective prudential oversight are a necessary but not sufficient condition for healthy and reasonably stable financial activity. The current relative stability of the world economy should not give reasons for governments to slow the pace of improvements in the international financial architecture that are designed to improve financial stability. Numerous problems remain unsolved. Indeed, the privatization of the capital account in emerging market countries (that is, the growth of private relative to official finance) which took place in the 1990s has been accompanied by a diversification of capital sources: FDI, portfolio investment, bank lending and a sharp increase in bond financing. The variety and complexity of financial instruments have also increased. Debt obligations can be denominated in foreign or local currency, with varying maturities (short-term or long-term) and repayment structures (principal amortization or bullet repayments upon maturity), offshore or onshore, secured or unsecured.

From a lender's perspective, debt and debt crisis resolution should not undermine the obligation of borrowers to meet their debts in full and on time. But at the same time creditors have a duty to exercise proper due diligence in their own lending decisions to assure themselves of the sustainability of their clients' creditworthiness. This is true for both the official and the private sector. But official and private creditors typically hold very different types of financial claims on debtor countries, and a fundamental tension exists between competing interests among the main groups of creditors because of their different goals and constraints.

Another point of contention between the private and the official sector is the comparability principle. Comparability seems to apply only in one direction – that is, from the Paris Club to the London Club but not from the London Club to the Paris Club. The principle of burden-sharing is not symmetrical. Although private-sector investors are now drawn into debt restructuring involving IMF lending, the reverse is not true. Official creditors such as national governments that comprise the Paris Club seem to have escaped the effects of some private-sector debt restructuring (as in the case of Russia).

We hope that this book will help not so much to solve some of these complex issues but at least to keep the debate open without having to wait for the next financial crisis.

References

Eden, Holger van, Albert de Groot, Elisabeth Ledrut, Gerbert Romjin and Lucio Vinhas de Souza (1999), 'EMU and Enlargement: A Review of Policy Issues', Working Paper, Economic Affairs Series, ECON 117 EN, Directorate General for Research, European Parliament, Luxembourg.

Eichengreen, B. (1999), 'Strengthening the Common Financial House', remarks delivered at the World Bank/Japanese Ministry of Finance Conference on Global Finance and Development, 2 March, forthcoming in a booklet edited by the Ministry of Finance.

Eichengreen, Barry, Paul Masson, Miguel Savastano and Sunil Sharma (1999), 'Transition Strategies and Nominal Anchors on the Road to Greater Exchange-Rate Flexibility', *Essays in International Finance*, No. 213, April, International Finance Section, Department of Economics, Princeton University, Princeton, NJ.

Frankel, Jeffrey (1999), 'No Single Currency is Right for All Countries or at All Times', NBER Working Paper No. 7338 (Cambridge, MA: National Bureau of Economic Research), September.

Gordon, Robert (1999), 'Has the New Economy Rendered the Productivity Slowdown Obsolete?', paper presented at the CBO panel of economic advisors (Washington, DC: Congressional Budget Office), revised, 14 June.

Masson, Paul R. (1999), 'Monetary and Exchange Rate Policy of Transition Economies of Central and Eastern Europe after the Launch of the EMU', IMF Policy Discussion Paper 99/5 (Washington, DC: International Monetary Fund).

Mishkin, F. (1999), 'Global Financial Instability: Framework, Events, Issues', *Journal of Economic Perspectives*, Vol. 13, No. 4, Fall, pp. 3–20.

Mussa, Michael, Paul Masson, Alexander Swoboda, Esteban Jadresic, Paolo Mauro and Andy Berg (2000), *Exchange Rate Regimes in an Increasingly Integrated World Economy* (Washington, DC: International Monetary Fund), April.

Obstfeld, Maurice (1998), 'The Global Capital Market: Benefactor or Menace?', NBER Working Paper No. 6559 (Cambridge, MA: National Bureau of Economic Research), May.

Obstfeld, Maurice and Alan M. Taylor (1998), 'The Great Depression as a Watershed: International Capital Mobility over the Long Run', in M. Bordo, C. Goldin and E. White (eds), *The Defining Moment: The Great Depression and the American Economy in the*

Twentieth Century (Chicago, IL: University of Chicago Press), pp. 353–402.

Rogoff, K. (1999), 'International Institutions for Reducing Global Financial Instability', *Journal of Economic Perspectives*, Vol. 13, No. 4, Fall, pp. 21–42.

Scammell, W. M. (1977), *International Monetary Policy: Bretton Woods and After* (Basingstoke, Hants: Macmillan).

Temprano-Arroyo, Heliodoro and Robert A. Feldman (1998), 'Selected Transition and Mediterranean Countries: An Institutional Primer on EMU and EU relations', IMF Working Paper, WP/98/82 (Washington, DC: International Monetary Fund), June.

PART I
REFLECTIONS ON THE ECONOMIES OF THREE MAJOR WESTERN PLAYERS

1 THE EUROPEAN ECONOMY: A REVIEW

John Forsyth

1.1 Introduction

The European economy's performance in the 1980s was, by common consent, disappointing. Growth in the European Union countries over the decade 1981–90 averaged 2.4 per cent, compared with 2.9 per cent in the United States and 4 per cent in Japan. Inflation in the EU averaged 6.6 per cent compared with 4.5 per cent in the United States and 1.9 per cent in Japan.

The problems were recognized and two major policy initiatives were developed to address them. The 1992 Single Market initiative aimed to complete the creation of a unified market for goods, services and the factors of production envisaged by the Treaty of Rome. It was hoped that the removal of the residual national barriers would imbue the European economy with greater dynamism. At the same time monetary coordination was developed through the exchange rate mechanism (ERM), leading to a convergence of inflation at a level set by the country with the best record of price stability, Germany. Plans were developed by the President of the European Commission, Jacques Delors, for monetary union which, it was argued, would further stimulate integration and competition in Europe. It would also embed price stability by institutionalizing German practice at the European level.

As a result, there was considerable optimism that the 1990s would see a resurgence of the European economy and commentators such as Lester Thurow argued that Europe would overtake the United States in growth and close the gap with Japan. To an important extent these prognostications reflected judgments as to the long-term competitiveness of the Asian and Rhine models of capitalism relative to the market-based Anglo-Saxon model. The 1990s called these judgments into question. Japan's growth has fallen to an average of 1.2 per cent and Germany's to 1.9 per cent, while the United States has averaged 2.5 per cent. All the Anglo-Saxon economies have grown faster than Japan and the major continental European economies.

This has led to a major reassessment of the vitality of the Anglo-Saxon model and growing acceptance of the neo-classical paradigm. It is worth noting that in the current debate over the future of the international financial architecture the neo-classical concerns over transparency and market efficiency are proving to command widespread assent. Critiques of both Asian and European economic performance also reflect neo-classical concerns with the efficiency of capital usage in Asia and of labour market efficiency in Europe. In contrast, debates over the US economy focus on the sustainability of the current expansion and the long-term viability of the 'new paradigm' as developed in Anglo-Saxon economies.

These global debates inevitably influence the discussion of the performance of the European economy. The major reforms planned in the 1980s were brought to fruition in the following decade with the completion of the 1992 Single Market programme and the creation of the euro. The macroeconomic performance of the European economy is still a cause for general concern, however, and the factors behind it remain a subject of vigorous debate between those who favour macroeconomic explanations and those who see the problems as microeconomic.

This review will focus on three issues: the macroeconomic performance of the European economy; the likely impact of the creation of the euro within Europe; and the significance of European developments for the global system.

1.2 Macroeconomic performance

Macroeconomic policy in the EU in the 1990s was dominated by two historic developments. The first was German reunification, which led to a rise in German interest rates as the Bundesbank acted to contain the potential inflationary effects of reunification. This rise in Deutschmark rates forced other participants in the ERM to raise interest rates, even though conditions in their domestic economies were very different from those in Germany. This caused serious strains in the financial markets and a lowering of growth rates. The strains in the financial markets led to Britain's exit from the ERM in 1992 and a general move to wider bands in 1993. The policy response was to press ahead with monetary union (the second historic development) and the associated Maastricht agreement on fiscal policy targets limiting public-sector debt to 60 per cent and deficits to 3 per cent of GDP. The economic rationale behind these targets was never clear but their political significance was never in doubt.

The Maastricht criteria meant that both monetary policy and fiscal policy were constrained in an unprecedented manner. The creation of a single European currency dominated economic policy after Maastricht even more than German reunification had before. The fiscal adjustment required was more demanding for some European countries than for others. Of the major countries, Germany and Italy were the most constrained – the former because of the fiscal impact of reunification and the latter by a long-established pattern of deficit financing.

Interest rates in most countries preparing for monetary union were held at levels above those required at home while German policy was restrictive. As the reunification boom fizzled out and German monetary policy was relaxed, however, the general level of interest rates fell significantly. This process accelerated as monetary union became imminent and a final convergence of interest rates took place. As a result, the creation of the euro has seen interest rates in a number of European countries fall to unprecedentedly low levels.

The 1990s were thus a decade of fiscal consolidation and monetary stabilization in Europe. The process has been seen as a consequence of Maastricht, which has received both the credit for the beneficial consequences and blame for the impact on growth. Inflation fell to an average rate of 2.8 per cent (from 6.6 per cent in the previous decade) and is now running at 1.7 per cent, a level which few would have thought possible in 1990. Growth has also fallen from 2.4 per cent to 2.0 per cent and unemployment in most EU countries remains very high by historical standards.

While Maastricht has been of central importance it should be noted that these trends of fiscal consolidation and monetary stabilization have been typical of advanced economies throughout the world. Their average inflation rate fell from 5.6 per cent to 2.3 per cent while growth fell even more, from 3.1 per cent to 2.4 per cent. These figures are heavily influenced by Japan and its special problems. If a comparison is made with the United States and the other advanced economies, it will be seen that they have achieved a similar fall in inflation while maintaining a significantly higher level of growth. Europe's relative success in reducing inflation and its failure to sustain growth are consistent with the argument that the Maastricht rules are biased towards price stability and against growth.

Within Europe there have been wide divergences in performance. Germany began the 1990s with a reunification boom which lifted growth to over 5 per cent, but its economy has grown at less than 1.5 per cent since 1992. Over the same period the country has seen a fiscal swing of some 4 per cent of GNP. An incipient recovery in 1998 was reversed as financial crises in Asia and eastern Europe weakened export demand, but prospects are now improving, in part because of the weakness of the euro. France began the decade with very low growth as interest rates were forced up by the restrictive German policy stance and the ERM. However, since the crisis of 1993, France has grown at a significantly faster rate than Germany, in part reflecting a much smaller fiscal swing of just over 2 per cent of GNP. This pattern of faster growth seems likely to continue. Italy has grown at a low rate over the past ten years and its average rate of 1.4 per cent reflects the very large fiscal swing of 9 per cent that was needed to meet the Maastricht criteria.

The UK began the decade with a recession which was linked to both ERM membership and a serious fiscal imbalance, but since leaving the ERM in late 1992 it has experienced growth at an average 2.7 per cent, which seems likely to be sustained even though sterling has appreciated substantially. Among the more peripheral European countries, such as Spain, Portugal, Ireland and Finland, there has been a marked acceleration of growth since the late 1990s, which can be linked to a fall in interest rates to historically low levels. In the case of Ireland, the boom has been further stimulated by depreciation against sterling, for the UK remains Ireland's key trading partner.

Macroeconomic factors can thus explain a good deal of Europe's economic performance in recent years. With such a diverse economy the adjustment of monetary policy to economic conditions is bound to remain more problematic than in most other economies. However, the persistence of unemployment rates in the range of 10–12 per cent in the euro area (when the United States and the UK have unemployment rates of around 4.5 per cent) and the low participation rates in many European countries do suggest that the inflexibility of European labour markets also provides a part of the explanation of Europe's low growth rate. Policies designed to protect employment have come to be associated with high unemployment and an inability to generate new jobs. The critique of continental European labour markets which is commonly accepted in the Anglo-Saxon economies does not command great support in Europe. In Germany Chancellor Gerhard Schröder's initial enthusiasm for reform has largely evaporated as a result of popular opposition – although, paradoxically, in France Prime Minister Lionel Jospin's public rejection of the critique has been accompanied by some significant reforming measures. Europe thus seems likely to be held back by inflexible labour markets, and high unemployment looks as if it will remain as a secular rather than a cyclical problem for many of its countries.

A more fundamental secular problem relates to the funding of pensions. These can be provided out of current revenue on a pay-as-you-go (PAYG) basis or be provided out of accumulated funds. PAYG schemes are typically used by government and are dealt with through the social security budget, while funded schemes typically relate to employment. Europe has both types of system. Britain, the Netherlands, Switzerland and Ireland have large pension funds. Germany, France and Italy have little in the way of funded schemes and rely on state provision.

With stable demographic structures the use of PAYG schemes will tend to be associated with a larger government budget relative to GNP and a smaller capital market, both of which are readily sustainable. But with an ageing demographic structure and a growing age dependency ratio the maintenance of a PAYG system will require raising taxes for the employed to meet pension obligations out of current revenue. The Organization for Economic Cooperation and Development (OECD) identified this as a major potential problem for its members in the late 1980s and began to quantify the scale of the liabilities. In the 1990s the IMF began to seek to assess fiscal liabilities on a consistent basis and swiftly concluded that unfunded pension liabilities should be included in the analysis as they represented a future claim on resources, as did funded debt.

The estimates which they produced for the major economies in 1986 showed very large variances, with France and Germany having unfunded liabilities of over 110 per cent of GNP while Britain, with limited state provision, had liabilities of around 10 per cent. It should be noted that these figures are highly sensitive to actuarial assumptions and that when the IMF repeated the survey in 1998, Germany was replaced in the analysis by Sweden. The figures are, however, very large in relation to the Maastricht debt ceiling of 60 per cent of GNP. They imply an off-balance-sheet deficit of a substantial scale as there is at present no budgetary accounting for the increase in these liabilities. There is a counterpart to the wide variance in the scale of unfunded pension liabilities in the scale of funded pension schemes. The distribution of both is bimodal, for countries with generous state provision have small funded schemes (since neither employers nor individuals have any incentive to accumulate funds to deal with retirement), while countries with limited state provision have large funded schemes (British pension fund assets are proportionally ten times greater than those of German schemes). When pension fund assets and unfunded state liabilities are aggregated the distribution becomes much closer to a normal one as it represents the aggregate present cost of retirement provision. It should, however, be pointed out that pension provision is typically more generous in countries operating on a PAYG basis as it has been possible to increase benefits with minimal current budgetary cost.

The Maastricht criteria for both debt and deficit levels in participating countries are seriously intellectually flawed as they take no account of this problem. They are also subject to serious moral hazard as they will penalize any country which shifts to funding, just as they favour countries which move to an unfunded basis (as happened to the France Télécom pension fund in the run-up to EMU). Reform, however, seems unlikely as France and Germany are the countries with the gravest problem and the Schröder government has already found that a very minor curtailment of state benefits to bring them in line with those typical of funded schemes has caused major political problems. The pension problem thus remains central to Europe's longer-term prospects. It also implies a growing difference in required tax levels between those countries with funded schemes and those using PAYG. This has important implications for tax harmonization plans.

1.3 The impact of the euro

The current pension problems provide grounds for caution over Europe's longer-term prospects, but it can be argued that in the shorter term the impact of the creation of the euro will have a dominating effect. This impact will be both structural and conjunctural. There is now a very large market across which exchange rate uncertainty has been eliminated. This will be convenient for large corporations, although it is not clear that it will have a decisive influence. Since James Tobin became concerned over the low cost of foreign exchange transactions, costs have collapsed and in the major currencies forward markets are deep and efficient. It is difficult to believe that any major companies do not have the capacity to manage the risks involved (or to seek to benefit from the opportunities offered). Major companies' willingness to engage in cross-border mergers does not seem to be fundamentally influenced by the existence of different currencies as companies are conversant with the management of such problems. Investment institutions typically regard exchange fluctuations as a potential source of return, and cross-border investment flows of equity and direct investment have grown rapidly in an environment of floating rates.

For smaller companies exchange risks represent a greater problem and European banks have been slow to extend to smaller customers the competitive service they offer to large companies. Small businesses, however, continue to operate across exchange rate barriers throughout the world.

Smaller countries may be some of the more important beneficiaries of monetary union in this respect, in that the lack of an efficient forward market has placed them at a disadvantage relative to the larger economies.

Consumers do not seem to have been deterred from cross-border purchases by exchange risk, as the growth of the European tourist industry would suggest. Both credit and cash cards now offer a user-friendly solution to the payment problem, which in a competitive market would be of minimal cost. In this respect e-commerce seems likely to be of more importance than the introduction of the euro as it increases the area over which prices can actually be obtained. The impact of the availability of information from Europe on the UK car market is having a major effect. Although the UK is not a participant in the euro, foreign travel has made the car-buying public in the UK conversant with exchange rate calculations.

In the capital markets, the effects seem likely to be minimal in the equity markets, where diversity of risk is regarded positively, but in the debt markets the effects will be very substantial. The creation of a very large market of homogeneous assets will provide less scope for management of exchange and interest risk, but greater scope and incentive for management of credit risk. This has already been reflected in the boom of euro issues which has been the counterpoint of the decline of the euro exchange rate.

The weakness of the euro should ensure a measure of recovery in the export-related sectors of the European economy. However, the problems inherent in the 'one size fits all' monetary policy suggest that there will be rises in inflation in a number of peripheral European economies such as Ireland's, which the European Central Bank (ECB), with its Europe-wide remit, will be bound to ignore. Whether fiscal policy will, within the Maastricht system, be able to respond sensibly is open to doubt. It can be argued that all large monetary systems suffer from the 'one size fits all' problem but within national economies there is typically a well-developed and politically uncontroversial system of fiscal transfers through the national budget. Europe does not yet have this system and there remains a diversity in its economy which must pose problems for inflation targeting. For these reasons the trade-off between price stability and growth may well remain poor while Europe is in what both ECB president Duisenberg and Bundesbank president Issing have implied is a transitional stage to full integration. These problems would be exacerbated by British participation as the ECB could not ignore British divergence in the way it can ignore divergence by smaller economies such as Ireland's.

1.4 European developments and the global system

Within the global system the creation of the euro seems likely to support the general trend to floating that has developed in recent years. European countries that were pegging their cross-exchange rates were predisposed to sympathize with countries pegging their exchange rates. But with something approaching benign neglect characterizing recent European exchange rate policy, it was not difficult for European G-7 members to join the United States in refusing to bail out countries which fall into payment difficulties as a consequence of maintaining exchange rate pegs in the future. Presumably different considerations will apply if they are candidates for euro membership.

Financial regulatory issues seem likely to remain with the Bank for International Settlements (BIS), as a regional body is no more credible than a national one in this area. The key new regulatory issues concern participation in the BIS negotiations. In the case of Europe, the ECB will have some difficulty in supplanting national regulators while national financial systems and interests remain so disparate. In the long term, however, the logic is that the ECB's role will grow.

Within the G-7 there has already been some reduction in European national participation where monetary issues are concerned. Yet until fiscal power is decisively transferred, national participation will remain a functional necessity, although in the longer term a structure parallel to the trade 'Quad' arrangement might emerge. In the transitional phase European power does not seem likely to be enhanced.

Within the financial markets the euro will necessarily play a central role, although the dollar seems likely to continue to offer greater liquidity based on the existence of a very large pool of homogeneous US treasury securities (which will have no parallel in the euro markets). This seems likely to keep the dollar as the dominant reserve asset even though the euro's role will grow. The structure of markets does not seem likely to change as a consequence of the creation of the euro, with New York and London remaining the dominant centres and other European centres suffering from a loss of critical mass in foreign exchange trading. This will tend to channel yet more of Europe's global business through London.

The creation of the euro should in time make European markets larger and more integrated. But in a period of rapid globalization the success of the European economy will depend on full engagement in the process, and it is vital that the euro is used as a means of facilitating global engagement rather than as an instrument of regionalization.

2 THE US ECONOMY IN THE 1990S: GOOD LUCK OR GOOD POLICIES ?

Barry Bosworth

2.1 Introduction

The US economy performed extremely well in the 1990s, particularly in comparison with other industrial economies. Between 1990 and 1999, real GDP grew at an average annual rate of 2.5 per cent, compared with 1.9 per cent for the European Union and around one per cent for Japan. Total employment grew by over 12 million, in contrast to job stagnation in Europe and Japan, and the unemployment rate is now at a 30-year low of 4.2 per cent of the workforce. By historical standards, this expansion is not particularly rapid, but its duration is most unusual, representing the second longest period of continuous gains in output and employment in the twentieth century.

What has propelled the expansion and is it sustainable? What has been the role of policy? Have US policy-makers been unusually skilful in steering the economy away from crises, or have they been operating in an extraordinarily benign economic environment? Are there serious threats to future growth in the form of a collapse of a stock market bubble or an unsustainable current account deficit?

In this brief essay I cannot hope to produce complete answers to all these questions, but I will try to provide some background information and interpretation of the economy's performance in recent years. Section 2.2 examines the proximate sources of growth in the US economy, which I think is fundamentally a demand-side boom made possible by a surprising lack of inflation pressures. The unexpectedly low and stable inflation rate in the face of ever-tightening labour markets is the subject of section 2.3. Section 2.4 examines the sources of a truly amazing turnaround in the US fiscal position, as the spectre of unending budget deficits has been transformed into a future of ever-growing surpluses. This is doubly surprising in view of the inability of President Clinton and the Congress to agree on any significant budgetary measures. Finally, in section 2.5 I examine the issue of the growing current account deficit and its potential for generating a future financial crisis.

2.2 Sources of growth

The US economic expansion has been driven by a strong recovery of investment from very depressed levels at the beginning of the 1990s and a binge of consumer spending. Both of these are most evident in the data on the saving–investment balance, shown in Table 2.1 and Figure 2.1. The net private investment rate has more than doubled from its 1991 low, and the boom in consumer spending has driven the household saving rate to zero. Again, both of these developments sharply distinguish the United States from Japan and Europe.

Investment

The decline in the investment rate over the second half of the 1980s has now been fully reversed and the share of GDP devoted to investment is near its historical peak. Computers and peripheral equipment represent only about 10 per cent of private investment and about 15 per cent of the growth since 1990. Yet in real terms, computers account for about half of the growth. The difference reflects the accelerated fall in computer prices. Expenditure on telecommunications and transportation equipment has also grown briskly, while investment in the more traditional areas of industrial equipment and

Table 2.1: Net saving and investment by sector, 1960–99 (% of net national product)

Sector	1960 –69	1970 –79	1980 –89	1990 –95	1996	1997	1998	1999
Saving	12.0	9.6	6.7	4.6	5.7	7.0	7.5	7.4
Private	11.0	10.9	10.2	8.6	7.4	7.3	6.4	5.4
Household	6.4	7.6	7.6	6.1	4.0	3.7	3.0	2.1
Government	1.0	-1.3	-3.5	-3.9	-1.7	-0.3	1.2	2.0
Investment	12.6	10.6	7.3	5.3	6.2	7.0	6.9	5.8
Private	9.5	8.9	7.5	5.1	6.7	7.6	8.5	8.3
Government	2.7	1.4	1.5	1.3	1.1	1.1	1.1	1.2
Net foreign	0.5	0.3	-1.7	-1.0	-1.6	-1.7	-2.6	-3.7
Statistical discrepancy	0.6	1.0	0.6	0.7	0.5	0.0	-0.6	-1.6
Capital consumption	10.9	12.3	14.2	14.1	13.9	13.8	13.9	14.1

Source: Bureau of Economic Analysis, Department of Commerce, National Income and Product Accounts.
Net saving excludes capital consumption allowances.

Figure 2.1: Private saving–investment balance, 1960–98

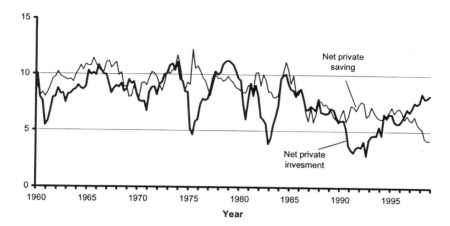

structures has been relatively stagnant. The investment boom has been fuelled by significant reductions in the cost of capital and a strong recovery in the rate of return on capital in the non-financial corporate sector. The return on capital followed a downward trend throughout much of the 1970s and 1980s; but by 1996, the after-tax return had returned to mid-1960s levels of about 7.5 per cent.

Current indicators suggest that the investment boom may be over and spending can be expected to grow more modestly in future years. The capital stock is currently growing in line with potential output. Any further increase would imply a rising capital–output ratio and the likelihood of a falling rate of return on capital. In fact, the rate of return drifted down in the last three years of the decade. Concerns about the rate of return on new investment are a primary reason for anticipating a future moderation of investment spending.

Consumer spending

Consumer spending has been the most consistent source of strength throughout the expansion, and it has far outpaced the growth in consumer incomes. As shown in Figure 2.2, there is a long-standing pattern of decline in the household saving rate extending back to the mid-1980s. Current explanations emphasize two factors: a large and sustained surge in the stock market, and declines in real rates of interest that have reduced the cost of debt service – particularly on home mortgages. The wealth–income ratio (Figure 2.3), which had been stable at about 4.5 since the mid-1960s, drifted up after 1985, but the most substantial increases were concentrated after 1996 and the

Figure 2.2: Personal saving, 1953–98 (% of disposable income)

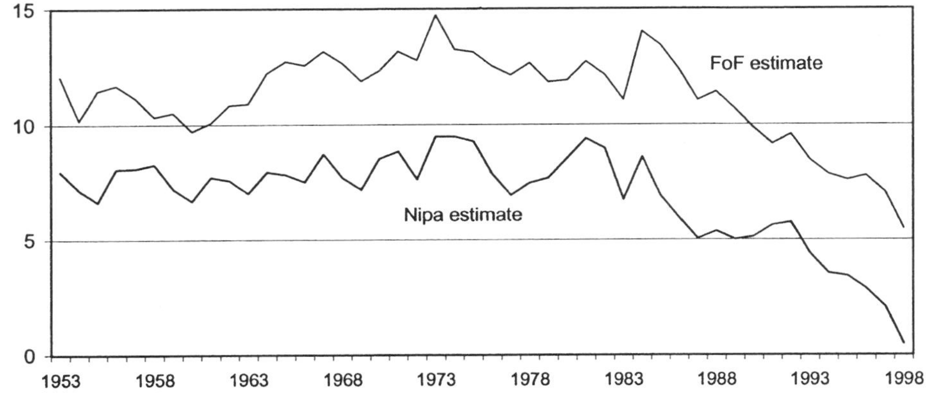

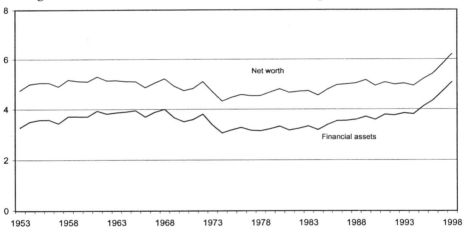

Saving (NIPA) is from the national accounts; Saving (FoF) includes the net accumulation of consumer durables and gov't employee pension accumulation.

Figure 2.3: Household wealth, 1953–98 (ratio to disposable income)

ratio has now moved above 6.0. Most of the recent empirical studies suggest that the marginal propensity to consume out of wealth is in the range of 0.03–0.04. With such an assumption, the rise in the wealth–income ratio can explain a large proportion of the decline in the household saving rate – as much as 5–6 percentage points. However, much of the fall in saving precedes the years of strongest increases in wealth.

The decline in interest rates also played a role in promoting consumption by reducing the costs of debt service. While homeowners typically finance their home purchases with long-term mortgages, there is no penalty for prepayment of that debt. Along with the decline in interest rates, the costs of refinancing a mortgage have also been reduced by regulatory changes and expanded competition in the mortgage banking industry. As a result, periods of interest rate reductions have trigged episodes of mass refinancing of mortgages. Home-owners typically use the refinancing as a opportunity to increase the mortgage amount and repay a portion of their consumer debt. They are left in a position to engage in another round of spending. Thus, average levels of consumer debt are not rising relative to income, but mortgage debt has expanded very rapidly. Mortgage interest charges are tax deductible and much lower than the charge on consumer credit balances. In effect, the development of an extensive and inexpen-sive market for mortgage refinancing provides a means of translating real estate gains into fairly immediate additions to consumer spending. It has also become a major channel by which monetary policy changes impact on the economy.

Looking ahead, the role of mortgage refinancing in promoting consump-tion has been short-circuited by the rise in long-term interest rates. As a result, the future trend of consumption is highly dependent upon future stock market developments. Several studies of the impact of stock market wealth on con-sumer demand have found long response lags, perhaps because consumers know enough to smooth out the short-run price variations. But without continued increases in equity prices, the income–wealth ratio will ultimately stabilize and the growth in consumption will slow to a rate more in line with that of income.

If equity prices should decline permanently by as much as 25 per cent – a frequently suggested magnitude of over-valuation – household wealth would be reduced by about 7.5 per cent. The result would be a cut in consumer spending by 1.3–1.8 per cent over a two-year period. The reduction would be larger relative to a baseline in which consumption has been a rising share of GDP. With these illustrative calculations, a stock market correction is equivalent to a demand-side shock of 1–1.5 per cent of GDP. Allowing for lags, the correction might be spread out over a two-year period, but it would be of a magnitude to severely tax the capabilities of monetary policy. The policy problem would be even more severe if the market correction were accompanied or caused by an acceleration of inflation.[1]

In contrast to the strong expansion of investment and consumer spending, the contribution of government spending has been negligible, and that of the trade sector consistently negative. However, the negative role of trade was largely due to a rapid increase in imports, since the growth of exports outpaced that of the economy as a whole until the collapse of the Asian market at the end of 1997.

---

[1] Empirical estimates of the effect of equity markets on consumer spending are extremely variable. For a recent exposition, see Ludvigson and Steindel (1999).

Table 2.2: Annual rates of change in prices, wages and productivity
(December to December % changes)

	1993	1994	1995	1996	1997	1998	1999*
Consumer Price Index	2.8	2.6	2.6	3.3	1.7	1.6	2.7
ex. Food and fuel	3.1	2.7	3.0	2.6	2.2	2.5	1.9
Producer prices							
Crude	0.4	-0.6	5.6	14.7	-11.7	-7.4	15.7
Finished	0.2	1.7	2.2	2.9	-1.2	-0.2	3.0
ex. Food and fuel	0.4	1.6	2.6	0.6	0.1	0.3	0.9
Employment cost							
Total compensation	3.6	3.1	2.7	2.9	3.3	3.4	3.4
Wages and salaries	3.1	2.8	2.9	3.3	3.8	3.7	3.5
ex. Sales occupations	3.0	2.9	2.8	3.3	3.7	3.1	3.6
Hourly earnings	2.6	2.7	2.9	3.9	3.7	4.0	3.5
Productivity growth*							
Non-farm	0.1	1.3	1.0	2.7	2.0	2.8	2.9
Manufacturing	2.2	3.1	3.9	4.1	5.0	4.8	6.4
Unemployment rate (annual average)	6.9	6.1	5.6	5.4	4.9	4.5	4.2

* Annual average.

2.3 Inflation

While domestic demand has been a major source of strength, the sustainability of the expansion owes much more to the passivity of inflation in the face of large and unexpected reductions in unemployment. In late 1994 the unemployment rate dropped below 6 per cent, a figure widely interpreted as the minimum consistent with non-accelerating inflation, and in subsequent years the Federal Reserve consistently under-estimated the economy's growth. The result was a largely unintended decline in unemployment to the current rate of 4.2 per cent. Yet, surprisingly, there have been no inflation consequences. As Table 2.2 shows, the core rate of price inflation has actually declined in the face of lower unemployment, and any acceleration of wage inflation has been offset by improvements in productivity.

Inflation performance, more than the strength of domestic demand, was the key to sustained expansion in the 1990s, and its reversal is the major potential threat to the continuation of growth. Passive inflation gives the monetary authorities latitude to respond in either direction to potential threats to expansion. An acceleration of inflation, however, would surely bring forth a more restrictive monetary policy, higher interest rates, a bursting of the bubble in equity markets and downward pressures on consumer spending. In a world of accelerating inflation, the Federal Reserve would not be able to easily offset negative shocks to domestic demand, raising the risks of a recession. Thus, an explanation for the lack of inflation pressures plays a critical role in any forecast of the future.

Most rationalizations of the restrained nature of recent inflation stress the confluence of a large number of factors, only some of which seem permanent. First, there has surely been an increase in the competitiveness of markets (particularly labour markets); a decline in the power of unions; deregulation of some key sectors of the economy, where cost-plus pricing contributed to wage increases; and the scaling back of alternatives to employment, such as unemployment insurance and welfare. In addition, workers are more aware of the competitive pressures of international markets, and employers are more able and willing to shift production to other locations. The least skilled workers also face increased competition directly through high rates of immigration. On the other hand, while employers cite increased competitive pressures in product markets, margins seem to have widened slightly in the 1990s. These institutional factors probably help explain why the 1990s were different from the 1970s; but as recently as 1988–9 the United States experienced a sharp acceleration of inflation when unemployment dropped to 5.5 per cent. The greater puzzle is what changed after 1989.

Second, the 1990s were a decade of highly favourable developments in the prices of the inputs other than labour. For example, the average price of imports (excluding computers) has fallen by 23 per cent since the end of 1990, and by 13 per cent since 1995. That reflects sharply lower commodity prices and an appreciation of the exchange rate. Even the 1997–8 economic crisis in Asia benefited the US economy by providing cheap imports at a time when a further surge in domestic demand made up for the loss of export markets. A series of negative inflation shocks, which have offset what otherwise would have been increased inflation pressures from tight labour markets, is currently the most popular explanation for the absence of inflation. But the transitory nature of such factors raises concerns about the future, because it suggests the unemployment rate is far below the level consistent with price stability over the longer term.

Third, some analysts see in the restrained behaviour of inflation the emergence of a new economy. This economy is based on better management and rapid innovations in the high-technology sectors that are contributing to major gains in productivity. These productivity gains have, in turn, offset the wage pressures of tight labour markets. The current data on productivity growth are decidedly mixed: growth was very rapid in the years 1995–8, but abnormally

Figure 2.4: Labour productivity, non-farm business, 1947–98

1992 = 100

Annual, 1947-92

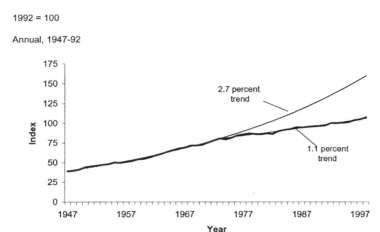

Quarterly, 1990-98

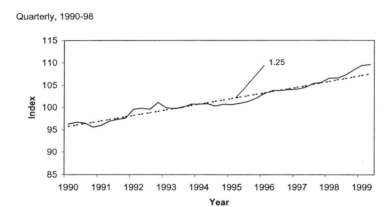

weak in the preceding years of the expansion. As Figure 2.4 shows, there is some evidence of an improvement in the trend growth rate in recent years. However, a recent study by Robert Gordon has argued that the improvement can be attributed to three factors:

(1) a normal cyclical factor;
(2) revisions in the price indexes that are not yet fully reflected in the historical data;
(3) the dominant influence of the computer industry on the output and productivity measures of durable manufacturing (see Gordon 1999).

Gordon finds that these three factors can account for all of the reported improvement. Thus, while the gains in productivity have contributed to the low rate of aggregate inflation, computers do not seem to have done much to raise the productivity of the computer-using industries. Gordon's paper is also useful in reminding us that a portion of slowdown in inflation as measured by the Consumer Price Index (CPI), about 0.5 percentage points, is simply due to methodological changes in the price indexes.

The restrained behaviour of inflation stands out as the most striking feature of the expansions. We lack a convincing explanation as to why it has been possible to achieve such low rates of unemployment without an outbreak of inflation. While it is difficult to attribute the improved trade-off to monetary policy, American monetary authorities have been willing to take full advantage of it, resisting the argument of those who pushed for a more restrictive policy after 1995.

2.4 Fiscal policy

Among the most dramatic developments of the past few years has been the reversal of the US fiscal outlook. For more than a decade, large and growing budget deficits were at the centre of any discussion of American fiscal policy. The inability of the Congress and President Clinton to cooperate on a pro-gramme of deficit reduction was central to a creation of a bitter and highly partisan paralysis of the federal government throughout the late 1980s and most of the 1990s. Yet today the outlook is for a future of large and rising budget surpluses; and, most surprising of all, that appears to have occurred without the Congress and the president changing policy in any considerable way.

Figure 2.5: Congressional Budget Office projections, unified budget, 1995–9

billions of dollars

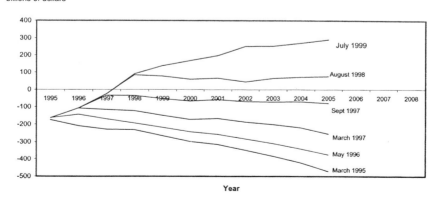

Source: Compiled by Robert Reischauer, the Brookings Institution.

Figure 2.6: Project budget balance, 1999–2009

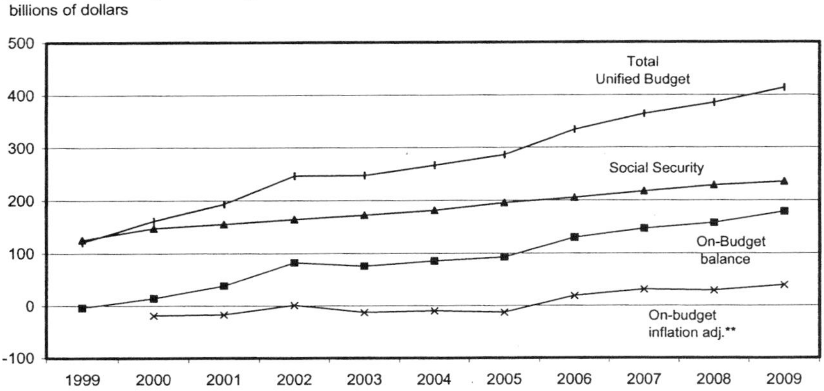

billions of dollars

Source: CBO, 2000.
Inflation-adjusted balance allows for discretionary spending to grow in line with inflation.

The magnitude of revision to the outlook is highlighted in Figure 2.5, which shows the progression of the ten-year budget projections, based on current policy, of the Congressional Budget Office (CBO) from 1997 to the present. As recently as early 1996, the outlook was for large and ever growing deficits that were expected to be about US$375 billion by 2005. Today, those same current policy projections show a surplus of US$300 billion by 2005, a turnaround of over 30 per cent of government outlays. Those revisions can be divided into three components: legislative actions, changes in the economic projections and technical re-estimates.

Except for actions taken in 1997, legislative changes have played a trivial role in the change of outlook. And even in 1997, Congress only acted in the sense of imposing discretionary spending limitations on future Congresses. Over the three-year period, the changes have been about equally split between revisions of the economic outlook and technical changes. In the summer of 1997, the CBO raised its estimate of the long-run growth rate from 2.0 to 2.3 per cent annually and lowered the projected bond rate by half a percentage point. In addition, revisions to the national accounts indicated a much higher proportion of the GDP going to taxable forms of income. The result was a shift in the projected balance for 2005 of more than one full percentage point of GDP.

The technical changes can be traced in part to lower rates of growth in the medical programmes, but the big surprise has been on the revenue side as personal income tax receipts were far above expected levels in 1995–8.[2] It has

---

[2] With indexation of the tax brackets for inflation, the effective tax rate (revenues as a share of GDP) was expected to be constant, allowing for a small amount of bracket creep due to real income growth. Since 1994, the effective tax rate has increased by two percentage points, yielding extra revenues of about US$175 billion annually.

been difficult to account fully for the surge in revenues. There is a substantial lag in the availability of detailed data on personal income taxes and there are two major competing explanations: a higher than expected flow of capital gains taxes, and a concentration of the aggregate income gains among high-income individuals with high marginal tax rates. At present, data are available only up to 1997, and they suggest that both factors have been important, but the biggest contribution is from unexpectedly high capital gains taxes (see Kasten, Weiner and Woodward 1999). Initially, the CBO treated the revenue surprise as a transitory phenomenon and reduced the effective tax rate in future years, but it is now projected to continue indefinitely. There are, however, no new projected surprises.

The current budgetary outlook is summarized in Figure 2.6. It is evident that the projected balance for the total budget is heavily dominated by the surplus in the social security account, which will continue until the baby boom generation reaches retirement. Both political parties have pledged to save the social security surplus, and those pledges are interpreted as necessitating a surplus or balance in the non-social security (on-budget) accounts.

Excluding social security, the Congress will find it difficult to achieve balance in the fiscal year 2000 budget and beyond, as the discretionary spending caps imposed in 1997 become progressively more difficult to meet. In essence, discretionary expenditures, representing about one-third of the budget, are capped at their current nominal values. Furthermore, the effective tax rate is assumed to stay at its current high level. On that basis, the on-budget surplus would be substantial in future years, exceeding US$100 billion annually after 2005. But if discretionary spending is assumed to simply grow in line with inflation, there is no significant surplus.

In summary, the solid performance of the economy and a series of fortuitous events have combined to eliminate the large budget deficits that have plagued the United States since the early 1980s, but the current projection of large future surpluses, outside of social security, is unlikely to be realized. However, even if only the surplus in social security is realized, the public debt will decline substantially as a share of GDP, more than reversing the increase of the 1980s.

2.5 Current account deficits

As shown in Figure 2.7, the decade-long economic expansion has been accompanied by a sizeable shift in the current account, from near balance at the beginning of the 1990s to a deficit of 3.9 per cent of GDP in the second quarter of 1999. Some perceive that imbalance as evidence of a country living beyond its means and borrowing from others to sustain its own consumption, and a predictor of future crises as foreign investors withdraw their funds from the US market.

Figure 2.7: The current account and the real exchange rate, 1970–99
percent of GDP

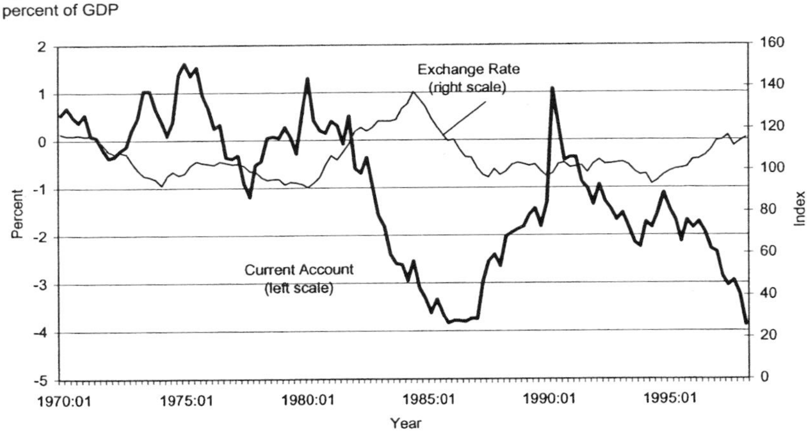

Source: National Accounts and Morgan-Guaranty.

But contrary to the popular conception, a current account deficit is not an indicator of a bad economy or bad policies. It is simply a reflection of underlying economic conditions – particularly the forces driving domestic saving and invest-ment. And from that perspective the news is mixed. First, on the investment side, the deficit is a reflection of an extraordinary recovery of private investment; and, while we might prefer the investment to be financed by domestic saving, it is certainly better to borrow from abroad than to forgo profitable investment opportunities. In part, therefore, the good investment opportunities have attracted foreign capital, driven up the exchange rate and contributed to a rising trade deficit.

Second, on the saving side there has been a large deterioration in household saving, but that has been more than offset by a large improvement in the public-sector balance, with the result that the national saving rate actually improved substantially during the decade. The only problem is that it did not grow as much as investment. If the 1991–3 period is used as a benchmark, the private investment rate has increased by 4 percentage points, the saving rate by 3 percentage points, and the current account by –3 percentage points. However, the statistical discrepancy has changed by –2 percentage points of national income, leaving us uncertain about the full source of offsets to the expansion of the current account deficit.

It is worth noting that the re-emergence of a large current account deficit in the late 1990s was quite different from that of the early 1980s. The deficit of the 1980s was primarily a reflection of a large decline in national saving. It vanished when the collapse of saving was followed by an equally large fall of investment. The 1990s evolved in a very different fashion as rates of both saving and investment increased. But, while the recovery of investment might be judged complete, national saving is still well below the rates of the 1970s.

In addition, the deficit of the 1990s was driven as much by developments in the global economy as by domestic conditions. Weak demand in other countries held down the demand for US exports, while the expansion of domestic demand and the willingness of the United States to maintain an open trading regime sustained the global economy through some difficult years. After 1995, the flight of capital from troubled economies to the United States pushed up the exchange rate and added a relative price influence to what had already been a substantial difference in income growth as a driving force behind the growth of the trade deficit. In this environment, it is hard to see how the United States or the global economy would have been aided by efforts to curtail US imports.

In future years, a benign scenario would envision recovery in other economies and growing investor confidence translating into a gradual decline of the US exchange rate and the trade deficit. The threat is that a sharp depreciation would add to inflation pressures and force a higher level of interest rates in the United States, terminating the expansion. However, the experience of the mid-1980s suggests that large exchange-rate changes create manageable problems for policy-makers. Current account deficits of the present magnitude are probably not sustainable over decades; but they are more a reflection of the relative strength of the US economy than a symptom of systemic failure.

The high stock market valuation, tight labour markets and unsustainable current account deficits are certainly threats to the continuation of the economic expansion; but the magnitude of risk does not seem out of line with past experience or beyond the capacity of economic policy. Barring an adverse shock, the economy continues to expand at a brisk, non-inflationary pace and the end of the expansion does not appear to be imminent.

References

Gordon, Robert J. (1999), 'Has the "New Economy" Rendered the Productivity Slowdown Obsolete?', paper presented at the CBO panel of economic advisors (Washington, DC: Congressional Budget Office), revised, June.

Kasten, Richard, David J. Weiner and G. Thomas Woodward (1999), 'What May Receipts Boom and When Will They Go Bust?' *National Tax Journal* Vol. 52 (September), pp. 339–47.

Ludvigson, Sydney and Steindel, Charles (1999), 'How Important is the Stock Market Effect on Consumption?', *FRBNY Policy Review* Vol. 20 (July), pp. 29–51.

3 A MEDIUM-TERM OUTLOOK FOR THE JAPANESE ECONOMY: REFORM IN THE CONTEXT OF AN AGEING POPULATION

Hidehiro Iwaki

3.1 Introduction

Japan has begun the process of transforming its economy. There is a growing consensus that the efficiencies and competitiveness of the market-place are the best way to increase productivity. There is increasing agreement too that in order to achieve this the economy needs to be restructured to allow the private sector and market forces to take over from the public sector (assisted by the private sector). This, in turn, calls for a comprehensive, but quick, restructuring programme.

One of the reasons why Japan experienced the asset boom of the late 1980s and the slowdown of the 1990s is that it failed to adapt structurally to the globalization of world markets and the increasing use of computers. As a result, capital that had missed an opportunity to invest turned to speculation, and the financial system failed to perform its role as an intermediary.

As the potential for labour and capital to boost Japan's economic growth declines because the labour force is no longer growing and demand has matured, total factor productivity will come to play an ever greater role in determining the rate of economic growth. And total factor productivity depends on how innovative products and systems are. To put it another way: the most important factor affecting Japan's economic growth will be total factor productivity, which depends in turn on how creative and imaginative Japanese companies are. This means that economic regulations and systems will have to be regarded as part of the infrastructure supporting free activity and that in order to stimulate creativity, economic activity will have to be seen as 'free unless specifically restricted'.

Economic freedom and fully functioning market mechanisms do not mean a return to primitive capitalism. Just as governments make mistakes, so do markets. Mankind has drawn on its collective wisdom and constantly improved and refined the market economy. Nevertheless, there is an urgent need to continue to cut information and transaction costs further and to make corporate disclosure and market rules more transparent. Progressive industrialized countries have already been through this process. It is not a voyage through uncharted waters. Nor is Japan the only economy trying to navigate a course through these waters.

This essay argues that Japan must reform its economy and make the transition to a market economic system driven by competition. Section 3.2, using NRI's medium- to long-term macroeconomic model (JMAP[1]) and assuming three different scenarios, simulates a medium-term forecast. This indicates that (1) if the status quo is maintained, Japan's Gross Domestic Product (GDP) will grow by an average of 0.5 per cent a year over the next five years; (2) even if public expenditure is increased, GDP cannot be expected to grow by more than 1.1 per cent; and (3) if a programme of economic restructuring is pursued, GDP may grow by as much as 1.7 per cent a year over this period. Section 3.3 shows that over the longer term, however, a declining birth rate, increasing longevity and a decreasing population threaten the economic situation. Therefore, as section 3.4 finds, sweeping reforms are particularly needed to ensure that the social welfare system (e.g. pensions, medical care and home care) can remain viable.

3.2 The need for reform

After maintaining a steady rate of increase of 3.8 per cent a year during the 1980s, Japan's real annual GDP growth rate fell to 1.2 per cent during the 1990s, according to estimates by the Nomura Research Institute. In fiscal years 1997 and 1998, following the increase in the rate of the consumption tax in April 1997, the rate of growth was in fact negative (−0.4 per cent and −1.9 per cent, respectively).

Similarly, the supply side suggests that the medium-term potential rate of economic growth also declined in the 1990s. The potential growth rate indicates the rate at which GDP will grow ('potential GDP') if all the factors of production (i.e. labour, capital, land and natural resources) are used as effectively as possible. If land and natural resources are assumed to be constants, potential GDP can be regarded as consisting of three factors: the potential input of labour, the potential input of capital and total factor productivity.

According to our estimate, during the 1980s potential GDP moved more or less in line with the real rate of annual economic growth (i.e. 3.7 per cent compared with 3.8 per cent). During the 1990s, however, the real rate of annual economic growth was no more than 1.2 per cent, in spite of the fact that potential GDP only declined to 2.6 per cent a year. The difference between the two (of 1.4 per cent) indicates the magnitude of the output gap that has opened up.

---

[1] JMAP stands for 'A Japanese Model for an Ageing Population'.

Given that Japan's potential input of labour is expected to decrease further as a result of the country's declining birth rate and the increasing longevity of its population, radical action on employment (including structural reform of the labour market) will be necessary if the labour force is not to continue to dwindle. Another important point is that in terms of two factors (labour and capital) Japan's rate of economic growth is bound to slow in the medium to long term. This means that total factor productivity is likely to become one of the main determinants of economic growth.

This section presents three medium-term scenarios (2001–2005) for the Japanese economy that take into account changes in total factor productivity and the need for structural reform of the labour market.

Three scenarios

As mentioned above, we use separate labour force participation rate functions for sex and age to make the effect of structural changes in the supply of labour as explicit as possible. In order to indicate supply and demand in the labour market, we estimate separate functions of the unemployment rate for each sex. These incorporate structural factors. Similarly, in order to show the relationship between economic growth and fiscal policy, we try to incorporate the central government general account (on the basis of fiscal statistics) and the general government balance between savings and investment (on the basis of a System of National Accounts, SNA). Finally, in order to show the relationship between macroeconomic growth and reform of the social security system, we have designed the model so that it calculates disposable household income.

Scenarios A and B assume basically the same economic structure as the one that currently exists. For example, it is assumed that the type of work available (the percentage of short-time workers), the structure of industry (the percentage of those working in service industries) and the number of crèches available are an extrapolation of the existing trend. The difference between the two scenarios is government expenditure. Scenario A assumes that this does not increase, that real public fixed capital formation is flat and that real government consumption declines by 1 per cent a year. Scenario B assumes that public fixed capital formation increases by 2 per cent a year and that real government consumption is flat.

Scenario C, on the other hand, assumes structural reform of the economy. As a result of this reform, the labour force stops shrinking and total factor productivity rises as private capital stock is scrapped and new capital investment and spending on research and development (R&D) increase. Scenario C also assumes that the number of people employed in service industries as a percentage of the total number of people in employment increases to 30 per cent and that the number of short-time women workers as a percentage of the total number of people in employment (excluding agriculture and forestry) increases to 40 per cent. It also assumes that the availability of more facilities (e.g. crèches) to help working mothers bring up a family leads to an increase in the female labour force participation rate. Similarly, it assumes that private R&D investment increases at the fairly high rate of 4 per cent a year and that private capital stock is scrapped at an annual rate of 6.5 per cent (rather than just the 4.5 per cent assumed in scenarios A and B – the average in the past).

Furthermore, in order to allow comparisons, all three scenarios assume that during the period covered (2001–2005) the volume of world trade expands at a uniform rate of 2 per cent a year. Finally, scenario C assumes that progress with structural reform leads to a recovery in confidence in the yen and that during the period covered, the yen appreciates against the US dollar at an average rate of 0.9 per cent a year.

The results

Feeding these assumptions into our medium-term macroeconomic model, we have simulated the medium-term outlook for the Japanese economy.

Scenario A assumes that the status quo is maintained. Spending on R&D is kept low, and excess plant and equipment are scrapped at only a moderate rate. As a result, the process of adjusting capital stock takes even longer. The simulation also indicates that during the period covered (2001–2005) private final consumption and private capital investment are both weak (0.5 per cent a year), while private residential investment declines by 1.3 per cent a year. Although domestic demand remains weak, external demand ensures that real GDP manages to grow slightly (0.5 per cent a year). On the supply side, there is no R&D-induced increase in total factor productivity, while the potential input of labour starts to decline as a result of a lack of progress in reforming the structure of the labour market. According to our calculations, during the period covered, the annual contribution from the potential input of labour is –0.2 per cent, while the potential rate of annual economic growth falls to 0.5 per cent. As a result, the output gap remains at its current high level. As far as the labour market is concerned, for structural reasons the unemployment rate continues to rise. The average for the period covered is 5.6 per cent.

In scenario B the simulation indicates that GDP increases at an average of 1.1 per cent a year. This is largely as a result of government expenditure and external demand, with real public fixed capital formation and the volume of world trade both growing by 2 per cent a year. Meanwhile, private capital investment grows at 0.5 per cent a year – the same rate as in scenario A. Similarly, our assumption that spending on R&D increases at the same rate as

GDP means that the potential rate of annual economic growth rises to 1 per cent as a result of the contribution from the potential input of labour and total factor productivity. However, it should not be forgotten that any attempt to force economic growth by relying too heavily on public spending runs the risk that the public finances may deteriorate further. This would happen if an increase in the national debt led to a rise in real interest rates, thereby discouraging companies from investing.

In scenario C, attempts to reform the structure of the economy meet with success. As a wider range of job types becomes available, as the service sector accounts for an increasingly large share of the economy and as more facilities become available to help working mothers bring up a family, the female labour force participation rate (particularly among women in the 30–45 age group) can be expected to increase. As a result, the simulation indicates that the labour force stops shrinking and that the input of labour contributes 0.2 per cent to the potential annual economic growth rate. Similarly, rising total factor productivity as a result of increased spending on R&D means that the potential annual economic growth rate can be expected to rebound to 1.7 per cent during the period covered in spite of the fact that a higher rate of disposal and a radical programme of abandoning idle plant and equipment tend to lower it.

The main points affecting demand are that there is an increase in the share of new information technology (IT) investment at the same time as capital stock is scrapped. IT investment has a beneficial effect on corporate profits, albeit with a certain time lag, and it can be expected to give a boost to private final consumption and private residential investment when distributed in the form of household income. Similarly, reform of the labour market and the social security system can be expected to have a positive impact on private final consumption by alleviating concern about the future and raising the propensity to consume.

During the period covered, private final consumption and private capital investment are expected to recover and grow at a rate of 1.8 per cent and 2 per cent a year respectively, while real GDP recovers and grows at a rate of 1.7 per cent a year. Given that 1.7 per cent is also the economy's potential annual growth rate, this means that demand and supply will be more or less in balance at the macroeconomic level.

In scenario C, unlike in scenarios A and B, our simulation indicates that the labour force increases by 1.5 million in 2005 as a result of an increase in the participation rate. Given that the demand for and supply of labour increase simultaneously, the simulation indicates that the annual unemployment rate (5.7 per cent on average) is roughly the same as in scenarios A and B.

A simulation of the annual savings rates in the various scenarios indicates that in scenarios A and B (the 'status quo scenarios') they remain virtually unchanged at roughly 13 per cent because annual private final consumption increases by only 0.5 per cent and 1 per cent respectively. In scenario C, on the other hand, in which structural reform leads to a recovery in private-sector activity, private final consumption recovers to grow at a rate of 1.8 per cent a year. As a result, according to our simulation, the annual savings rate falls to about 12 per cent by 2005 from its current level of around 13 per cent.

Savings–investment balance of the government sector

After peaking at 3 per cent in 1993, the gap between domestic savings and investment (as a percentage of nominal GDP) narrowed for three years in a row, only to widen again to 2.2 per cent in 1997 as a result of the economic slowdown in Japan and a rise in exports stimulated by a weaker yen.

In contrast, the government sector's excess investment increased sharply in the 1990s, with that of general government (central government, local government and the social security fund) reaching 3.4 per cent in 1997 after recording an excess for five years in a row. The main reasons for the government sector's growing excess investment have been low tax revenue as a result of the prolonged economic slowdown and increased expenditure as a result of the numerous large stimulus programmes which the government has resorted to combat the slowdown.

Because the budget deficit has accumulated, the government's long-term debt has ballooned, so that central government debt alone was nearly 60 per cent of nominal GDP in 1998. This sharp rise has affected interest rates in the form of a risk premium. The effect is also transmitted to the economy via incomes and real interest rates.

In scenario A, revenue (e.g. from taxation) increases only slightly because, although spending on public works is capped, the economy grows at only 0.5 per cent annually. As a result, excess investment continues at 4.3–4.4 per cent a year even after 1999 and begins to rise again in 2005 as increases in expenditure (e.g. on social security) outpace increases in taxation.

In scenario B, real annual economic growth of 1.1 per cent ensures that tax revenues increase. However, aggressive fiscal policy leads to a rise in long-term interest rates with the result that the government's excess investment continues to increase, reaching an even higher level (4.6 per cent of nominal GDP) than in scenario A in 2005, after which it levels off.

In both scenarios A and B, albeit to a slightly different extent, the government-sector savings–investment balance fails to improve. As a result, government-sector debt begins to increase, and long-term central government debt reaches 67 per cent (scenario A) and 64 per cent (scenario B) of nominal GDP by 2005.

In scenario C, on the other hand, spending on public works increases at the same rate as GDP. As a result, expenditure and revenue also grow at roughly the same rate. Meanwhile, the government sector's excess investment gradually begins to improve after peaking at 4.9 per cent of nominal GDP in 2002, while the national debt also begins to shrink after peaking at 65.2 per cent of nominal GDP in the same year.

3.3 Macroeconomic effects of an ageing population

Of the various medium- to long-term trends affecting the Japanese economy, the one it is feared could have a negative impact, especially on growth, is the demographic trend: more people will live longer, while the population as a whole will decline. As the birth rate declines, Japan's population is ageing rapidly – a trend that is expected to continue for the foreseeable future. In 1998 more than 20 million Japanese were aged 65 or over, and in 1999 they accounted for 16.7 per cent of the population. This figure is expected to continue to rise, reaching 22 per cent in 2010.

The total fertility rate in Japan has declined to 1.38 per woman (1998) as more women find employment and decide either not to marry or to marry late. As there is little likelihood that these trends will reverse, the only way that the birth rate can rise is if more provision is made to help working mothers to bring up a family. Even if action is taken, however, it will take time, so perhaps it should be assumed that the lower-bound estimate of the birth rate is more likely to be accurate.

Not only is the proportion of younger people declining and that of older people rising as a result of Japan's declining birth rate, but the population as a whole is also declining. By 1998 the rate of population increase had fallen as low as 0.3 per cent, and in 2007, according to the median estimate of the country's future population, the overall population is expected to start to decline. According to the lower-bound estimate, however, this is expected to happen sooner – in 2004. According to the median estimate, Japan's population will continue to decline over the longer term, falling some 3.5 million by 2020 (i.e. at a rate of 236,000, or 0.19 per cent, a year) and continuing to decline thereafter.

Japan's declining population and the increasing proportion of old people impact on the macroeconomy by reducing the supply of labour as well as the demand for housing and consumer goods and services. As the rate of increase in the labour force participation rate (one of the factors determining potential GDP) declines, the potential rate of economic growth will also decline. Although the entry of more women and elderly people into the labour force will alleviate this impact, Japan's labour force will fall by 320,000 (i.e. at a rate of 0.1 per cent a year) by 2005 if this effect is stripped out.

If the potential rate of economic growth does decline as a result, the expected rate of growth will also decline. If that happens, capital investment will be affected, and Japan's capital stock will become increasingly obsolete. There is then the risk of a vicious circle where, as Japanese industry becomes increasingly less competitive, Japanese companies cut back further on capital investment. The only way to break this circle is to (1) induce an increase in the supply of labour, (2) provide incentives for companies to become more competitive by replacing their capital stock, (3) stimulate latent demand and create new jobs by easing restrictions and (4) encourage companies to raise productivity by becoming more competitive and technologically innovative.

The declining birth rate and increasing longevity will also place an enormous burden on Japan's social security system, especially its pension, medical care, and home care systems. At the moment, the cost of these systems is borne largely by those currently in work, while the elderly receive the benefits. However, the ratio of those in work to the elderly is expected to decline from 3.1: 1 in 1999 to 2.3: 1 by 2010. Unless social security contributions are raised or benefits cut, the deficits on each of these accounts will increase, threatening the social security system as a whole.

The balance on each of these accounts has a dramatic macroeconomic impact by virtue of its effect on public finances. The greater the burden on the state, the greater the upward pressure on interest rates as more government bonds have to be issued. Similarly, the private sector will cut back on current consumption because of fears that taxes will have to be raised at some stage to cover these costs. The threat to the social security system also has a macroeconomic impact through its effect on households' and companies' propensity to save. Households can be expected to adopt a less defensive attitude to savings if the threat to the social security system recedes.

Increasing longevity also tends to increase the ratio of the combined tax and social security burdens to national income. Unless this ratio is sustainable, there will be a significant macroeconomic impact by virtue of the effect on corporate and household behaviour. In the following sections we have tried to calculate the long- to medium-term balances of the pension and healthcare systems in order to judge whether the current systems are under threat and to evaluate in quantitative terms the possible impact on them of the various reform proposals that have been made.

3.4 Reforming the Japanese public pension system

Japan's public pension system has a number of shortcomings. First, it is coming under threat from the nation's increasing longevity. If the current system continues, the Employees' Pension System is expected to go into deficit in 2008 as the number of people retiring continues to increase. The second shortcoming is a significant intergenerational inequality caused by the asymmetrical age structure of Japan's population. Over an average lifetime, someone born in 1940 can expect to receive pension pay-outs equivalent to 169 per cent of what he has contributed towards his pension, whereas someone born in 1970 can expect to receive only 85 per cent (i.e. less than he has contributed). There is also inequality in the treatment of households in which both husband and wife have worked (and therefore contributed to a pension scheme) and those in which the wife has been a full-time housewife. Under the present system, the former bear some of the cost of funding the latter's pension. The system's third shortcoming is that employees and the self-employed are covered by different pension schemes with no continuity between them. There is therefore no 'neutral' system.

The biggest problem is whether or not the pension system is sustainable. At the last reassessment (in 1994), it was calculated that, in order to prevent the system from going into deficit, pension contributions (which are paid jointly by the employee and the employer) would have to be increased to 29.8 per cent of an employee's standard monthly salary by 2025. According to population projections made in 1997, however, the working-age population is now expected to be lower than had previously been expected while the number of elderly people is expected to be higher. On this basis, pension contributions will have to be increased to 34.3 per cent of an employee's monthly salary by 2025 if the system is not to go into deficit.

A further consideration is the fact that, as a result of weak economic growth, pension funds have achieved lower rates of return than projected. This has had a negative effect on pension finances. If these are not to go into deficit, the way in which the Employees' Pension System works will have to be reviewed sooner or later. The Ministry of Health and Welfare has already submitted its latest (1999) reassessment proposal to the Diet, and this is expected to become law in fiscal 2000.

The ministry, by reducing pay-outs, hopes that its current (1999) proposal will curb increases in pension contributions and put the pension system on a sounder financial footing. It aims to do this in three ways: first, by gradually raising the age of eligibility to 65 (this will apply to all pensioners – both men and women – as well as to both the basic state pension and the earnings-related element step by step by 2030); second, by reducing pay-outs on the earnings-related element by 5 per cent; and, third, by limiting the rate at which pay-outs can increase by relating it to a sliding scale based on the cost of living (rather than wage inflation). (However, a sliding scale based on wage inflation will be used to determine – or 'assess' – the first pay-out a pensioner receives.)

In addition, it is proposed that contributions remain at the current rate of 17.35 per cent of an employee's monthly salary for the time being (with half being paid by the employer and the other half by the employee) but be increased to 18.65 per cent by October 2004, after which they would be increased by increments of 2.3 per cent every five years until they reached a maximum of 25.2 per cent in 2019. It is also envisaged that by 2004 the state's share of the cost of funding the basic pension would be increased from one-third, as at present, to one-half.

We have carried out a simulation to see whether the Employees' Pension System could be funded on the basis of the ministry's proposal. In order to do this, we altered the timetable for pension contributions and pay-outs and made the same macroeconomic assumptions as those used by the ministry in its recalculation of pension finances.

In our simulation of the first case, the number of people receiving an old-age pension (including double-counting cases in which people receive more than one pension) increases by some 16.81 million by 2020, and the number of people receiving a pension as a proportion of those contributing to one rises from 20.7 per cent to 51.9 per cent. As the average pay-out per pensioner increases by 1.6 per cent a year, total pension pay-outs increase to about ¥72 trillion by 2020. Even if pension premiums are raised to 25 per cent or more by 2020 and total contributions rise to ¥49 trillion, the pension system will still go into deficit in 2008, and the deficit will continue to increase from then on.

In our simulation of the second case, the number of people receiving an old-age pension as a proportion of those contributing to one declines from 51.9 per cent (the level in the first case) to 49.4 per cent. This is because the number of people receiving a pension declines (men: by about 600,000; women: by about 190,000) following the raising of the age of eligibility. Similarly, the disappearance of the sliding scale linked to wage inflation once the amount of a pay-out has been decided and the 5 per cent reduction in the earnings-related element has been made means that the average pension pay-out in 2020 is reduced from ¥2,961,000 to ¥2,866,000. As a result, total pension pay-outs in fiscal 2020 are 7.7 per cent less than would otherwise be the case, a saving of ¥5.6 trillion.

In addition, the improvement in pension finances means that the Pension Reserve Fund also increases, while the improved return that this achieves also contributes.

In short, this means that if the ministry's proposal is adopted (and its own macroeconomic assumptions are applied), the pension system should remain more or less in surplus until 2030.

3.5 Conclusion

This essay has shown that unless market reforms are undertaken quickly, Japan will remain on a path of slow growth. Economic reforms, however, are complicated by the ageing of the population, which makes the urgency of expanding the labour force and enhancing the competitiveness of enterprises ever more pressing.

The current pension reform means that, unless our macroeconomic assumptions are quite wide of the mark, raising the age of pension eligibility to 65 and abolishing wage-inflation indexing should be enough to ensure that the system can be sustained until 2030. However, unless macroeconomic conditions after that are much more favourable than we can reasonably expect, it is unlikely that the system can be sustained without making further changes in either the age of eligibility or the size of contributions and pay-outs. If we add to this the risk that population projections may have to be lowered again, more radical reform of the public pension system may be necessary to ensure its sustainability.

Any such reform would have to take into account not just the question of how to sustain the system but also broader issues. In particular, there is an urgent need to carry out pension reform as part of a comprehensive programme of structural reform of the economy. This is because creating a pension system that is neutral between different forms of employment (i.e. that does not discriminate between employees and the self-employed) and fair to all generations would improve the supply of labour and the liquidity of the labour market, thereby boosting macroeconomic growth.

PART II

ASSESSMENT OF AND RESPONSES TO FINANCIAL TURMOIL

4 THE ASIAN FINANCIAL CRISIS OF 1997–8: A CASE OF MARKET FAILURE, GOVERNMENT FAILURE OR INTERNATIONAL FAILURE?

Edward K. Y. Chen

4.1 AN ECLECTIC MODEL OF THE ASIAN FINANCIAL CRISIS

The Asian financial crisis triggered by the fall of the Thai baht on 2 July 1997 after speculative attacks on the currency resulted in a region-wide economic meltdown, with drastic currency devaluations, widespread insolvency and difficulty for financial institutions and businesses, shattered financial markets, sharp depreciation of asset values, economic downturn and surging unemployment. The unprecedented scale, depth and severity (as well as the contagious and self-reinforcing nature) of the crisis took almost all by surprise.[1] There had been at different times and in different regions debt crises, currency crises, banking crises and stock market crashes. But at no other time had all four types of crisis happened simultaneously. This explains why the Asian financial crisis has attracted so much attention from policy-makers and theorists alike. They all ask: what caused the crisis?

There has been a proliferation of writings on the causes of the Asian financial crisis. The predominant school attributes the crisis to the problems of economic fundamentals and policies in the Asian economies (Krugman, 1998a). This can be summarized as a case of government failure in individual economies. In this school of thought, overcapacity, exchange rate misalignment (overvaluation) and institutional weaknesses in the financial sector were the major problems. However, it can be argued that the macroeconomic fundamentals (including exchange rate regimes) were generally sound in the Asian economies before the outbreak of the crisis.[2] The exchange rates were fairly stable and not seriously overvalued on a trade-weighted basis,[3] fiscal deficits were either under control or non-existent, inflation and unemployment remained low and growth

[1] Even Krugman (1994) predicted only a slowing down of East Asian economic growth on the basis of small productivity increases in these economies. He did not predict a financial crisis, nor did he foresee the severity of the economic downturn.
[2] See McKinnon (1998) and Bosworth (1998).
[3] See Rana (1999).

rates relatively high, and even current account deficits were not alarming in terms of their size and cause. In Latin America current account deficits prior to the crisis there in the early 1980s were not only larger but also of a different nature, and were due to overconsumption. In Asia, by contrast, they were the result of rapid capital formation due largely to the surge of foreign direct investment. Hence, the current account deficits were balanced by the inflow of capital. Also, such deficits had existed for a number of years during which economic growth continued to be rapid.[4]

If one speaks only about economic fundamentals, one would certainly be unable to explain the crisis in Hong Kong and Singapore, and to a large extent Taiwan. In the case of Hong Kong and Singapore, not only were their foreign exchange reserves huge (close to $100 billion for each) but their regulatory and supervisory frameworks for financial institutions were of world standard. Hong Kong had suffered from current account deficits since 1995 (–3.5 per cent of GDP in 1995, –2.4 per cent in 1996 and –3.9 per cent in 1997), but the overall balance of payments had been positive thanks to capital inflows. In any case, such current account deficits, which were relatively small and arose mainly because of over-investment rather than overconsumption, should not have caused a currency crisis along the lines of the so-called 'first generation' models of financial crisis. Thus the so-called 'first generation' model of crisis caused by chronic flow deficits is not applicable in explaining the Asian financial crisis.[5]

Market failure or government failure

It is undeniable that excessive private-sector borrowing in foreign currencies was a major factor contributing to the crisis. But this was an immediate rather than a fundamental cause because there must be reasons for heavy borrowing by corporations and circumstances under which it occurred. State intervention and cronyism have been identified as the underlying reasons for excessive private-sector borrowing. It can certainly be argued that state intervention is inevitable in the face of pervasive failure in the capital markets (Stiglitz, 1993). State intervention makes the capital markets work better and therefore improves the performance of the whole economy.

Stiglitz (1993) gives a detailed description of seven causes of financial market failure:

---

[4] Reisen (1997) maintains that, on the basis of long-term and cyclical considerations, current account deficits even as high as 8 per cent of Thailand's GDP were sustainable. Indonesia, hit the hardest by the crisis, had only a 4 per cent current account deficit beforehand.

[5] This is why there is another school of thought that places the emphasis on the weaknesses of the prevailing international financial architecture (Chen, 1998a and 1998b; Radelet and Sachs, 1998).

(1) Monitoring financial institutions is a public good and as such there is an undersupply of monitoring.
(2) Monitoring, selecting projects and lending produce externalities within the financial sector and across markets in the entire economy.
(3) Financial disruption produces negative externalities that extend well beyond financial markets.
(4) Many financial markets are missing and incomplete in the sense that there are relatively few commodities that one can buy and sell forward. Also, many of the risks people would like to insure against cannot be insured against, and people cannot borrow as much they would like at the going interest rate or even at any interest rate.
(5) Imperfect competition usually exists in financial markets despite the fact that there may be a large number of financial institutions. Information is not perfect in financial markets and lending is not only based on interest rates but also on the likelihood of repayment.
(6) Pareto inefficiency exists even under competitive market conditions because there is a divergence between private returns and social returns in financial markets.
(7) There are many uninformed investors in financial markets because they do not have the information (which can be complex and expensive to obtain) on the basis of which they could make rational decisions. Or, even if they have the information, they do not process it correctly.

In the light of these pervasive market failures, it is necessary for the government to intervene in financial markets. In developing countries, one way to facilitate this intervention is for the government to enter into close partnership with financial institutions and private corporations.

Today the close interconnection between the state, the financial sector and the corporations is labelled as cronyism. But yesterday, when the Asian economies were enjoying miraculous economic growth, it was regarded as close cooperation or as an efficient and effective business partnership, a distinctive feature of the Asian economic growth model. Today's cronyism could be an expedient way (as in the past) to overcome market failures in the financial sector. It is said that close cooperation between the state, the financial sector and the corporations has 'reduced financial costs and made economic agents less risk-averse and encouraged them to plan for longer-term goals' (Kumar and Debroy, 1999). In the face of market failure, state intervention and linkages between banks, the state and the corporate sector are necessary to reduce systemic risks.

In developing countries, banks have been the major source of funds for corporate expansion. Capital markets are underdeveloped and market failures prevail. In East Asia, budgetary surpluses have made it unnecessary for governments to borrow. The absence of a government securities market means that there is no benchmarking for risk-free interest rates. It also follows that a market for corporate bonds would not be able to develop easily. Corporate expansion has therefore to depend on private borrowing, and cross-ownership and cross-directorship between banks and firms can be regarded as a strategy to deal with market failure in the financial sector. In the circumstances of market failure, corporations in the private sector would most likely misuse credits. They tend to overborrow and to have high debt–equity ratios. In this case, the government is not a part of the problem. The government's fault lies in its failure to detect the problem at an early stage or to resolve it effectively when it is discovered. This high leveraging of private corporations has little to do with cronyism embedded in a particular culture. It is largely the result of market failures.

There are two additional reasons for the dependence on commercial borrowing by corporations in developing countries. First, asymmetric information leads to two basic problems in the financial sector: adverse selection (undesirable projects are most likely to be chosen) and moral hazard (borrowers have incentives to undertake high-risk and undesirable activities) (Mishkin, 1996). The asymmetric information problem is particularly acute because of the relatively weak supervisory and regulatory institutions and an inadequate ability to enforce transparency. Equities markets are therefore less likely to be developed, because of the high risks that investors have to face. Private businesses therefore resort to borrowing from banks and other financial institutions. But banks, facing the information asymmetry problem, tend to take the lower-risk projects, which results in an inadequate supply of funds to the economy as a whole. Some private businesses then use their connections and position to acquire the funds they need. Market failure therefore gives rise to cronyism.

Another interesting idea has been developed by Kumar and Debroy (1999) using a microeconomic approach. It is hypothesized that firms in developing countries are revenue maximizers à la Baumol rather than profit maximizers. Under revenue maximization, a higher-level output (and also greater investment in capacity) is produced. When decreasing returns begin, capital is paid less than the value of its marginal product because firms want to maintain or even increase their payment to labour which has been scarce, especially skilled labour. With declining profitability, it would be difficult to raise capital from the capital markets. Capacity increases could then be financed only by borrowing from banks. This is especially the case where interest rates are repressed. If domestic interest rates are high, firms will borrow in those foreign currencies that are subject to lower interest rates. This gives a partial explanation of what happened in many parts of Asia before the financial crisis.

The lesson we learn is that financial liberalization in developing countries should also include development of efficient capital markets for the financing of corporate expansion. In this case, supervision and regulation of capital markets will be as important as in the banking sector.

International failure

What we have discussed so far has been confined to the domestic environment of most Asian countries before the financial crisis. We have argued that the root of the crisis was the pervasive market failure in the financial markets. Governments have actually been doing a reasonably good job in coping with the market failure. But government failure is a consequence of government ineffectiveness in many cases to deal with market failure, and is therefore not the primary source of the Asian financial crisis. Certainly, weaknesses in the domestic financial institutions are important factors in the outbreak of the financial crisis. However, the international financial system also play an important part in explaining the crisis. In fact, some domestic financial weaknesses were related to or accentuated by the deficiencies in the international financial architecture. Only by taking these external or international factors into consideration can we adequately explain the crisis in those Asian economies where economic fundamentals were very sound, foreign exchange reserves were huge, foreign debt was non-existent and banks were in good financial health.

One can go so far as to argue that financial crises are products primarily of the prevailing international financial system, which is actually a dollar-standard system established after the gold standard came to an end in the early 1970s. Money supply has grown extremely fast since then, and with the liberalization of trade and investment this supply has been internationalized in developed and developing countries. Today, the volume of foreign exchange spot transactions is over 70 times the total value of the international trade in goods. Foreign exchange transactions now are therefore almost all investment-related. But it is difficult to know how much of these transactions is for speculation rather than for long-term investment. At the same time, the debt and securities markets have grown dramatically with the continuous emergence of new and sophisticated financial instruments, in particular the derivatives products. In 1997, contracts for derivatives products amounted to US$40,940 billion (Bank for International Settlements, 1998), which was four times their value in 1992 and 3.7 times the total value of international trade in goods in 1997.

The deepening and widening of the financial sector have also increased the global importance of non-bank financial institutions that are more risk-taking and less subject to monitoring and supervision. Financial liberalization has evidently increased the exposure of emerging countries to the risks posed by these institutions and the concomitant cross-border flows of short-term capital. Domestic banks in many East Asian countries were over-guaranteed and under-regulated, and it could equally be true that international banks also suffered from the same problem. Multinational banks engaging in cross-border activities are not monitored by any international body, but in the event of default by their large customers they can count on multilateral organizations to bail them out. This was what actually happened during the early stages of the Asian financial crisis. For every borrower, there is a lender. International banks that lend heavily to domestic banks and businesses in the form of foreign currency-denominated loans without making a careful credit risk analysis should also bear some responsibility for the outcome.

In sum, the international financial system established since 1973 has not been able to evolve in a way that can cope with the rapid changes in the global financial sector. Specifically, the IMF has not been able to deal with the prevailing international financial operations and their problems. The IMF was founded in 1945 in order to help the operation of a system of fixed exchange rates based on a fixed relationship between the dollar and gold. The IMF had to find a new *raison d'être* after the collapse of the Bretton Woods system (Feldstein, 1998). Its new roles were to provide short-term credits to countries suffering from current account and debt problems and to monitor those countries' macroeconomic adjustments. These were the purposes of the IMF's involvement with Asian countries during the financial crisis of 1997–8 as well as with Latin American countries in crisis in the 1980s. The IMF was reasonably successful in stabilizing the Latin American situation. Clearly, however, the Asian crisis was difficult, and the IMF was not as successful.[6] Figure 4.1 shows that the primary causes of this crisis were market failure in the financial markets, which was not corrected effectively by government intervention, and the failure of the international financial system to cope with the rapidly evolving post-Bretton Woods world economy. Unlike in the Latin American experience, macroeconomic instability was largely not an issue. It is thus understandable that the conventional IMF prescription, imposing strict monetary and fiscal discipline on countries that were rescued, did not work well in the Asian crisis.

4.2 FINANCIAL SYSTEMS AND FINANCIAL REFORMS

The Asian financial crisis revealed the weaknesses of the financial institutions and systems in many Asian economies. This raises an important question: why was two decades' financial liberalization and reform in Asian economies unable to help build a sound financial system?

In the literature on economic development, discussions of the role of the financial sector have been dominated by the McKinnon-Shaw hypothesis

[6] See, for example, Feldstein (1998) and Bosworth (1998). For an interesting discussion of the IMF's prescription and its application throughout the world, see NRI (1998).

Figure 4.1: Causes of the Asian financial crisis

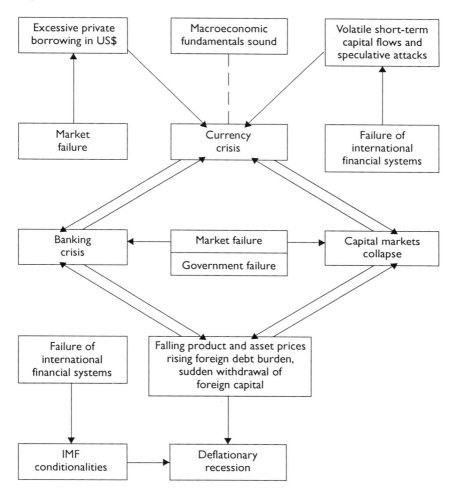

developed in the early 1970s.[7] Financial repression in various forms (in particular interest rate repression, state-controlled credit allocation, subsidized credits, state ownership of banks, underdevelopment of capital markets and restrictions on capital flows) is a major obstacle to economic development, resulting in misallocation of funds and a mismatch of savings and investment. Many governments of developing countries take this hypothesis seriously. Financial reforms in South America in 1974–82 (called the Southern Cone

[7] See McKinnon (1973) and Shaw (1973). For an earlier discussion in the same vein, see Goldsmith (1969).

experiment) were the first attempt to put the McKinnon-Shaw hypothesis into practice. Unfortunately, this test led to disastrous consequences. It became clear even then that it was not advisable to transfer the OECD countries' financial systems to developing countries wholesale. An initial argument in support of this conclusion was that macroeconomic stability must be a precondition for financial reforms and liberalization (McKinnon, 1988; Fry, 1988). Evidently, macroeconomic stability is only one of the many important factors affecting the success or failure of financial reforms. In general, the sequencing of reforms must be a crucial consideration. In the decade following the failure of the Southern Cone experiment, the development economics literature focused on the issue of sequencing. This literature was summarized in a most comprehensive way by McKinnon (1991).

The sequencing for successful financial liberalization in developing countries consists of four steps. First, an appropriate macroeconomic policy should be implemented in order to ensure fiscal balances, current account balances, and relatively low levels of inflation and unemployment. Second, domestic financial markets should be liberalized – in particular, interest rates should be determined by market forces, credit subsidies should be removed, state banks should be privatized, and portfolio and reserve requirements should be relaxed. Third, in the foreign sector the exchange rate for current account transactions should be liberalized. Lastly, the capital account in international transactions should be liberalized in order to allow for completely free international capital flows.

There is no question that sequencing is an important factor in financial liberalization in developing countries, and the McKinnon summary makes good sense. But experience in the real world shows that there is no inexorable law governing the correct sequencing of financial reforms. In the recent history of financial liberalization, Chile, Turkey and New Zealand followed a relatively rapid approach without paying much attention to the sequencing discussed above. They met with various degrees of success.[8] On the other hand, Malaysia, South Korea, Thailand and Taiwan adopted a cautious and gradual approach to introducing financial reforms. Yet these countries could not avoid the contagion of the Asian financial crisis. Indonesia undertook a 'big push' approach, liberalizing most of the controls over and restrictions on the financial sector within a relatively short time. The capital account was also liberalized at an early stage of financial reform. Until the time of the Asian financial crisis in late 1997, Indonesia's financial liberalization was as successful as that of other Asian economies that had adopted a very different approach. Indeed, there are somewhat convincing arguments that a 'big bang' approach is needed for effective implementation of financial reforms. This is because bottlenecks and

---

[8] For an analytical survey of the experience of financial reforms in the past two decades, see Caprio, Jr, Atiyas and Hanson (1994, ch. 5) and Williamson and Mahar (1998).

inefficiencies in a financially repressed economy are all interconnected. A 'big bang' approach of hitting the heads of all the nails is necessary to prevent lags and slack in the response of the repressed financial sector to reforms. Moreover, the financial sector and the real sector are interconnected. Financial reforms should be accompanied by economic restructuring and readjustments in the real sector.

Some thus hold the view that the capital account should not necessarily be the last step in the liberalization process. They would go so far as to argue that liberalization of the capital account might be an impetus for domestic financial-sector reforms. Like it or not, in this highly globalized world economy, *de facto* liberalization of capital accounts is a fact of life and a growing trend.[9] It has also been argued that opening the capital account itself cannot be blamed for the macroeconomic instability faced by Chile during its financial reforms in 1977–82.[10] We have learned from the theory and the empirical evidence of financial reform in the past two decades that sequencing is an important policy matter in the implementation of financial reforms. But there are certainly other, equally or more significant determinants, and, most importantly, there cannot be a set of universal rules governing the sequencing of financial reforms in developed and developing countries alike.

Since the early 1990s, the focus of research on financial liberalization has shifted from sequencing to institutional factors that must have an important part to play inasmuch as no unique sequencing of financial reforms can be deduced from the empirical evidence. Among the earliest studies in this vein, Villanueva and Mirakhor (1990) raised the issue of institutional reforms as preconditions for financial liberalization. Institutional reforms of financial infrastructure would include legal and accounting systems aligned with international standards, abilities and facilities to appraise and control credit risks; and capabilities and facilities to collect and disseminate financial and economic information. Other institutional requirements would include the establishment of efficient and effective supervisory and regulatory agencies to oversee the operation of financial institutions and capital markets and also the grooming of a banking sector that is both robust and sufficiently competitive. A further precondition must be the availability of financial experts to cope with the demand created by the establishment of a financial sector with modern institutions and sophisticated supervisory and regulatory agencies. The success of financial reforms in Hong Kong and Singapore can to some extent be explained by their open-door policy towards the recruitment of experts internationally and their efforts in developing local human resources.

---

[9] For an exposition of policy issues related to financial reforms based on recent history, see Caprio, Jr et al. (1994, ch. 13).
[10] Salvador Valdes-Prieto, 'Financial Liberalization and the Capital Account: Chile, 1974–84', in Caprio, Jr et al. (1994, Ch. 12). For a recent study, see Masuyama (1999).

With regard to the structure of governance, earlier studies focused more on the public sector, while more recently the focus has been on private-sector corporate governance. There is a growing literature about it, but it is not the intention of this essay to explore this particular area of institution-building in financial reforms.[11]

The importance of institutions in economic development and therefore financial liberalization is not a new discovery.[12] What is interesting is that many of the institutions that were at one time regarded as the pillars of economic growth in East Asia have been blamed for the outbreak of the Asian financial crisis. It is important to make a distinction between formal and informal institutions and to be mindful of the facts that (a) formal and informal institutions are interconnected and success in establishing one type of institution depends on the other, and (b) formal institutions can usually be transferred and established within a relatively short time but informal institutions are country- and culture-specific.[13] The formal institutions are what we have described above: the political system and the economic system, the governance structure of public, financial and private organizations and corporations, human resources development, the legal framework etc. In many cases, the establishment of these formal institutions involves only the endorsement by government of legal or administrative documents or at most the setting up of agencies and offices with bureaucrats or quasi-bureaucrats.

The crucial question is whether these formal institutions actually operate effectively in accordance with their intended objectives. The answer lies in whether they are compatible with the informal 'institutions' such as history, customs, norms, beliefs, traditions, political ideology, economic philosophy etc. A democratic constitution may not imply a democratic government if the prevailing political ideology is non-democratic. A market economy may not be driven by free market forces if there are obstacles to the operation of efficient markets. The existence of supervisory and regulatory agencies may not imply the compliance of financial institutions to international rules and regulations. Financial liberalization, therefore, may not mean that operations in financial markets are free from political influence and cronyism. An elaborate legal framework is no guarantee of contracts always being enforced. An important lesson we have learned from the Asian financial crisis is that there are indeed pervasive market failures in the financial sector in developing countries, and those market failures have given rise to significant distortion in the allocation of credits and in saving and investment behaviour.

[11] A thorough study (yet to be published) can be found in Farrar (1999).
[12] See North (1981, 1990, 1995).
[13] A research project on how initial conditions (formal and informal institutions) influenced the course of financial liberalization in Asia before the financial crisis of 1997–8 is being undertaken by the East-West Center (Honolulu). See Lee (1999).

Prevailing informal institutions give rise to some culture-specific remedies to the situation, for example by forging a close partnership between the state, banks and private corporations, resulting in the underdevelopment of capital markets. Financial liberalization *à la* McKinnon-Shaw would undermine the original financial system and the economy at large even if formal institutions too are encouraged to develop. The crux of the matter is that culture-specific informal institutions do not work in harmony with newly created formal institutions. This of course does not imply that financial liberalization should not be implemented in developing Asian economies. But financial liberalization should be 'tuned' to local institutions and culture. At the same time, local institutions and culture can be changed slowly so that they can work more harmoniously with the new institutions.

It is now time to discuss building a new international financial architecture.

4.3 BUILDING A NEW INTERNATIONAL FINANCIAL ARCHITECTURE

A 'new' IMF

The idea of a new international financial architecture is not new. This catchy phrase was used as early as 1988, when finance ministers and central bankers attending the meetings of the IMF and the World Bank saw the need to strengthen the international financial system. As a matter of fact, economists and policy advisers had begun to discuss the building of a new international financial structure soon after the breakdown of the Bretton Woods system in the early 1970s. In recent years, the architecture initiative stemmed from the G-7 summit in Naples in 1994, just before the Mexican financial crisis. Obviously the debate intensified after that crisis, and even more after the Asian financial crisis of 1997-8.

In 1998, a new international financial architecture became a pressing issue. According to Michael Camdessus, Managing Director of the IMF, five principles must govern it (IMF, 1998):

(1) The operation of financial institutions and financial markets must be as transparent as possible so that the IMF can effectively monitor financial developments in all member countries.
(2) The supervisory and regulatory frameworks for overseeing the banking and financial sectors must be strengthened. At the same time, international standards in accounting, legal systems, auditing and payment systems etc. should be adopted.
(3) There must be greater involvement of the private sector in global capital markets with a view to stabilizing capital flows and avoiding moral hazard.

(4) Financial liberalization should continue, but attention must be paid to the pace and sequencing of reforms.
(5) International financial markets should be modernized in the same way as domestic markets.

These principles are undoubtedly very important. But they are hardly controversial, and contain no new insights about the building of a new international financial architecture. They ignore core issues such as the building of a new institutional governance structure for overseeing the global financial markets and regulating the international financial system. This is perhaps understandable, because no one expects that the managing director of the IMF would put forward a proposal to undermine the IMF's own existence. But the truth is that the building of a new international financial architecture would necessarily imply the creation of new institutional frameworks or the establishment of new institutions. The very fact that the IMF failed to prevent the Asian financial crisis and almost stifled the speedy recovery of some Asian economies suggests that its role and institutional set-up must be reviewed.

The conceptualization of an international financial architecture with an emphasis on crisis prevention and crisis response has been undertaken by Stanley Fischer, First Deputy Managing Director of the IMF. Fischer (1998) proposes five requirements for crisis prevention:

(1) The flow of timely, accurate and comprehensive data to the public through the Special Data Dissemination Standard of the IMF should be encouraged. This is transparency.
(2) The supply of data to the IMF by member countries should be ensured so that it can engage in effective surveillance of capital flows and detect trouble spots as early as possible.
(3) Domestic financial systems should be strengthened on the basis of a set of best practices promulgated by the IMF. In 1997, the 25 core principles of the Basle Committee on Banking Supervision were introduced.
(4) The operation of domestic and international financial markets should be improved.
(5) The liberalization of a country's capital account should be handled prudently. The IMF is now at work on amending its charter so that the liberalization of capital movements is a part of its tasks.

Fischer's points indicate that the IMF has to find new roles in the international financial system, even though he is still satisfied with its organizational structure. One suggestion has been made, for example by Jao (1999) and the Nomura Research Institute (NRI, 1998), to strengthen the work of the IMF by increasing its cooperation with the Bank for International Settlements (BIS) and the World Bank. A more drastic proposal would be to form an agency that monitors international capital movements and banking supervision by pooling some of the existing resources of the IMF, the BIS and the World Bank.

Even if for political and other reasons it would be difficult, if not impossible, to restructure the IMF, the existing membership of the G-7 should be reviewed. Judging from the severity and contagiousness of the Asian financial crisis, the developing countries' financial advancement has an important part to play in the global financial sector. There is no reason why the G-7 should still confine itself to the major developed countries. It is now high time that the G-7 be expanded to include countries such as China, South Korea and Brazil. Perhaps Hong Kong and Singapore should participate as observers along with Russia. This proposal for a G-10 plus 3 is a necessary step in the building of a new international financial architecture after the Asian financial crisis. The loosely organized G-22 cannot be a substitute for an expanded G-7.

Control over short-term capital flows

The recent financial crisis provides strong evidence for the importance of a controlled liberalization of short-term capital. With a changing international financial environment (the globalization of capital, the rapid development of capital markets in emerging countries, the sophistication of financial instruments and an obsolete international financial architecture), even economies such as those of Hong Kong and Singapore that have very sound economic and financial fundamentals were not immune to speculative attacks. On the other hand, countries such as China and India, whose financial systems are not advanced, were not subject to speculative attacks because their capital accounts were (and are still) not liberalized. Taiwan and Malaysia, which quickly adopted measures to control short-term capital flows after the crisis, were able to recover relatively quickly from the crisis. Thus, until the international financial architecture is rebuilt, controlled liberalization of short-term capital flows is recommended for most, if not all, emerging markets.

Although we agree that the free market system must be advocated, we should nonetheless be mindful of the possibilities for market manipulation. Even in the United States, anti-trust laws against unfair competition are important safeguards for the market system. In 1980, when the silver market was manipulated, the US regulatory authorities had to stop the activities of the Hunt brothers. In emerging markets, the situation is much more serious. The financial markets and foreign exchange markets are very small relative to those in the developed countries. While financial markets have become globalized, the laws and regulations governing financial flows are still national. There is a

Table 4.1: Capital inflows into Indonesia, the Philippines and Thailand, 1990–97 ($bn)

	1990–4[a]	1995–6	1997 (Q1–Q3)	1997 (Q4)
FDI	5.0	10.8	9.4	0.9
Portfolio investment	3.6	12.9	8.8	−5.6

[a] Average.

Source: IMF, *International Financial Statistics*, various issues.

need for a concerted effort by a group of countries or the world as a whole to oversee the globalization of financial markets. In this connection, the Japanese initiative for an Asian Support Fund should not have been dismissed so readily.

The hedge funds that were significant 'participants' in the Asian financial crisis have grown from almost nothing in the early 1990s to more than 4,000 funds with assets of $400 billion. Their capacity to leverage up to nearly 20 times their capital makes them so mighty. The Long-Term Capital Management (LTCM), with $4.8 billion in capital and a debt of $100 billion, has an exposure larger than the external debt of South Korea (Tsang, 1998). It is reasonable to argue that a 'transparent' and 'fair' approach to market information is by itself not enough to prevent emerging markets from suffering significant capital outflows caused by hedge funds (NRI, 1998). Notwithstanding some institutional weaknesses in the financial sector, their economic setback in Indonesia, the Philippines and Thailand during the Asian financial crisis was caused largely by the sudden withdrawal of huge amounts of foreign capital (Table 4.1), which was unwarranted in view of the then prevailing economic conditions.

Drastic measures have to be undertaken – whether they be the partial foreign exchange controls adopted by Malaysia after the Asian financial crisis or Chile's levy on short-term capital, which has been removed recently after the achievement of its goals. Even the Tobin tax (Tobin, 1978) is not entirely unrealistic.

The volatility of short-term capital flows should be controlled in some form in the financially less sophisticated economies. Transparency helps but it is not the ultimate solution.

Exchange rate regime

In many studies of the Asian financial crisis, the fixed or managed fixed exchange rate system is regarded as the major contributory factor. It is usually pointed out that, had the Asian countries adopted a more realistic exchange rate policy, the crisis could have been avoided or at least been made much less severe and that their exchange rates should have been devalued much earlier. Although there is much truth in this argument, it is not necessarily true that a flexible exchange rate regime is superior to a fixed exchange rate system in emerging economies. Today, an independent floating system prevails in the developed world. But globally it accounted for the system of only 51 of 181 countries as of 30 June 1997 (Pilbeam, 1998: 306). Exchange rate stability is a blessing for most of the small open economies, and even for many large countries.

Recent currency crises have led to a revival of discussion of the Williamson target zone system. For each of the major currencies Williamson (1985) suggested a method to calculate the 'fundamental equilibrium effective exchange rate' (FEEER). He proposed that the exchange rate should be allowed to fluctuate, say ±10 per cent on either side of it.[14] It is best for a group of countries to engage in a cooperative effort to intervene in the foreign exchange market and manage the exchange rate. This proposal is evidently against free market principles. But one must also consider the likelihood that, under a flexible system, exchange rates will tend to diverge from economic fundamentals. This is especially the case with small and open emerging economies that are subject to massive short-term capital flows as a result of globalization and financial liberalization. Excessive volatility in exchange rates can be very disruptive to economic activity and growth.

There are certainly theoretical, practical and political difficulties in the implementation of a managed fixed exchange rate system such as the target zone.[15] But it should not be rejected outright. In the 1980s, the United States did take a lead in intervening to manage the exchange rates of major currencies under the Plaza Accord (1985) and the Louvre Accord (1987). In building an international financial architecture, the search for an exchange rate system for the major currencies is certainly a crucial issue.

4.4 SUMMARY

The Asian financial crisis has turned the building of a new international financial architecture into a pressing issue. The failure of international organizations contributed to the crisis in conjunction with market failure and government failure. It is unfortunate that, as the crisis was soon brought more or less under control and confined to Asia, the enthusiasm for rebuilding the international financial architecture quickly dissipated. Let us hope that it will not require the outbreak of another major financial crisis to bring about new initiatives for rebuilding it.

[14] See Jao (1999).
[15] For a critique of the target zone system, see Frenkel and Goldstein (1986).

References

Bank for International Settlements (1998), *Annual Report*.

Bosworth, B. (1998), 'The Asian Financial Crisis', *The Brookings Review*, Summer.

Caprio, Jr., Gerard, Izak Atiyas and J.A. Hanson (eds) (1994), *Financial Reform: Theory and Experience*, Cambridge University Press, New York.

Chen, Edward K.Y. (1998a), 'Asian Financial Crisis: Causes and Implications', speech at Conference on Asian Financial Crisis, Shanghai, 2 February.

Chen, Edward K.Y. (1998b), 'Asian Financial Crisis and Greater China Economic Cooperation', Speech at the International Conference on Greater China Economic Cooperation, Macau, 23 February.

Claassen, E.M. (ed.) (1991), *Exchange Rate Policies in Developing and Post-Socialist Countries*, International Center for Economic Growth, San Francisco.

Farrar, John H. (1999), 'The New Financial Architecture and Effective Corporate Governance', Conference on 'Challenges for the New International Financial Architecture: Lessons from East Asia', 4–5 June, University of Hong Kong.

Feldstein, Martin (1998), 'Refocusing the IMF', *Foreign Affairs*, March/April.

Fischer, Stanley (1998), *The IMF and the Asian Crisis*, Second Annual Forum Funds Lecture on Public Policy, UCLA, 20 March.

Frenkel, J.A. and M. Goldstein (1986), *A Guide to Target Zones*, IMF Staff Papers, Vol. 33, No. 4.

Fry, Maxwell J. (1988), *Money, Interest, and Banking in Economic Development*, Johns Hopkins University Press, Baltimore, MD.

Goldsmith, Raymond (1969), *Financial Structure and Development*, Yale University Press, New Haven, CT.

International Monetary Fund (1998), '1998 Annual Meeting Overview', and 'Managing Director's Opening Address', *IMF Survey*, 19 October.

Jao, Y.C. (1999), 'The New Financial Architecture and Its Implications for Hong Kong', Conference on 'Challenges for the New International Financial Architecture: Lessons from East Asia', 4–5 June, University of Hong Kong.

Jomo, K.S. (ed.) (1998), *Tigers in Trouble: Financial Governance, Liberalization and Crises in East Asia*, Hong Kong University Press, Hong Kong.

Krugman, Paul (1994), 'The Myth of Asia's Miracle', *Foreign Affairs*, November/December.

Krugman, Paul (1998a), 'What Happened to Asia?', Krugman's website, *http://web.mit. edu. krugman*, January.

Krugman, Paul (1998b), 'Will Asia Bounce Back?', speech for Credit Suisse First Boston, Hong Kong, March.

Kumar, Rajiv and B. Debroy (1999), *The Asian Crisis: An Alternate View*, ADB, Manila, July.

Lee, Chung (1999), 'Financial Systems and the Financial Crisis in Asia', paper presented at the Conference on Comparative Study of Financial Liberalization in Asia, 23–24 September, East-West Center, Honolulu, Hawaii.

Masuyama, Seiichi (1999), 'Introduction: The Evolution of Financial Systems in East Asia and Their Responses to Financial and Economic Crisis', in Masuyama, et al. (eds).

Masuyama, Seiichi, Donna Vandenbrink and Chia Siow Yue (eds) (1999), *East Asia's Financial Systems: Evolution and Crisis*, NRI and ISEAS, Singapore.

McKinnon, Ronald (1973), *Money and Capital in Economic Development*, The Brookings Institution, Washington, DC.

McKinnon, Ronald (1988), *Financial Liberalization and Economic Development: A Reassessment of Interest-rate Policies in Asia and Latin America,* Occasional Paper No. 6, International Center for Economic Growth, San Francisco, CA.

McKinnon, Ronald (1991), *The Order of Economic Liberalization: Financial Control in the Transition to a Market Economy,* The Johns Hopkins University Press, Baltimore, MD.

McKinnon, Ronald (1998), 'Exchange-Rate Coordination for Surmounting the East Asian Currency Crises', *Asian Economic Journal,* Vol. 12, No. 4.

Mishkin, F. S. (1996), 'Understanding Financial Crises: A Developing Country Perspective', Annual World Bank Conference on Development Economics, World Bank, Washington, DC.

Montes, Manuel F. (1999), 'Diagnoses of the Asian Crisis', in Ippei Yamazawa (ed.), *Strengthening Cooperation Among Asian Economies in Crisis,* IDE/JETRO, Tokyo.

Moreno, R. (1996), 'Models of Currency Speculation: Implications and East Asian Experience', *FRBSF Economic Letter,* No. 96–13, April.

North, D.C. (1981), *Structure and Change in Economic History,* W.W. Norton, New York.

North, D.C. (1990), *Institutions, Institutional Change and Economic Performance,* Cambridge University Press, Cambridge.

North, D.C. (1995), 'The New Institutional Economics and Third World Development', in John Harris et al. (eds), *The New Institutional Economics and Third World Development,* Routledge, London.

NRI (1998), *Nomura Asia Focus,* Autumn, Nomura Research Institute.

Pilbeam, Keith (1998), *International Finance,* 2nd edn, Macmillan, London.

Radelet, Steven and Jeffrey Sachs (1998), 'The Onset of the East Asian Financial Crisis', Harvard Institute for International Studies, 30 March.

Rana, P.B. (1999), 'The East Asian Financial Crisis: Issues Related to Exchange Rate Policies', *East Asian Economic Perspectives,* ICSEAD, Kitakyushu, Vol. 10, March.

Reisen, Helmut (1997), 'Sustainable and Excessive Current Account Deficits', UNU/WIDER Working Paper No. 151, Helsinki, May.

Shaw, Edward (1973), *Financial Deepening in Economic Development,* Oxford University Press, New York.

Stiglitz, J.E. (1993), 'The Role of the State in Financial Markets', Proceedings of the World Bank Annual Conference on Development Economics, World Bank, Washington, DC, October.

Tobin, James (1978), 'A Proposal for International Monetary Reform', *Eastern Economic Journal,* Vol. 4, No. 314.

Tsang, Donald (1998), 'Globalization, Capital Flows and Free Markets: Lessons from Hong Kong', speech before the J.F.K. School of Government, Harvard University, 13 October.

Villanueva, Delano and Abbas Mirakhor (1990), *Strategies for Financial Reforms: Interest Rate Policies, Stabilization, and Bank Supervision in Developing Countries,* IMF Staff Papers, Vol. 37, No. 3, September.

Williamson, John (1985), *The Exchange Rate System,* Institute for International Economics, Washington, DC.

Williamson, John and Molly Mahar (1998), *A Survey of Financial Liberalization,* Essays in International Finance, No. 211, November 1998, Department of Economics, Princeton University, Princeton, NJ.

5 CAPITAL CONTROLS: A VIEW FROM MALAYSIA

Zainal Aznam Yusof
Denis Hew
Gomathy Nambiar

5.1 INTRODUCTION

On 2 July 1997, the Bank of Thailand announced the flotation of the baht. This event triggered a region-wide phenomenon, forcing slides in the currencies of neighbouring countries, including the Malaysian ringgit.[1] In 1998 the financial crisis entered a new phase, spreading beyond Asia to Russia[2] and Latin America and becoming a full-blown global crisis. The spread of the crisis brought into focus the downside risks of globalization and the deepening integration of the world financial market. Of the ASEAN countries, Indonesia was the most severely affected, followed by Thailand and then Malaysia. The Philippines and Singapore were the least affected.

In Asia, concern was increased by the sharp fall in the yen against the dollar and the growing sentiment that if the yen fell too far, China could devalue the renminbi, provoking a new round of competitive devaluation. The weakness of the Japanese economy and its financial system contributed to the depth of the fall in regional activity. Meanwhile, the intervention by Hong Kong authorities in the market came under heavy criticism.

These events led to much debate, especially with regard to the fact that the IMF blamed the inherent structural weakness of many of the East Asian countries for the crisis. The massive capital outflow witnessed in 1997 – the five most severely affected economies of East Asia experienced net private outflows estimated to be US$12 billion – was said to be a natural phenomenon representing the reaction of market forces.

This paper responds to the IMF's diagnosis by arguing that the macro-economic fundamentals in Malaysia were strong and therefore that the country's economy did not deserve to be sanctioned by the market. Malaysia had no other

The views expressed in this paper are entirely the writers' own and should not be taken as having institutional support.
[1] See Chen in this volume, chapter 4.
[2] See Granville in this volume, chapter 9.

choice but to introduce capital controls on 1 September 1998. The central bank of Malaysia, Bank Negara Malaysia (BNM), announced the introduction of selective capital controls to insulate the economy from the continuing financial turmoil. Malaysia's decision led to a debate on the merits of capital controls in the presence of fixed exchange rates and highly unpredictable capital flows. Section 5.2 of this chapter reviews the economic situation of Malaysia. Section 5.3 explains how Malaysia responded to the financial turmoil. Section 5.3 describes the Malaysian capital controls experience, and section 5.5 other international experience with capital controls. The conclusion focuses on the implications for the international financial architecture in the light of the Malaysian experience and makes tentative recommendations on how to reform that architecture.

5.2 THE MALAYSIAN ECONOMIC SITUATION

Before the onset of the crisis, Malaysia's macroeconomic indicators were favourable relative to those of its neighbours. It had a succession of budget surpluses, which helped to lower public debt, contain inflation, boost savings and also encourage private-sector growth. The external current account deficit, although high when the crisis began, was largely financed by foreign direct investments (FDI). In addition it had a reasonable level of foreign exchange relative to its short-term debts. This situation contrasted sharply with the situation in Thailand and Indonesia, where growing current account deficits were financed from unbridled private sector offshore borrowing, mostly short-term in nature.

As the international crisis deepened, Malaysia's capacity to withstand the impact of the external shock began to falter as its foreign exchange reserves of US$24 billion provided only a limited cushion. The first time the ringgit came under heavy speculative pressure was in May 1997. The pressure intensified in July following the devaluation of the Thai bath, and the ringgit reached 4.88 against the dollar on 9 January 1998, or 48.8 per cent lower than the average exchange rate of RM2.5 to the dollar in 1997. The outward flight of private capital and the weakening currency dampened the stock market. On 12 January 1998, the Kuala Lumpur Stock Exchange (KLSE) saw its composite index crash to a low of 477.57 points, which wiped out almost RM580 billion or 65 per cent of the total market capitalization recorded when the index was at a high of 1271.57 points in February 1997.

Meanwhile the banking system saw a reduction in liquidity as fund outflows from the equity and money markets exerted upward pressure on interest rates. In July 1997, the three-month Kuala Lumpur Inter-Bank Offered Rate (KLIBOR) rose to a high of 8.6 per cent from 7.5 per cent at the end of June. For the rest of the year the three-month rate hovered within a range of 7.86–10 per cent. The three-month rate soared to 11.03 per cent in April 1998. At the same time the average base lending rates continued an upwards trend into the first half of 1998. The average base lending rates of commercial banks and finance companies were maintained at 12.7 per cent and 14.7 per cent respectively by end of June 1998. The statutory reserves requirement was kept at 13 per cent. Tight quarterly loan growth targets of 15 per cent were imposed in 1998, compared to 25 per cent in 1997. BNM raised its three-month intervention rate from 8.7 per cent at the end of 1997 to 11 per cent in February 1998.

Economic activity slowed, with real GDP growing by 5.6 per cent in the final quarter of 1997, compared to 9.5 per cent for the same period in 1996 (Table 5.1). In 1998, real output growth declined by 7.5 per cent after a decade of expansion. Output contraction of 10.9 per cent in the third quarter was reported, followed by another quarter of output contraction at 10.3 per cent. This contractionary impact was also partly attributable to the government's earlier policy response designed to restore investor confidence and stabilize financial markets. In compliance with the IMF's prescriptions, the stance of both fiscal and monetary policies was tightened in order to help remove excesses in the economy and strengthen the fundamentals.

In December 1997, the government announced an 18 per cent cut in spending from the 1998 budget allocation to complement its earlier decision to halt ongoing construction projects and defer implementation of several mega-projects, including the Bakun hydroelectric dam, the Putrajaya Administration Centre Phase II, the northern regional international airport and the Kuala Lumpur Linear City. The deferred projects were estimated to cost a total of about RM65 billion.

At the same time, the Malaysian ringgit which had earlier registered some gain against the dollar, once again depreciated owing to unfavourable regional developments. By the end of August of 1998, the local currency had declined by 13.3 per cent against the dollar compared to 3.625 at the end of March 1998, when it had risen by 34.0 per cent from the lowest level of 4.88 in January 1998. The equity market in turn lost RM300 billion in terms of market capitalization when the KLCI hit a low of 262.7 points in September 1998, which wiped out the gains of RM170 billion made in February 1998.

The banking sector saw the level of non-performing loans (NPLs) rise speedily, primarily owing to the revision in NPL guidelines amidst reduced margin and falling loan demand. Earlier, in March 1997, BNM had instituted credit controls on sectors such as property, shares and consumption as a step to contain asset inflation. In October 1997, the government announced measures to strengthen the banking system, including tightening the non-performing loan ruling period from six to three months beginning with the financial year 1998. In August 1998, the sector as a whole registered a net NPL of 15.8 per cent or RM66 billion – a steep increase over the 2.2 per cent or RM14 billion in

Table 5.1: Malaysia's quarterly GDP, 1996–9 (% growth rate)

Year	1996				1997				1998				1999	
Sector/Quarter	Q1	Q2	Q3	Q4	Q1	Q2	Q3	Q4	Q1	Q2	Q3	Q4	Q1	Q2
Agriculture, forestry and fishing	-3.7	6.3	10.7	4.4	1.9	3.9	-1.5	-2.1	-2.1	-6.9	-4	-4.8	-3.5	8.7
Mining and quarrying	15.8	5	-2.7	-4.8	-0.6	2.6	1.9	8.1	0.6	0.3	1.2	5.1	-2.3	-6
Manufacturing	18.2	18.9	18.3	17.4	11.8	9.6	11.3	9.2	-5.8	-10.3	-18.9	-18.6	-1.1	10.4
Construction	12.1	16.1	18.1	18	17.5	10.8	7.3	7.8	-14.5	-19.8	-28	-29	-16.6	-6
Services														
Electricity/water/gas	17.2	11.7	8.4	2.2	-4.3	-6.1	-7.1	-4	0.2	4.6	2.9	4.3	2.4	3.7
Wholesale/retail/hotels	12.3	7.5	6.2	6	7.3	9.5	10.2	5.2	2.8	-1.9	-8.1	-4.7	-1.1	-0.6
Transport/ storage/comm.	8.1	2.9	7.3	11.1	10.5	16.8	14.6	5.2	6.4	2.9	-1.8	-3.4	2.5	0.5
Finance/insurance/real estate	19.9	14.8	15.4	18	19.8	22.4	19.8	14.3	5.9	-2.6	-8.9	-10.4	-6.4	0.9
Other services	10.1	8.6	7.3	5.8	5.9	7.3	7.6	8.1	7.4	5.5	1.9	0.3	1.9	1.1
Government services	17	-9.1	1.9	1.7	24.3	8.7	4.8	0.1	-14.9	12.4	4.4	5.4	14.5	1
Less Imputed bank service	27	22.7	22.5	21.3	26.1	29.9	27.3	20	7.2	0.4	-4.7	-4.4	0.7	3.1
Plus Import duties	8.4	-2	4.5	21.5	2.4	7.9	8.8	4.5	-32.5	-39.4	-48.5	-44.5	-0.2	36.7
GDP	*12.2*	*8.8*	*9.7*	*9.5*	*8.6*	*8.4*	*7.7*	*5.6*	*-3.1*	*-5.2*	*-10.9*	*-10.3*	*-1.3*	*4.1*

Source: Department of Statistics Malaysia, Bank Negara Malaysia.

August 1997. During the first eight months of 1998 net new loans dropped to RM1 billion compared with RM60 billion in the same period of 1997. Annual loan growth moderated sharply to 7.5 per cent at the end of August 1998, which was far below the targeted year-end growth of 15 per cent. The rapidly rising NPLs, bigger loan loss provisions, the higher cost of funds and lower loan disbursement inevitably not only choked the profitability of the banking sector but also eroded its capital base.

The effect of the tight macroeconomic policy stance, therefore, proved very destructive, and it was seen that any further attempt to stabilize the financial markets by tightening fiscal and monetary policies would serve only to worsen the economic situation and increase social difficulties. At this point, Malaysia decided to abandon the IMF's prescription and opt for an alternative action plan called the National Economic Recovery Plan (NERP).

5.3 RESPONDING TO THE CHALLENGES: POLICIES FOR RECOVERY AND GROWTH

On 7 January 1998, a National Economic Action Council (NEAC) was established to deal with the financial crisis. It comprised elected cabinet members, a cross-section of executives in the private sector and technocrats. The NEAC met and solicited the views of the private sector, public sector and NGOs during the first half of 1998 on the impact of the crisis and the way to respond to it.[3] The NERP was unveiled in July 1998, with currency stability as a primary objective. This culminated in the government imposing capital controls on 1 September 1998 in order to guard the economy from global financial instability. The six key objectives of the NERP were as follows:

1. Stabilizing the ringgit
2. Restoring market confidence
3. Maintaining financial market stability
4. Strengthening economic fundamentals
5. Continuing the equity and socio-economic agenda
6. Revitalizing affected sectors

As part of the National Economic Recovery Plan, monetary policy was loosened from the beginning of August 1998. The BNM 3-month intervention rate was lowered in stages from 11 per cent to 10.5 per cent, 10 per cent, 9.5 per cent, 8 per cent, 7.5 per cent, 7 per cent, 6.5 per cent and most recently to 6 per cent.

[3] The NEAC consists of 24 members. The NEAC executive committee, whose chairman is Dato' Seri Mahathir, consists of five members, and the NEAC Working Group, whose executive director is Tun Daim, has seven members.

The Statutory Reserve Ratio (SRR) was reduced from from 8 per cent to 6 per cent and then to 4 per cent and the base lending framework (BLR) was revised. The banking sector was encouraged to lend by the provision to it of resources to achieve a minimum annual loan growth target of 8 per cent. Restrictions on loans to acquire property, shares and cars were liberalized and special funds were provided to finance the priority sectors.

In 1999, the broad monetary aggregate M3 increased by 2.1 per cent in the second quarter, compared with −1.3 per cent for the same period in 1998. The increase in M3 reflected mainly the expansionary effect of external operations. The net international reserves of BNM rose by US$3.4 billion in the second quarter of 1999 and amounted to US$31.1 billion at the end of June (about six months of imports). The increase reflected the higher trade balance, net inflows of portfolio capital and proceeds from sovereign bond issue of US$1 billion. As of 14 August 1999, the international reserves of BNM had risen to US$31.9 billion.

BNM maintained positive real interest rates throughout 1998 and the first half of 1999. In the second quarter, responding to general concern that high interest rates were hampering the economic recovery, BNM reduced the intervention rates to 6.5 per cent in April, to 6 per cent in May and then to 5.5 per cent in order to boost private investment and consumption activities. The average bank lending rate (BLR) declined to 6.79 per cent and 7.95 per cent by August from the July end-levels of 7.24 per cent and 8.5 per cent. In addition, as part of efforts to stimulate domestic demand, with effect from 28 July 1999 the minimum annual income eligibility criterion for credit cards was reduced to RM18,000 from RM24,000. BNM also accelerated the consolidation of the banking sector. On 29 July 1999, it was announced that six large domestic financial groups would be created from the 58 existing banks but the final number of banks may be larger as concerns were expressed by the banking community about BNM's lack of flexibility on the consolidation exercise – in particular, the composition of the banking groups and the short time-frame. Hence, flexibility was introduced into the blueprint of the bank merger exercise in October 1999 when BNM allowed Malaysia's 55 financial institutions to pick their own merger partners – i.e. the shareholders of the banks are now given responsibility to initiate and drive the merger process. The deadline for the submission of merger proposals was the end of January 2000 and the completion of the merger exercise has been extended by 9 months to December 2000. By 31 January 2000 BNM had received ten bank merger proposals, four more than the original six proposed anchor banks.

For the first half of 1999, inflation increased by 3.3 per cent, against 5 per cent for the same period in 1998 and 4 per cent in the previous quarter. Excluding volatile food prices, the adjusted consumer price index (CPI) recorded an increase of 1.7 per cent in the second quarter of 1999, against 2.4 per cent in the first quarter. For the whole of 1999 inflation was expected to be contained below 4 per cent.

As part of the NERP, the government also embarked on a policy of fiscal stimulus leading to a budget deficit of RM16.1 billion or 6 per cent of the GNP in fiscal year 1999. Preliminary estimates for the national budget for 1999 show an expansionary budget with an allocation of RM67.4 billion. Operating expenditure is estimated to be around RM47.2 billion, with development expenditure at RM20.2 billion. Infrastructure expenditure has been given strong emphasis in order to stimulate the economy. Expenditure for various social sectors, including health, education, low- and medium-cost housing, rural roads and clinics, were given priority so as to cushion the adverse effects of the financial crisis.

Taking into account the additional financial allocation for the Seventh Malaysia Plan, public-sector expenditure is expected to add further stimulus to the economy for fiscal year 2000. For the remaining part (1999–2000) of the Seventh Plan an additional RM22 billion has been allocated for development expenditure, raising the allocation for the plan period (1996–2000) to about RM88 billion.

Public-sector consumption recorded a positive growth of 8.7 per cent in real terms in the second quarter of 1999 on the back of higher government expenditure on supply and services as well as defence.

Private investment expenditure, however, continued to be slow, because of excess capacity faced by selected industries, particularly those in construction-related materials and transport equipment. For the second quarter, private consumption grew by 3 per cent, in contrast to the contraction of 4.1 per cent in the first quarter of 1999.

During to its the heavy reliance on bank financing, the corporate sector was hit hard by the rise in interest rates following the onset of the crisis, a condition exacerbated by the sharp decline in demand and the collapse in the value of assets used as collateral. A three-pronged strategy was initiated for addressing the liquidity needs of weak financial institutions and corporate borrowers and also for facilitating the restructuring and consolidation of the banking system.

First, Danaharta was established as an asset management company in May 1998 to acquire NPLs from banking institutions in order to strengthen their balance sheets and enhance their ability to lend. Secondly, Danamodal was set up in August 1998 with the objective of addressing constraints faced by shareholders of banking institutions in raising additional capital. Thirdly, it was recognized that the availability of finance is a critical factor in enabling viable businesses to continue to function. In this respect the Corporate Debt Restructuring Committee (CDRC) provides the platform for borrowers and banking institutions to work out debt restructuring packages without resorting to legal means. The CDRC complements Danaharta and Danamodal in accelerating

Figure 5.1: Linkages between Danaharta, Danamodal and the CDRC

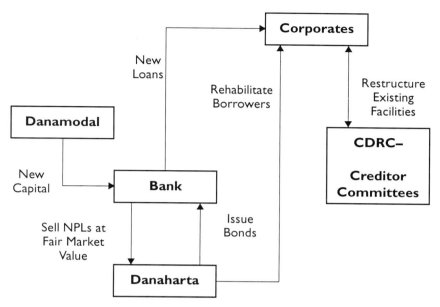

the pace of economic recovery by providing an approach for banking institutions to play a greater role in the rehabilitation of the corporate sector. The linkages between Danaharta, Danamodal and the CDRC are depicted in Figure 5.1.

Malaysia has made steady progress in implementing its financial and corporate sector restructuring programme. Danaharta has acquired and managed loans of about RM40 billion from the financial system, representing 2,000 loan accounts, as of 30 June 1999. From the banking system alone, Danaharta has acquired and managed NPLs amounting to about RM30 billion, or 34 per cent of total NPLs in the banking system. As a result the net NPL ratio moderated to 7.9 per cent on six-month classification as of 30 June 1999 and remained at that level as of the end of July 1999, after peaking at 9 per cent on six-month classification as of the end of November 1998. In addition the average monthly rate of increase in non-performing loans moderated to 1.75 per cent for the first half of the year from an average monthly increase of 10.1 per cent in 1998. Although RM15 billion had been allocated to Danaharta to fund its NPL acquisitions as of 30 June 1999, only RM8.6 billion had been utilized.

Danaharta also started its loan and asset management process and began as well to dispose of some of the assets acquired from financial institutions. During the second quarter, the Danaharta managers conducted a restricted tender exercise for its foreign currency loans with a recovery rate of 55 per cent; this was successfully completed in August 1999.

Since its inception, Danamodal has injected RM6.4 billion into ten banking institutions. The capital injection by Danamodal has improved the average risk to weighted capital adequacy ratio (RWCAR) of the ten recapitalized banking institutions from 9.8 per cent as of the end of August 1998 to 13.9 per cent as of the end of May 1999. As of the end of August 1999, Danamodal's capital injection was reduced to RM5.7 billion from the previous month's level of RM5.9 billion upon the repayment of capital by some banking institutions.

In the case of CDRC, considerable progress has been made, taking into consideration that CDRC only facilitates the restructuring of debts of over RM50 million that involve more than three banking institutions. As of the end of August 1999, CDRC had accepted 62 cases with debts totalling RM34.9 billion, of which 11 restructuring schemes involving debts of RM11.2 billion had been completed and were being implemented. At the same time 12 cases involving debts worth RM2.9 billion had been rejected. Corporate restructuring was also being undertaken hand in hand with financial restructuring in several cases under the purview of CDRC.

In the first quarter of 1999, the Malaysian economy might have bottomed out with GDP growth of –1.3 per cent, and there were some preliminary signs of recovery. The second-quarter growth of 4.1 per cent confirmed that Malaysia was on the path of recovery. Analysis of the supply side pointed to growth being propelled by the strong rebound in the manufacturing sector and to a lesser extent by a pick-up in domestic demand for transport equipment and construction-related materials. The agriculture sector also recorded strong gains on the back of an increase in crude palm oil production.

On the demand side, exports served as a catalyst of economic growth, driven by manufactures of semiconductors and electronic components. The latter account for slightly over 50 per cent of Malaysian exports. Exports expanded by 14.2 per cent during the quarter against an increase in imports of 8.8 per cent. The increase in imports represented the first increase in dollar terms since the third quarter of 1997. The trade account recorded a surplus for eight consecutive quarters amounting to RM18.1 billion. For the first half of 1999, the trade surplus increased to RM33.7 billion, compared with RM22.4 billion in the first half of 1998.

In addition to the favourable performance by the export sector, both public-sector expenditure and to a lesser extent private consumption expenditure looked to continue to pick up in the second half of the year. Private investment expenditures were expected to remain sluggish, as they had been over the last two quarters of 1998. Both private investment and private consumption shrank by more than 10 per cent in 1998. Stock prices plunged by nearly 70 per cent and stock market capitalization fell by more than 200 per cent of GDP at one stage. This enormous wealth loss has translated into weak consumption and investment demand. In addition, the excess capacity in the economy and continued global uncertainty could deter private investment from turning positive in 1999 or even in 2000.

As for the second half of 1999, growth is estimated to be around 6–7 per cent, thanks to continuous export-driven growth and a strong fiscal stimulus. For the full year of 1999, a growth of between 3.7 per cent and 4.2 per cent is expected, which was significantly higher than the official forecast of one per cent.

5.4 CAPITAL CONTROLS: THE SOLUTION

Capital controls were introduced on 1 September 1998, 14 months after the outbreak of the crisis, with the aim of protecting the Malaysian economy from further deterioration in the world economic and financial environment. The measures taken were as follows:

- The ringgit exchange rate will be fixed to the dollar at 3.80.
- On external accounts, transfers require prior approval.
- On general payments, import payments must be settled in foreign currency, and payments in ringgits to non-residents for ringgit-asset investments must be made in ringgits through external accounts.
- Trade settlements must be made in foreign currency.
- Investments abroad exceeding RM10,000 require prior approval.
- Residents are not allowed to obtain ringgit credit facilities from non-residents.
- Import and export of ringgit currency are restricted to RM1,000 per person. There are no limits on the import of foreign currencies by resident and non-resident travellers. The export of foreign currencies by non-residents is permitted, up to the amount of foreign exchange brought into Malaysia.
- A one-year witholding rule for the repatriation of portfolio capital is imposed.

No capital controls were imposed on the following:

- Current account transactions (the only amendment is that all trade transactions are to be settled in foreign currencies and no longer in the domestic currency).
- Repatriation of interest, dividends, fees, commissions and rental income from portfolio investments and other ringgit assets.
- Foreign direct investment (FDI) inflows and outflows, including income and capital gains.

Capital controls are directed only at speculative short-term capital flows or 'hot money', not long-term FDI; they are not intended to disrupt trade-related transactions: current account convertibility is maintained. (See Figure A2 in the Appendix on the weekly movements of the RM/US$ exchange rate and the Kuala Lumpur Composite Index (KLCI) from September 1998 to October 1999.)

On 4 February 1999, some adjustments were made to the capital controls. Portfolio investors were allowed to repatriate their capital and profits as well as to encourage new capital inflows. There were two categories of capital funds: those funds in Malaysia prior to 15 February 1999 and those that came on and after that date. The original capital brought in before 15 February 1999 was allowed to be repatriated subject to a graduated levy, which was based on the duration of the investment. For capital repatriated within a period of up to seven months from the date of entry into Malaysia (since the announcement on 1 September 1998), the levy was 30 per cent. For the period exceeding seven months and up to nine months, the levy was 20 per cent; for the period exceeding nine months and up to 12 months, the levy was 10 per cent; and after 12 months no levy would be imposed on the capital. No levy would be imposed on repatriation of profits made within the 12-month holding period. All profits made after this 12-month holding period would be subject to a repatriation levy of 10 per cent. Dividend, interest and rentals would not be subject to a levy.

For funds brought in on and after 15 February 1999, the principal was allowed to be repatriated without levy. However, profits would be subject to a levy of 30 per cent if they were repatriated within a period of up to 12 months from the date when profits were made. The levy was reduced to 10 per cent if the profits were repatriated after 12 months from the date profits were made.

The imposition of capital controls in Malaysia was not well received by the international community. Capital controls are seen as having a limited role in balance-of-payments management and their implementation as neither desirable nor effective.[4] Alesina and Milesi-Ferretti (1994) have found that countries with a fixed or managed exchange rate, low per capita income and high ratios of government consumption to GDP are more likely to maintain certain controls. In the same paper, the authors point that countries with more independent central banks and balanced current accounts are less likely to maintain such controls. Other studies, by Bartolini and Drazen (1997) and Laban and Larrain (1997), which cite the experiences of the United Kingdom, Italy, New Zealand and Spain, emphasize that the liberalization of capital outflows often increases capital inflows.[5]

Johnston and Tamirisa (1998), however, concede that although most studies provide some useful insights into the consequences of capital account liberalization and support the hypothesis that capital account liberalization has a

---

[4] See Johnston and Tamirisa (1998) and EDRC (1998).
[5] Ibid.

positive impact on economic growth, there is almost no discussion on the potential macroeconomic effects of removing capital controls. In particular, most studies are silent on the danger of full capital account liberalization before the domestic financial system has been suitably strengthened. They are silent too about how it can encourage volatile capital flows that can create an environment leading to serious economic problems – and, potentially, financial crises. Only a limited number of studies have emphasized caution in capital account liberalization. For instance, Rodrik (1998) and Bhagwati (1998b) have found no significant relationship between liberalizing capital flows and economic growth; they argue that liberalizing capital flows and free trade cannot be handled on the same level. Stiglitz (1998) has also begun to urge caution at the early stages of capital market liberalization.

The general consensus is that capital controls have numerous negative effects. It is said that a parallel market or black market in foreign exchange will develop and that trade distortions will be observed, as exporters will have an incentive to under-invoice their receipts and vice versa for importers. It is also said that there will be a stronger incentive to manipulate transfer pricing of goods and that capital controls will generate a huge bureaucracy to enforce them, and this in turn will increase red tape and opportunities for corruption. Moreover, it is argued that, it becomes difficult once capital controls are in place to lift them and that the longer they are maintained, the greater the likelihood of economic distortions and graft.

But despite this long list of negative effects, few of them seem to have materialized in Malaysia, such as black market activities or an increase in trade distortions. It is true, however, that short-term portfolio investors have complained: they feel that their transaction costs have increased with the repatriation levy and that the administrative process is cumbersome. Also, the need to keep detailed records of all inflows, both transactions made before and after the imposition of capital controls, and the apportioning of profits to the right portfolio, has proved to be time-consuming.

With regard to the exchange rate, it is argued that with no market mechanism in place to determine it, the fixed rate has become overvalued relative to neighbouring countries, thus causing a loss of export competitiveness. The actual peg at RM3.80 to the dollar is actually undervalued, making Malaysian exports more competitive relative to those of neighbouring countries and spurring an export-led recovery. And the current view is that the ringgit should be revalued at between RM3.20 to 3.50 to the dollar in order to prevent huge current account surpluses from flooding the economy with excess liquidity that may be channelled into non-productive sectors.

Assessing the impact and effectiveness of capital controls is not that easy, as Dooley (1996, pp. 669–70) sums up:

Empirical work on the 'effectiveness' of capital controls has suffered from the lack of a widely accepted definition of what constitutes an effective control programme. At one end of the spectrum, effectiveness has been defined as differences observed over extended time periods in the average behaviour of selected economies' variables between countries with capital controls and countries without them. At the other extreme, effectiveness has been defined as a government's ability to maintain an inconsistent macroeconomic policy regime indefinitely.

With regard to the Malaysian experience, a useful starting point may be to review the modifications made to capital controls on 15 February 1999, permitting portfolio investors to repatriate their capital and profits subject to a graduated levy of 10–30 per cent depending on the duration of the investment. This modification appears to have stemmed an expected massive capital outflow, following the first anniversary of capital controls in Malaysia – to no more than RM1.2 billion on 2 September 1999 compared with an earlier official estimate of RM5 to RM7 billion. (See Table A1 in the Appendix on the 'Flow of funds through external accounts/special external accounts' from 5 March 1999, to 29 September 1999.)

The reasons why capital outflows have been lower than projected can be explained by various factors, one being the levy system, which helped to spread the outflow pressure of short-term funds more evenly over the interim period of 15 February to 1 September 1999. Also Malaysia's strong economic recovery provided short-term portfolio investors with the expectation of much higher returns on their investment. Additionally, investors may have expected that the authorities would possibly announce further modifications or even remove the existing capital controls. Another factor which may have played a role was the announcement of the reinstatement of Malaysia in Morgan Stanley Capital International's (MSCI) stock indices in February 2000.

On 21 September 1999, the government introduced further modifications and changed the existing two-tier levy system on profits on portfolio investment (that is 30 per cent on profits repatriated within one year from 15 February 1999 and 10 per cent after one year) to a flat 10 per cent levy. This was done in response to appeals from foreign fund managers that the two-tier levy had created problems in calculating prices and determining the exact amount of levy applicable to their investment. This particularly affected fund managers who have continuous portfolio investments in Malaysia and repatriate their profits regularly.

This latest set of modifications has raised a number of concerns. The capital gains tax of 10 per cent could lead to tax evasion measures. It will raise the required rate of return on investments in Malaysia relative to other private-sector investment and may slow the rate of private capital inflows. And although capital mobility has been increased for foreign portfolio investors, the fear is that the modifications may not boost liquidity in the stock market, as market participants remain cautious. A sluggish domestic stock market caused by higher transaction costs will raise the cost of borrowing for Malaysian companies, and this will stifle the growth of the corporate sector. Moreover, the discretionary powers of the government on capital control policy (such as increasing the tax rate) add to market uncertainty.

5.5 LEARNING FROM OTHER CAPITAL CONTROLS EXPERIENCES

It may be useful at this stage to review other forms of capital controls in order to see how the Malaysian capital controls experience could be further improved.

Box 5.1 summarizes some of the prevailing lessons drawn in the literature from past forms of capital controls. These suggest that capital controls in Malaysia could take the form of prudential controls in the future, as were instituted in 1995, or could even evolve along the Chilean model (see below). The composition of capital flows is obviously important. Short-term capital flows are highly volatile and complicate macroeconomic management. Therefore Malaysia should aim to achieve an appropriate balance between short-term and long-term capital inflows. In this context, the Chilean model offers some useful practical insights.

The Chilean model

In the late 1980s and early 1990s, Chile experienced a surge in capital inflows that created a conflict between the authorities' internal and external objectives. The problem was how to maintain a tight monetary policy without hindering Chilean export competitiveness. In 1991, the central bank of Chile attempted to resolve this dilemma by imposing a one-year unremunerated reserve requirement on foreign loans which was designed to discourage short-term borrowing without affecting long-term investments. Under this system, the rate of unremunerated reserve requirement was increased (from 20 per cent to 30 per cent) and its coverage was extended in several steps to cover most forms of foreign financing except FDI. In addition, bond-issuing restrictions were placed on borrowers (that is domestic firms and banks) in order to reduce risky borrowing and protect against an unnecessary build-up in external debts.

The Chilean experiment between 1991 and 1997 can be seen as an attempt to control the composition of foreign borrowing without hindering the volume of inflows to the country. Le Fort and Budnevich (1996) suggest that the Chilean capital controls were effective because, in the absence of effective capital

Box 5.1: Lessons from past capital controls

- Controls on capital outflows are less effective. Spain, which introduced controls on short-term capital outflows during the ERM crisis in 1992, modified the controls within 13 days and scrapped them within two months of implementation after discovering that their requirements were tending to affect foreign trade transactions adversely. This experience was also shared by Portugal which introduced controls for four months (September–December 1992) but did not reintroduce them during subsequent episodes of exchange rate tension within the ERM.
- Controls on inflows can alter maturity composition and the volume of capital flows, although the evidence on this has been disputed by some. Chile and Colombia appear to have managed to alter the maturity composition of capital flows.
- Price-based controls are more efficient than quantitative restrictions.
- Distinguishing between short-term (portfolio) flows and long-term (FDI) flows can be difficult to administer in practice.
- Prudential banking regulation is a preferred instrument which can have effects similar to restrictions on capital movements, for example by requiring that all inflows of funds from abroad be included in the definition of eligible liabilities for statutory and reserve requirements, as Malaysia did when it confronted large short-term inflows in 1995. Or countries can put a limit on the external liability position of each banking institution, as seems to be the case with Taiwan.
- Changes are needed in the architecture of the international financial system in view of the excessive volatility, strong contagion effects and increased moral hazard in international financial markets.

Source: World Bank Report (May 1999) and Eichengreen et al. (1998).

restrictions, it would have been impossible to keep domestic interest rates above comparable international rates. Their argument implicitly assumes that a mix of sound macroeconomic policies and sustained growth ruled out a 'peso problem' explanation for the interest rate differential. However, the evidence on the effectiveness of Chilean capital controls in reducing the short-term external debt is somewhat ambiguous (Table 5.2). These data on the evolution of Chile's external debt show that the introduction of capital controls affected the maturity composition of net capital outflows only after 1995, when controls were strengthened. When controls were introduced in 1991, the short-term

Table 5.2: Evolution of Chile's external debt ($m)

Year	Short-term	Total external debt	Short-term debt total/debt (%)	Debt/GDP Year (%)
1988	3,462	18,914	18.3	78
1989	4,367	17,914	24.7	63
1990	5,027	19,070	26.4	63
1991	3,957	18,116	21.8	53
1992	5,496	20,263	27.1	47
1993	5,665	21,364	26.5	47
1994	6,497	24,109	26.9	46
1995	6,254	24,559	25.5	36
1996	4,356	24,701	17.6	34
1997	3,078	27,639	11.1	35

Source: International Monetary Fund, 'Chile's Experience with Capital Controls', *Annual Report on Exchange Arrangements and Exchange Restrictions*, Annex IV.

component of the external debt dropped five percentage points but increased again in 1992 before declining to 17.6 per cent and 11.1 per cent of total external debt in 1996 and 1997 respectively.

Table 5.3 seems to lend support to the view that capital controls have had some effect in limiting the short-term component of Chile's external debt. At the end of June 1997, loans with less than one year to maturity represented 43 per cent of Chile's total exposure, which is relatively low compared with other countries listed in the table. Colombia had followed similar policies and also had a relatively small share of short-term loans, reinforcing this point.

There is, however, disagreement about the effectiveness of the Chilean model. Cardoso and Laurens (1998) find that the introduction of capital controls had some temporary effect on the composition of external financing. Their regression results suggest that capital controls were effective in the six months following their introduction but ceased to be effective thereafter.[6] While (1999) pointed out that during the 1994–5 Mexican crisis, Chile was less affected than other Latin American countries, and this could be attributed to its lower proportion of short-term debt. Therefore Chile's inflow tax appears to be a useful capital control tool which can be used during times of volatile capital flows.

In 1998, the Chilean authorities reduced the unremunerated reserve requirement to zero, as they were no longer concerned about massive capital inflows into emerging markets.

[6] See 'Chile's Experience with Capital Controls', *IMF Annual Report on Exchange Arrangements and Exchange Restrictions*, Annex IV.

Table 5.3: Chile's debt in comparative perspective, end June 1997

Country	Total	Up to 1 year	1 to 2 years	Over 2 years	Un-allocated	% S-T debt[a]
Venezuela	12,148	3,629	421	6,717	1,381	29.9
Hungary	10,851	4,018	964	3,653	2,216	37.0
Colombia	**16,999**	**6,698**	**1,423**	**8,503**	**375**	**39.4**
Chile	**17,573**	**7,615**	**673**	**8,698**	**587**	**43.3**
Mexico	62,072	28,226	2,659	24,647	6,540	45.5
Poland	9,249	4,274	436	3,223	1,316	46.2
Slovak Rep.	3,656	1,710	304	1,514	128	46.8
Turkey	25,060	13,067	2,516	8,087	1,390	52.1
Czech Rep.	11,378	6,078	967	3,508	825	53.4
Argentina	44,445	23,891	1,662	15,207	3,685	53.8
Russia	69,091	38,308	3,811	24,959	2,013	55.4
Malaysia	28,820	16,268	615	8,248	3,689	56.4
South Africa	22,889	13,247	1,249	6,132	2,261	57.9
Philippines	14,115	8,293	326	4,001	1,495	58.8
Indonesia	58,726	34,661	3,541	17,008	3,516	59.0
Brazil	71,118	44,223	2,193	19,555	5,147	62.2
Thailand	69,382	45,567	4,592	16,491	2,732	65.7
Peru	8,013	5,368	278	1,946	421	67.0
South Korea	**103,432**	**70,182**	**4,139**	**16,366**	**12,745**	**67.9**
Uruguay	4,370	3,020	104	1,196	50	69.1
Hong Kong	222,289	183,115	4,417	24,974	9,783	82.4
Taiwan	25,163	21,966	236	2,598	363	87.3
Singapore	211,192	196,600	1,719	9,818	3,055	93.1

[a] Per cent short-term debt.

Source: Bank for International Settlements.

The South Korean model

The South Korean capital controls programme placed significant restrictions on foreign direct investments as it adopted a course of sequenced liberalization. The sequencing of reforms led to early liberalization of commercial credit and short-term flows while it maintained restrictions on long-term inflows. Foreign direct investment through merger and acquisition was not permitted and the approval of the authorities was required for the establishment and extension of domestic branches of foreign enterprises.[7] For non-financial institutions, approval from the Bank of South Korea was needed. Portfolio investments in domestic equities were also restricted through a 20 per cent limit on the percentage of any listed firm that non-residents could hold. As the South Korean capital

[7] See *Exchange Arrangements and Exchange Restrictions*, Annual Report, 1997, pp. 461–66.

controls were focused on long-term rather than on short-term investments, we should find the opposite effect to that of the Chilean programme on external debt. Table 5.3 confirms this intuition. As we saw above, Chile's short-term borrowing represented 43 per cent of total borrowing while the corresponding figure for South Korea was 68 per cent. Furthermore, if we rank emerging economies by relative weight of short-term borrowing, Chile and South Korea appear at the opposite ends of the spectrum.

To some extent this observation gives support to the call by the Malaysian prime minister for the need to regulate short-term capital, as South Korea was one of the affected countries during the crisis. The South Korean case illustrates the vulnerability of an economy that started a series of reforms in order to liberalize its capital account. Liberalization brought a high level of unhedged short-term foreign currency debts to South Korea, consequently setting the stage for currency attacks, even though the macroeconomic fundamentals were relatively favourable at the onset of the crisis. The unregulated capital account poses special risks because it permits borrowing in foreign currency and strips the authorities of their ability to act as lenders of last resort: central banks cannot print foreign currency, and their capacity to provide commercial banks with the foreign exchange they need to make good on their foreign obligations is limited to their stock of international reserves. This argument provides part of the rationale for the need for prudential regulation in terms of short-term flows.

The Taiwanese model

Taiwan had various forms of capital controls and financial restrictions in place prior to the Asian financial crisis:

- Qualified foreign institutional investors (QFIIs) such as banks, insurance companies, fund managers and other foreign investment institutions require a month to obtain approval from the Taiwanese authorities and can invest only up to US$600 million per approval. Such supervision and restrictions allow gradual and systematic foreign portfolio participation in the Taiwanese stock market.
- Principal and profit repatriation is subject to a tax clearance certificate. Taxes of 20–35 per cent on dividends and 20 per cent on interest income are applied on remittances by foreigners.
- Limits are set on banks' foreign currency deposit ratios (FCDRs) which vary depending on the liquidity levels of the banking system; that is, banks are set limits on the amount of NT dollars that they can use for foreign exchange trading. This mechanism may curb the operations of hedge funds, which need liquidity to move their funds freely.

- Foreign banks are not allowed to open offshore accounts for Taiwanese citizens, which limits capital flight. The expansion of foreign bank branches is restricted and their deposit bases are limited.
- Total foreign ownership of a listed Taiwanese company by QFIIs cannot exceed 30 per cent.
- Taiwanese citizens are required to seek approval to take out more than US$5 million from the country; Taiwanese companies can take out up to US$50 million without approval from the relevant authorities.

Taiwan's capital controls are not as extensive as China's, and these controls appear so far not to have caused severe economic distortion within the country. Taiwan does not control the following:

- The use foreign currencies for trade purposes.
- Long-term capital flows from foreign direct investment.
- Repatriation of capital or profits from foreign direct investment.

The benefit of the Taiwanese model is that it allows discrimination in terms of foreign investment. Only approved foreign institutional investors are allowed, and once they meet the criteria for being a QFII, they can participate relatively freely in the Taiwanese market. In Taiwan's case, market forces appear to operate relatively freely despite having capital controls. Meanwhile, speculative short-term capital inflows and their disruptive effects on exchange rates and the stock market are minimized.

5.6 THE TOBIN TAX

Since the financial turmoil, the 'Tobin tax'[8] has often been discussed. This calls for a small levy on all foreign exchange transactions (including foreign exchange transactions related to trade) and seeks to improve the efficiency of financial markets in allocating resources by discouraging short-term inflows. It would be applied not only to short-term capital inflows but also to long-term inflows. However, by having a very small tax the impact on long-term inflows could be minimized.

Nonetheless the Tobin tax is a tax on all foreign trading, and as such it has many weaknesses:

---

[8] Tobin, J. (1978), 'A Proposal for International Monetary Reform', *Eastern Economic Journal*, No. 4, pp. 53–9.

- Its introduction would require agreement on a global scale.
- Global finance has become so sophisticated that it would be administratively very difficult to monitor, control and tax all foreign exchange transactions.
- The cost of operating a 'Tobin tax' could turn out to be enormous.
- Determining the magnitude of the tax rate is difficult: too small a tax rate will not deter currency speculators if capital gains exceed the tax; too large a tax rate may disrupt the operations of financial markets.

One variant of the 'Tobin tax' supports a small tax on all cross-border transactions. A tax of this nature would be less distortive than the Tobin tax and easier to implement; it would also be a disincentive to short-term inflows. It could be treated as a transitory device designed to provide countries with a smooth process of integration into the world economy.

5.7 CONCLUSION

The main point of the Malaysian experiment with selective capital controls since September 1998 has been to create a 'breathing space' so that domestic policies can reduce macroeconomic disequilibria and financial distortions to manageable proportions. Thus, the implementation and progress of reforms since September 1998 support the foregoing view that the selective capital controls measures imposed by Malaysia were a means and not an end in itself or an alternative to reforms. Malaysia is still assessing the effectiveness of capital controls measures and considering further modifications. It has been only a year since the imposition of capital controls, and any serious study would call for a comparison between the pre- and post-capital controls periods in order to assess both the direct and the indirect effects, as was the case with the Chilean model. But the earlier indictment that capital controls would be disastrous for Malaysia has been proved to be incorrect.

This chapter has argued that capital controls as a stabilization tool in countries with under-developed financial systems have been ignored. Malaysia is the only country affected by the Asian financial crisis to have implemented capital controls in response to it. In Malaysia's case, selective controls did provide a reasonable measure of certainty at a time of unprecedented turbulence by allowing the government to revitalize the economy via fiscal expansion and an 'easy' monetary policy, which was later advocated by the IMF for Indonesia, South Korea and Thailand.

This chapter has also shown that a Chilean-style inflow tax helped to alter the structure of capital towards more medium- to long-term capital, in contrast to the South Korean style of capital control restrictions on long-term capital such as FDI which reversed the debt structure in favour of short-term inflows, with disastrous economic consequences. The Chilean model of taxing capital inflows or the Malaysian model of levies on capital outflows would be worthy of consideration by countries with an inadequate financial infrastructure or prudent regulatory framework as a way to cope with the risks associated with volatile inflows.

Removing restrictions on capital account transactions while the financial system and regulatory framework remain underdeveloped, as was the case with Indonesia and Thailand, has proved dangerous. This led to unregulated unhedged short-term capital inflows which were financing unproductive projects and resulted in a collapse of the financial system during the crisis. Countries such as China, Taiwan and Chile which had some form of capital controls, withstood the recent turmoil better than Hong Kong, the bastion of free marketeers, or Mexico, which was under an IMF programme.

The IMF has been promoting capital account liberalization by linking it with trade liberalization – it regards them as going hand in hand. But Bhagwati (1998a) argues that although the benefits from international free trade have been well documented, the evidence to support the benefits from capital account liberalization is unpersuasive and limited. He believes that trade liberalization should not be linked to capital liberalization, as the former is not subject to herd behaviour, market panics, stock market crashes and destabilizing speculation. Bhagwati argues further that this 'Capital Myth' is perpetuated by a powerful network that includes senior officials from the IMF, the World Bank and the US Treasury who have what he calls the 'Wall Street-Treasury complex', a view of the world that does not go beyond the interests of Wall Street.

In the light of these objections, there is a need to develop detailed guidelines for capital account liberalization in order to help a country to decide whether or not to open up its capital account.

Eichengreen (1999) recommends that medium- to long-term capital in the form of FDI should be liberalized first as it is less destabilizing. Frankel and Rose (1996) find in their empirical study that FDI is less likely to trigger a financial crisis, as the costs of liquidating tangible assets are much higher than those for liquidating portfolio capital. Eichengreen and Mussa (1998) argue that it is critical for financial liberalization (including capital account liberalization) to be accompanied by policies aimed at limiting financial risk. They mention that there must be rigorous prudential regulation and supervision of domestic financial institutions and capital markets by national authorities. They point out too that the lender-of-last-resort facility must be designed cautiously in order to avoid or at least minimize moral hazard. Moreover, an environment of implicit government guarantees must be avoided so as to discourage excessive short-term capital inflows. Banks and non-bank financial intermediaries must manage their balance sheet risks prudently – this includes adopting proper credit risk analysis and avoiding dependence on short-term foreign denominated debt. There must be a strong system of corporate governance so that corporate borrowers manage their financial risk properly.

The G-22 reform proposals on the international financial architecture include measures such as more transparency, uniform reporting and accounting procedures, better risk assessment, increased surveillance and strengthening domestic financial institutions. But none of these reforms consider the difficulties faced by developing countries, especially those in East Asia.[9]

The causes of financial instability do not differentiate between emerging economies and industrialized countries. Nor is there any mechanism allowing a real dialogue among industrialized countries, emerging market economies and poor countries. The social impact of financial crises – social safety nets and other social issues – is too often ignored, but social consequences do affect economic recovery, and their long-term implications for the economy are still unfolding.

Reform of the global financial architecture should, at the minimum, enable Asian governments to establish mechanisms and/or a common fund to protect their economies from international financial turmoil. The role of the IMF in resolving the crisis is over-emphasized. Other international financial institutions and alternative regional mechanisms, such as an Asian Monetary Fund (AMF), could play a significant role in crisis resolution. There is a critical need for a permanent funding agency with a standby regional financial support mechanism to provide liquidity quickly to 'hot spots' within East Asia in order to foil speculative currency attacks. The need for such a stabilization fund is all the more critical now with the recent inflow of 'hot money' into the region as foreign investors are caught up in the euphoria of a rapid economic recovery leading to sharp rises in regional stockmarkets. Hence, the establishment of an Asian Monetary Fund should be encouraged as a emergency stabilization funding agency that is able to inject capital into distressed Asian countries during times of financial crisis. Such an Asian-focused stabilization fund would complement the IMF in a way similar to the Manila-based Asian Development Bank (ADB), which supports the World Bank. This would also fend off accusations that an AMF would undermine the activities of the IMF, and it would also contribute to the financial stability of the East Asian region. An AMF could collaborate closely with the ADB, creating Asian-focused twin institutions that support the IMF and the World Bank in their efforts to maintain financial and economic stability in the region.

Japan could initially be the core donor via its Miyazawa fund, and East Asian economies with huge foreign reserves such as China, Hong Kong and Taiwan should participate as donors to an AMF. Given the significant build-up

[9] These proposed reforms were drawn from 'Comments on the Reports on the International Financial Architecture', International Monetary Fund, August 1999.

of their foreign reserves during the crisis, the ASEAN countries should also consider making contributions to an AMF.

Prudential regulation of the financial system as recommended by the G-22 reports should be targeted not only at developing countries but also at developed countries. As many of the hedge funds are based offshore, the US government should step up regulation among US commercial banks that lend to hedge funds and other speculators. The Long-Term Capital Management (LTCM) experience has shown the tremendous influence hedge funds can yield in global financial markets aided by the imprudent involvement of many of the world's top banks. In the case of the LTCM, it was allowed by its bankers to run up a balance sheet position of US$120 billion against a capital of only US$4.8 billion, a leverage of nearly 25 times its capital. This shows the striking feature of financial globalization – that is, the extraordinarily large amounts of capital that can be generated for speculation by a small number of non-bank institutions such as hedge funds. These hedge funds should be regulated; they should be made to be more transparent in their operations and to observe strict corporate governance. Collusion between banks and hedge funds should be forbidden and the leverage margins of banks to hedge funds should not exceed a certain limit. In other words, there should be international standards that introduce strict corporate governance and prudential regulations on financial institutions in both the developing and the developed world.

APPENDIX

Table 5.A1: Flow of funds through external accounts/special external accounts, March-September 1999

1999: week to	Net portfolio cumulative inflow (RM m)
5 March	−21.73
10 March	18.53
17 March	21.21
24 March	37.29
31 March	74.22
7 April	62.35
14 April	398.10
21 April	424.04
28 April	554.05
5 May	1,089.33
12 May	1,436.33
19 May	2,063.73
26 May	2,372.46
2 June	2,831.32
9 June	2,913.52
16 June	2,881.12
23 June	2,934.94
30 June	3,879.48
7 July	4,213.76
16 July	4,700.95
21 July	4,561.69
28 July	4,606.22
4 August	4,389.82
11 August	4,160.09
18 August	3,592.60
25 August	3,897.21
1 September	2,766.68
8 September	1,621.49
15 September	674.66
22 September	−394.79
29 September	−1,323.17

Source: Bank Negara Malaysia.

References

Alesina, A. and Gian Maria Milesi-Ferretti (1994), 'The Political Economy of Capital Controls', in L. Leiderman and A. Razin (eds), *Capital Mobility: The Impact on Consumption, Investment and Growth*, Cambridge University Press for CEPR.

Bartolini, L. and Drazen, A. (1997), 'Capital Account Liberalisation as a Signal', *American Economic Review*, Vol. 87 (March), pp. 134–54.

Bhagwati, J. (1998a), 'The Capital Myth: The Difference between Trade in Widgets and Dollars', *Foreign Affairs*, Vol. 77, No. 3, pp. 7–12.

Bhagwati, J. (1998b), 'Free Thinker: Free-trader Explains Why He Likes Capital Controls', *Far Eastern Economic Review*, 15 October.

Camdessus, M. (1998), Report of the Managing Director to the Interim Committee on Strengthening the Architecture of the International Monetary System, International Monetary Fund, 15 September.

Caramazza, F. and Aziz, J. (1999), 'Fixed or Flexible? Getting the Exchange Right in the 1990's', International Monetary Fund, *Economic Issues*, No. 13.

Cardoso, J. and Laurens, B. (1998), 'The Effectiveness of Capital Controls on Inflows: Lessons from the Experience of Chile', Unpublished, Monetary and Exchange Affairs Department, International Monetary Fund.

Colomiris, C. (1998), 'The IMF's Imprudent Role as Lender of Last Resort', *The Cato Journal*, Vol. 17, No. 3.

Corsetti, G., Pesenti, P. and Roubini, N. (1998), 'What Caused the Asian Currency and Financial Crisis?' Asia Crisis Web Homepage at *www.stern. nyu.edu/~nroubini/asia/AsiaHomepage.html*.

Delhaise, P.F. (1998), *Asia in Crisis: The Implosion of the Banking and Finance Systems*, John Wiley & Sons (Asia) Pte Ltd.

Dooley, M.P. (1996), *A Survey of Literature on Controls over International Capital Transactions*, IMF Staff Papers, Vol. 43, No. 4, December.

Driscoll, D. D. (1996), *The IMF and the World Bank: How Do They Differ?*, IMF paper, August.

Driscoll, D.D. (1998), *What is The International Monetary Fund?*, IMF paper, September.

Economist Survey (1999), 'Global Finance', *The Economist*, 30 January.

EDRC Briefing Notes No 4, October 1998, 'Exchange Controls: The Path to Economic Recovery in Asia?' Asian Development Bank, Economics and Development Resource Centre.

Eichengreen, B. (1999), 'Towards a New International Financial Architecture: A Practical Post-Asia Agenda', Washington, DC: Institute for International Economics.

Eichengreen, B. and Mussa, M. (1998), 'Capital Account Liberalization and the IMF', *Finance and Development*, December, Vol. 35, No. 4.

Eichengreen, B., Mussa, M. with Dell' Ariccia, G., Detragiache, E., Milesi-Ferretti, G.M. and Tweedie, A. (1998), 'Capital Account Liberalization: Theoretical and Practical Aspects', *IMF Occasional Paper 172*, IMF, Washington, DC.

Eichengreen, B. and Mathieson, D. (1999), 'Hedge Funds: What Do We Really Know?', International Monetary Fund, *Economic Issues*, No.19, September.

Feldstein, M. (1998), 'Refocusing the IMF', *Foreign Affairs*, March/April.

Fischer, S. (1998a), 'The Asian Crisis and the Changing Role of the IMF', *Finance and Development*, June.

Fischer, S. (1998b), 'The IMF and the Asian Crisis', International Monetary Fund, 20 March.

Frankel, J.A. (1999), 'The International Financial Architecture', Policy Brief No. 51, Brookings Institution, Washington, DC.

Frankel, J. and Rose, A. (1996), 'Currency Crashes in Emerging Markets: An Empirical Treatment', *Journal of International Economics*, Vol. 41, pp. 351–66.

Giannini, C. (1999), 'The IMF and the Lender-Of-Last-Resort Function: An External View', *Finance and Development*, Vol. 36, No. 3, September.

Greenspan, A. (1998), 'Remarks by Chairman Alan Greenspan – The Structure of the International Financial System', at the Annual Meeting of the Securities Industry Association, Boca Raton, Florida, 5 November.

Grilli, Vittorio and Gian Maria Milesi-Freretti (1995), *Economic Effects and Structural Determinants of Capital Controls*, IMF Staff Papers, Vol. 42, September, pp. 517–51..

International Monetary Fund (1999a), 'Comments on the Reports on the International Financial Architecture', International Monetary Fund, Washington, DC, August.

International Monetary Fund (1999b), 'Progress in Strengthening the Architecture of the International Financial System', International Monetary Fund, Washington, DC, 5 September.

International Monetary Fund (1999c), 'The IMF's Response to the Asian Crisis', IMF paper, External Relations Depatment of the International Monetary Fund, Washington, DC, 17 January.

International Monetary Fund, *World Economic Outlook*, December 1997, May 1998, September 1998, December 1998, April 1999 (electronic copy), International Monetary Fund, Washington, DC.

Johnston, B. and Tamirisa, N, (1998), '*Why Do Countries Use Capital Controls?* IMF Working Paper WP/98/181, International Monetary Fund, Washington, DC, December.

Krueger, A. (1998), 'Whither the World Bank and the IMF?' *Journal of Economic Literature*, Vol. 36, December, pp. 1983–2020.

Laban, R. and Felipe Larrain (1997), 'Can a Liberalisation of Capital Outflows Increase Net Capital Inflows?', *Journal of International Money and Finance*, Vol. 16, June, pp. 415–31.

Lane, T. (1999), 'The Asian Financial Crisis: What Have We Learned?', *Finance and Development*, Vol. 36, No. 3, September.

Le Fort, Guillermo and Budnevich, C. (1996), 'Capital Account Regulation and Macro-economic Policy: Two Latin American Experiences', The Jerome Levy Economics Institute of Bard College, *Working Paper No. 162*, Washington: The Jerome Levy Economics Institute of Bard College

Masson, P. R. and Mussa, M. (1997), *The Role of the IMF: Financing and Its Interaction with Adjustment and Surveillance*, Pamphlet Series No. 50, International Monetary Fund, Washington, DC.

Ministry of Finance (Japan) (1998), 'Internationalization of the Yen – Interim Report', 12 November.

Miyazawa, K. (1998), 'Towards a New Financial Architecture', Speech by Mr Kiichi Miyazawa at the Foreign Correspondents Club of Japan, 15 December.

Radelet, S. and Sachs, J. (1998), 'The East Asian Financial Crisis: Diagnosis, Remedies, Prospects', Harvard Institute for International Development, 20 April.

Rodrik, D. (1997), 'Has Globalization Gone Too Far?', Institute for International Economics, Washington, DC.

Rodrik, Dani (1998), 'Who Needs Capital Account Convertibility?' in Peter Kenen (ed.), *Should IMF Pursue Capital Account Convertibility?*, Essays in International Finance Section, No. 207, Department of Economics, Princeton University, May.

Rohwer, J. (1998), 'Taiwan's Secret Weapon', *Fortune*, 26 October.

Roubini, N. (1998a), 'The Case Against Currency Boards: Debunking 10 Myths about the Benefits of Currency Boards', Asia Crisis Web Homepage at *www.stern.nyu.edu/ ~nroubini/asia/CurrencyBoardsRoubini.html*.

Roubini, N. (1998b), 'An Introduction to Open Economy Macroeconomics, Currency Crisis and the Asian Crisis', Asia Crisis Web Homepage at *www.stern.nyu.edu/~nroubini/ NOTES/intromacro.html*.

Rubin, R. (1998), 'Strengthening the Architecture of the International Financial System', Remarks from Office of Public Affairs, Treasury, 14 April.

Sachs, J. (1997a), 'IMF Orthodoxy Isn't What Southeast Asia Needs', *International Herald Tribune*, 6 November.

Sachs, J. (1997b), 'International Monetary Failure', *Time Magazine*, 8 December.

Sachs, J. (1997c), 'IMF is a Power Unto Itself', *Financial Times*, 11 December.

Shinohara, H. (1999), 'On The Asian Monetary Fund', Japan Institute for International Monetary Affairs, *IIMA Newsletter*, No. 4, 31 March, pp. 13–24.

Stiglitz, J. (1998), 'The Role of International Financial Institutions in the Current Global Economy', Address to the Chicago Council on Foreign Relations, Chicago, 27 February.

Tobin, J. (1978), 'A Proposal for International Monetary Reform', *Eastern Economic Journal*, No. 4, pp. 53–9.

PART III

IN SEARCH OF AN EXCHANGE RATE REGIME

6 PRACTISING EXCHANGE RATE FLEXIBILITY

Olivier Davanne and Pierre Jacquet

6.1 INTRODUCTION

In the wake of the severe currency crises that have hit the world economy since the early 1990s, the debate between exchange rate floaters and fixers has, at least temporarily, narrowed down to a few options. Problems in emerging markets have clearly exposed the costs of excessive exchange rate rigidity. Similarly, in industrial countries experience with the European monetary system has led to the obvious conclusion, in line with Mundell's trilemma, that fixed but adjustable exchange rate systems cannot be viable without effective capital controls. Over the last few years, a general consensus has emerged on how to manage the international monetary system. Specifically, countries face a limited choice of exchange rate policy options:

- Most large countries, including the most advanced emerging countries, embrace floating, with occasional ad hoc interventions, whether coordinated or not;
- Fixed exchange rate regimes should be ruled out, unless they take the extreme form of currency boards or full monetary union (which includes dollarization, that is, adopting a foreign currency as the only legal tender, and the type of multilateral, cooperative monetary union put in place by the European Union);
- Fixed but adjustable exchange rates may remain an option for poorer, less developed countries, under the condition that they be backed by capital controls.

In this chapter, we review these options and argue that, although it marks indisputable progress as compared to earlier practices, the above menu is incomplete, unnecessarily restrictive and can and should be substantially improved. Our main point is that the consensus rightly prescribes exchange rate flexibility but does not address the central question of how to practise it. In our discussion, we shall explore why and how G-3 countries and emerging markets should monitor and manage exchange rate flexibility. Section 6.2 discusses the *raison d'être* of the consensus and reviews its main options. The following two sections explore ways to manage exchange rate flexibility usefully through a system of adjustable reference parities in emerging markets and through a mechanism of exchange rate monitoring in countries with a floating currency, especially in the G-3. Section 6.5 discusses institutional implications and the role of the G-7 and of the International Monetary Fund (IMF) as far as the surveillance of markets and economic policies are concerned. A final section summarizes our conclusions and recommendations.

6.2 THE CONSENSUS REVISITED

Recent experience has vindicated the inconsistency triangle originally exposed by Mundell (1968) between free capital mobility, fixed exchange rates and national monetary policy autonomy. As a result, there has been a clear, consensual move away from fixed exchange rates and, mostly, towards flexibility. The option of resorting to capital controls to back exchange rate stability does not receive much support. It is largely ruled out for industrial countries. There is, as far emerging markets are concerned, a crucial distinction between controls on capital outflows, which receive little support, and controls on capital inflows which seem more appropriate in view of the difficulties, in these countries, of managing large inflows of capital from abroad, and the risk of their reversal. Except in less developed countries, capital controls are not seen in the current consensus as a desirable ingredient of exchange rate regimes.

In this section, we first document the demise of fixed rates, before turning to some issues raised by exchange rate flexibility. We then discuss the alternative route of renouncing monetary sovereignty. While Europe was able to launch the European monetary union (EMU), this is not a likely option for other industrial countries for the time being; but some economists today argue that currency boards are the most attractive option for many developing countries.

The end of fixed rates

The crises of the 1990s have highlighted several difficulties with fixed exchange rates, especially when they are rigidly managed. First, the 1992–3 crisis of the exchange rate mechanism of the European monetary system (EMS) illustrated the role of speculation. As major European countries gradually dismantled remaining capital controls, the EMS became vulnerable to speculative capital flows. As long as the *de facto* alignment of weak currency countries' monetary policies with that of the Bundesbank was deemed to be credible, notably anchored on the prospect of ultimate monetary union, the EMS remained stable. Indeed, it exhibited remarkable stability between 1987 and 1992.'The Danish 'no' to the referendum about monetary union membership in the spring of 1999, however, followed by France's clear lack of enthusiasm in the September referendum, together with legitimate questioning about the relevance of German monetary policy for countries confronted with recessionary forces and high interest rates, brutally restored uncertainty about the final outcome (EMU). It also unleashed the triangular inconsistency, opening a period of speculative attacks on weaker EMS currencies, and leading to the eventual widening of fluctuation margins from 2.25 per cent to 15 per cent around the central parity on 2 August 1993.

The EMS crisis brought home one of the major implications of capital mobility, namely the role of private-sector expectations. In this case, there was a presumption that, in the face of increased economic hardship, monetary authorities would find it difficult to stick to their preferred policy – shadowing the Bundesbank – and would sooner or later succumb to the option of auto-nomous behaviour. This belief was enough to feed speculation, even against currencies that were clearly not blatantly misaligned. In a world of free capital mobility, fixing the exchange rates invites pure speculation. Instead of assessing the current fundamentals, speculators speculate about the sustainability of current policies; they can also anticipate that monetary authorities might give up when faced with the costs of fighting speculation. A speculative attack then becomes self-fulfilling.

Second, crises in emerging countries also contributed to the disqualification of fixed exchange rate systems (even when they allow for readjustments) or various forms of nominal anchoring (for example, through a fixed rate of monthly devaluation, chosen to less than compensate for the inflation differential with the anchor currency). These crises, from Mexico to Thailand, have illustrated the costs of real exchange rate overvaluation and the difficulty of reacting in time with an appropriate nominal devaluation before a speculative crisis plays havoc with the currency and the financial system. In countries where the exchange rate is used as an anchor to help reduce inflation, real overvaluation may be initially helpful as a constraining force, but it rapidly becomes a problem. Fixed exchange rates sooner or later turn into a credibility contest between monetary authorities and markets; short of timely parity changes, they lead to serious misalignments, finally setting the stage for speculative crises and devaluations. But timely parity changes cannot happen: so much credibility is staked on defending the parity that no government is ever willing to adjust it early enough lest it be interpreted as a breach of resolve. Thailand, Mexico or the UK before September 1992,[1] among others, provide examples of this recurrent difficulty.

[1] Although, in the exchange rate mechanism of the EMS, a decision to devalue the pound would have had to be a collective one and not just a British one.

The costs of preventing necessary exchange rate adjustments from taking place can be enormous. Real overvaluation helps import disinflation; but it is costly, unless it is wisely used as a subsidy to capital imports, speeding up development (as Spain did after joining the European Union) and translating into productivity gains that can alleviate the loss of competitiveness. But even then, the accumulated misalignment must be corrected at some point, and correction never comes smoothly.

This is not the only problem with fixed exchange rates. They also create moral hazard to the extent that investors wrongly live under the illusion that there is no exchange rate risk, and invest excessive amounts in consequence. In a context of high capital mobility, countries carelessly pile up short-term foreign debt denominated in hard currency. If and when the domestic currency becomes overvalued, the sheer size of foreign currency denominated liabilities will play against a timely devaluation. But, eventually, the currency will have to be devalued and the debt burden rockets. A solution to this moral hazard could be found in a strict monitoring of the country's financial markets and economic policies by the international community, notably the IMF. But exchange rate rigidity is a strong impediment to effective monitoring, as was amply illustrated in the case of Mexico in 1993, Thailand in 1997 and Brazil in 1998. A timely, critical assessment of national policies would interfere with the credibility of the exchange rate target and would require a hefty risk premium to compensate for a risk of devaluation, thus contributing to economic duress and validating the initial critiques. As a result, IMF officials refrain from overtly critical assessments, both through actual pressures and through self-restraint. Effective monitoring requires flexibility.

One of the welcome features of the current consensus is that fixed rate regimes have given way to increased flexibility. At the same time, there is a broad agreement that free float is not the best option. The consensus therefore recognizes the challenges of exchange rate flexibility, even though it has remained remarkably silent on how to address them.

The challenges of flexibility

Floating carries major defects. In developing countries, the exchange rate is a crucial price. Floating rates leave policy-makers without an indicator and a constraint and economic agents without any external anchor to their expectations. In countries which lack a strong institutional policy base, namely many developing countries, the option of anchoring the domestic economic policy on an internal anchor, such as an inflation target and central bank independence, simply does not exist, or is not credible. In such countries, floating accommodates the lack of policy discipline, but also by this very token makes it possible, thus maintaining the country in a sort of self-sustained bad policy trap.[2] Floating therefore does little to contribute to develop policy proficiency and can even help sustain inappropriate policies. This is one of the reasons why many developing countries resorted to nominal exchange rate anchoring in the 1980s. Now that the dangers of regimes with nominal exchange rate anchors, notwithstanding their contribution to disinflation, have been largely exposed, there is a need to devise a system that could combine the benefits of the nominal anchor and the requirements of flexibility. Free float, obviously, is not such a suitable system for countries in which the institutional policy base is lacking.

Two further aspects deserve emphasis. First, a floating exchange rate leaves developing countries with unclear relative price signals that cannot but be detrimental to investment and development. For small, open developing countries that necessarily rely a lot on foreign trade and savings, flexible exchange rates are not an attractive option. Even for the larger ones, flexible rates expose them to wide swings in their real exchange rates and can bring undue costs to their economy, even if it is properly managed at the domestic level. Second, exchange rate instability in emerging countries can have a very negative and lasting impact on the availability of external finance. There is a need to compensate, with a potentially hefty risk premium, foreign investors or local investors who rely on foreign finance for an increased exchange rate risk. Overall, the cost of capital and the level of investment are likely to be severely affected in emerging countries that do not try to limit exchange rate volatility.

In the more developed regions, including industrial countries and major emerging countries, the consensus rightly points out that what ultimately matters is the quality and credibility of domestic policies. Inflation targets and independent central banks are supposed to do more to stabilize exchange rates than any set of exchange rate policies. But even there, two factors also argue for still managing floating. First, as discussed below, foreign exchange markets are not efficient, exchange rates do not reflect fundamentals and there will be excessive nominal and real exchange rate volatility[3] with potentially high costs for resource allocation due to erroneous signals even if national economic policies are sound. Unanticipated exchange rate movements abruptly change the conditions of price competition. This uncertainty may affect trade and investment decisions and lead to substantial resource misallocation.

Second, excessive fluctuations of the exchange rates of key currencies play

---

[2] While fixed exchange rates involve some moral hazard, one could also say that floating rates involve moral hazard – albeit of a different sort – since they provide insurance against bad policies. The response to moral hazard is neither in fixed nor in floating rates, but in a mixture of flexibility and monitoring.

[3] The overvaluation of the US dollar in 1984 and the first months of 1985 is a case in point.

havoc with economic and financial stability worldwide.[4] Preventing such fluctuations should be seen as an international public good. This suggests that the management of key exchange rates should be considered an important objective for multilateral action. Due to the nth-currency problem (with n currencies, there are n-1 exchange rates), if all countries pursue their own exchange rate objective in an uncoordinated fashion, the chance is that conflict and instability will result. Such lack of coordination opens the door to beggar-thy-neighbour policies, actual or imaginary, that may bear on the politics of international trade and investment and lead to protectionist pressures. Floating between major currencies also helps maintain the consistency between internationally uncoordinated economic policies; but it makes the lack of coordination more palatable, thus implicitly increasing the difficulty of such coordination and leading to a lesser perception of its usefulness. It is hardly appropriate, as a policy response, for a globalizing world that calls for increased coordination. Our central point here is that managing the float is a problem of coordination, and that does not make it any simpler.

These defects of floating exchange rates substantiate the case for more formal exchange rate arrangements, such as target zones, between major industrial countries. As a result, some leading economists have recently advocated the radical option of a renunciation of monetary sovereignty, either through a currency board (see Dornbusch (1999)) or through the dollarization of the economy (see the debate between Hausmann (1999) and Sachs and Larrain (1999) on the merits and problems of dollarization). We now turn to a brief discussion of these options.

Is monetary sovereignty still relevant?

The option of unilaterally abandoning monetary sovereignty cannot be seriously envisioned for developed economies. It could not be accepted politically, and it would not make much sense economically in countries that have the necessary institutions for conducting monetary policy and have to face idiosyncratic shocks. Monetary union, as a scheme through which countries do not abandon sovereignty but exert it at a higher level by sharing it, makes more sense, although it is open to the criticisms implied by the literature on optimum currency areas. But, for political reasons as well, the option is not open to the G-3 countries. The success of the EMU was based on a very specific set of political characteristics, and crowned a process that had evolved over three decades. EMU may expand over time, but hardly provides a reproducible model for the rest of the world.

---

[4] Some even see in the fluctuations of the US dollar/yen exchange rate the major factor behind the Asian crisis. See McKinnon (1998).

Various proposals for the setting up of target zones between major industrial countries have attracted attention and support as useful blueprints to manage exchange rates. Most of them, however, tend to ignore the constraint of political feasibility. If the target is left unspecified and the band too large, the target zone by itself is akin to floating and gives little indication about exchange rate management. In other variants, monetary authorities have to stake their credibility to a specific, visible commitment. The consensus view does not support the ambitious proposals for hard bands, because by making the commitments explicit and by staking the government resolve to identifiable parity references and fluctuation bands, they sooner or later come down to a credibility contest between governments and markets. Hard bands require a strict commitment by governments to maintain exchange rates within agreed margins around a specified parity. They are vulnerable to the weakness exposed by the EMS crisis and require a very tight and formalized cooperation of monetary policies. The time is not ripe to harness the kind of political support that would be needed for such a scheme to emerge. Hence, the consensual conclusion for G-3 countries is that the best that can happen is more of the same – namely, floating occasionally managed in a coordinated or uncoordinated way through interventions or, rarely, through ad hoc coordination. We share the consensus reservations with hard bands, but we also think that there is more to target zones than the hard band version (see section 6.5).

The choice is greater for developing countries. Here, the case for currency boards may look straightforward: capital mobility requires monetary policy credibility if the exchange rate is to remain stable. There is simply not enough institutional capacity in developing countries to provide the necessary credibility. Hence, it is worthwhile for them to abandon the pretence of autonomous policy-making and to rely instead on the credibility of foreign monetary policy. This leads to a substantial decline in the interest rate premium. The objection that foreign monetary policy may not be adapted to domestic circumstances is not convincing, because the lack of institutional maturity suggests that domestic monetary policy is not up to the task anyhow, and this is sanctioned on capital markets by hefty risk premiums.

While currency boards may work for some time in some countries (e.g. Argentina, Estonia and others), they have inevitably imposed high costs and forced painful adjustment on banking sectors as lax domestic monetary policy was suddenly replaced by the binding constraint of foreign monetary policy. The important point is that a condition for currency boards to be successful and promote economic development is that financial restructuring and institution-building take place. But as institutions strengthen, this may change the perception of the cost/benefit analysis of the currency board and lead to questions about the credibility of the commitment to maintain it over time. Currency boards should therefore be regarded as useful, transitory devices or, alternatively, as intermediate steps towards full monetary union with outside partners. For example, some east European countries might try to anticipate EMU membership by setting up a currency board with Euroland. Premiums still occasionally imposed on the Argentinian peso demonstrate that the credibility of the currency board is not perfect. For a country such as Brazil, one wonders how any move towards a currency board could be made credible. Sooner or later, even currency boards are bound to face a severe test of credibility: as long as the currency exists, its value can change and speculation can develop. In our view, notwithstanding their possible transitory benefits and their role as possible intermediate steps towards full monetary integration, currency boards do not bring any systemic relief to the defects of excessive rigidity. On the contrary; they are but a fixed exchange rate system pushed to the limit, a huge gamble with uncertain long-term benefits, an invitation to ultimate brinkmanship both from monetary authorities and from market speculators.

Beyond the consensus

What we called the consensus thus leaves two major questions without an answer. First, how should a floating regime, if and when adopted by emerging countries, be managed? In the current consensus view, managed floating may well be for many the preferred option. But without a blueprint, the policy choice has little operational content. This is a central issue for countries looking at effective development strategies and in need of an external anchor to stimulate domestic change, institutional building and sound economic policy-making. The exchange rate regime matters in a very fundamental way; mistakes can be responsible for very costly setbacks.

Second, how should the double issue involved in floating among G-3 countries, namely excess exchange rate volatility and insufficient economic policy coordination, be addressed? It is useful to highlight the shortcomings of the current international macroeconomic environment.

Floating has left major countries without any collective discipline in terms of macroeconomic policy interaction – let alone coordination. Partly as a result, the sustainability of current exchange rates is very much in doubt for the dollar, the yen and the euro. The recovery in Europe, in Japan, in Asia, the fate of the bubble in Wall Street, are vulnerable to pronounced exchange rate instability. It is time to care about an effective monitoring of exchange rate movements. It will not solve the coordination problem, but it will raise awareness that the domestic economic policies of G-3 countries are tightly interdependent and that the non-cooperative equilibrium can and should be improved upon.

Both for emerging markets and for industrial countries, we believe that the menu of options included in the consensus view is too limited and that there is room for significant improvement, still taking on board the recent and valuable insights on which the consensus is based. For emerging markets, we will argue that there is a fourth option to the exchange rate problem that could be attractive to some countries. It is possible to tie monetary policy through a sort of feedback rule that would make a system of adjustable reference parities credible and viable. For G-3 countries, we believe that more research on fundamentals and on equilibrium exchange rates, if properly conducted and used as a basis for debate and interaction between monetary authorities and the markets, can provide the basis for a mechanism of monitoring that could considerably help stabilize expectations in line with fundamentals. This is a first, modest but promising step towards managing G-3 exchange rate flexibility. The following sections develop these ideas.[5]

6.3 THE FOURTH OPTION

As we have seen, the international consensus is strongly critical of the fixed-but-adjustable exchange rate regimes that played such a prominent role in the financial crises of the 1990s. However, one can argue that recent problems had more to do with the way these systems were managed than with the stability of exchange rates *per se*.

Exchange rate crises in the 1990s, both within the EMS and in developing nations, have clearly sanctioned the failure of rigid, automatic policies used to ward off speculation, backed by the total use of exchange rate reserves and a massive increase in interest rates that could backfire into a recession. These policies are obviously unconvincing and fail to restore confidence in currencies, for speculators doubt their effectiveness and sustainability. They can even spell disaster when the measures fail (no more exchange reserves, loss of all monetary or even political credibility). As a result, it is very difficult in such conditions to prevent an exchange rate adjustment from happening under a speculative attack.

Elastic flexibility as an antidote against speculation

There are subtler and more effective ways to manage such systems and preserve exchange rate stability, however. The French exchange rate policy from summer 1993 to spring 1995 provides an interesting example of what could be called an elastic policy.

After the widening of the fluctuations margins of the EMS exchange rate mechanism on 2 August 1993, the French government, against market expectations, decided not to use the monetary policy autonomy thus restored to

---

[5] Our proposals here expand on Bergsten, Davanne and Jacquet (1999).

promote growth as a priority. Indirectly, through a series of coded messages, monetary authorities informed markets that French interest rates would be maintained significantly above German ones so long as the franc–Deutschmark parity did not return to the EMS central rate. The interest rate policy was thus aligned with that of Germany, maintaining a stable and reasonable risk premium destined to encourage the purchase of francs. This monetary policy stance provided the kind of signal that markets prompt in questioning the authorities' exchange rate commitments were ready to heed, and was thus able to pull the franc back up to its pivotal rate within the EMS as early as late 1993. As a result, French monetary policy entered a period of calm after 12 months (September 1992 to August 1993) of recurrent currency crises.

This elastic policy, terminated in spring 1995, was a remarkable success in terms of exchange rate management.[6] It succeeded because it responded to a so-called second-generation currency crisis (see Eichengreen, Rose and Wyplosz (1994) for a description). The market did not question the medium- or long-term sustainability of the franc to Deutschmark parity, but wondered whether the French authorities could continue to pay for the costs in the short term. The remarkable results of European central banks' post-1993 approach to exchange rate management has been highlighted by Bartoloni and Prati (1998). Their analysis 'points to the usefulness of this policy for other countries that target their exchange rates'. One of the lessons of this whole experience is that even sustainable parities may have to be defended against markets' speculation and that defence, if properly orchestrated, can be successful.

Obviously, there were many specific factors behind the success of the elastic policy in the French case. Economic fundamentals were much stronger than in emerging countries, and EMU prospects substantially enhanced the credibility of the French commitment in favour of stable exchange rates. Notwithstanding these differences, however, we believe that this example has a much broader significance and serves to illustrate some very general lessons on the feasibility and effective way of preserving relative exchange rate stability under fire from the markets. In particular, two distinct features of the elastic policy stand out in comparison with the traditional, unsuccessful approach to maintain exchange rate stability.

First of all, when confronting downward exchange rate pressure, authorities should assess whether the parity that comes under attack is really sustainable. If it was managed correctly in the past, there is in principle no reason for questioning it, unless a current, new economic shock calls for a change. Any problem with sustainability, however, calls for timely readjustments. This is a major departure from current practices, in which monetary authorities stake so

---

[6] Of course, this does not address the question of whether the priority given to the exchange rate was appropriate in the first place, in a period (summer 1993) marked by hesitant growth and rising unemployment.

much in preserving the exchange rate target that they fail to take due and timely action with respect to necessary readjustments.

Second, a gradual, feedback-based, defence mechanism needs to be used to defend the sustainable parity. What we described as the elastic policy consists in defending the parity in a flexible way (no hikes in interest rates at unbearable levels, protection of exchange rate reserves), by resorting to something like the French mechanism as soon as the exchange rate has clearly overshot its target.[7] Interest rates can be pegged transparently to foreign rates, augmented with a significant and well-defined risk premium that takes into account the characteristics of the country concerned. This risk premium is maintained or increased so long as the currency has not regained its target. If necessary, this defence mechanism can be backed by interventions on the exchange market. Now, there are obviously costs to the economy, in terms of interest rates that end up being higher than they should be, but these costs are due to market – rather than policy – failure, and giving in would result in letting the currency depreciate from a sustainable, equilibrium level, thus accepting both costly misalignment and uncertainty.

A new class of fixed-but-adjustable rates: adjustable reference parities

Such a system, which we have called a system of adjustable reference parities (see Davanne (1998) and Bergsten, Davanne and Jacquet (1999)), is clearly a member of the fixed-but-adjustable family of exchange rate regimes (when exchange rates are allowed to fluctuate around a reference parity itself commonly subject to adjustment). As analysed above, however, such a system avoids all the drawbacks of its more traditional cousins, which lack flexibility and have failed so far. Here, two layers of flexibility deserve discussion: the nature and management of the reference parity, and the flexible response of monetary policy when the exchange rate departs from its reference parity.

A reference parity defined as a basket

How to choose the reference parity? A parity of reference must imperatively be defined as a basket of currencies that reflects the structure of external trade. The latter should at least include dollars, euros and yens.[8] One of the factors that triggered the Asian crisis was the loss of competitiveness for countries that had pegged their currencies to the single dollar between 1996 and 1997, a period during which the dollar had dramatically appreciated against the yen.

---

[7] For example, if the currency shifts more than 2% below its target.
[8] We can also imagine that the IMF might build representative indexes on currencies of emerging nations that could be taken into account in the baskets of reference, next to the US dollar, the euro and the yen.

We insisted earlier, and this is one aspect of flexibility, that parity readjustments are not ruled out by definition and should even be treated in a routine way. The possibility of a readjustment gives the market a clear incentive to monitor closely the fundamental economic position of the country and the compatibility of the current exchange rate with balanced economic growth in the medium to long term. Notwithstanding occasional changes, the reference parity should be adjusted as a flexible crawling peg, and the gradual devaluation – or revaluation – should be known in advance. The goal would be to maintain the parity of reference at sustainable middle- and long-term levels.[9]

Defining the exact terms for adjustment should be one of the key issues discussed at the IMF article IV annual examination. Section 6.5 examines general institutional issues and in particular to the IMF's role with regard to exchange rate policies.

A flexible, but price-stability-oriented, monetary policy response

We emphasized above that the defence of a parity judged as sustainable should be very progressive in order to avoid the trap of excessively high interest rates and the loss of international reserves.

But there is a caveat: the capacity to tighten up the monetary conditions during economic overheating could be severely curtailed if stabilizing exchange rates were to become too strong a priority. An incipient rise in interest rates is liable to lead to heavy capital inflows, which substantially limits the extent to which interest rates can rise, except for huge sterilized interventions in the foreign exchange market. In such circumstances, the appropriate response may be to let the currency appreciate against the reference parity. Should economic growth be too strong, a reference-parity-based exchange rate policy should not deter authorities from determining interest rates and keeping a lid on inflation. The optimal response in terms of currency appreciation will crucially depend on the economic context.

For example, if the risk of overheating is due to household consumption – the Mexican situation in the early 1990s – the best and most obvious response is a tighter fiscal policy that avoids both an increase in interest rates and an exchange rate appreciation. The latter would penalize the export sector even though it is not the source of the current difficulties and would contribute to an

---

[9] Such a crawling adjustment policy does not broaden margins for manoeuvre for monetary policy. Planning a future exchange rate devaluation cannot be an effective response when faced with an economic slowdown. The favourable effect on competitiveness is deferred, while interest rates should progress initially so as to convince investors to keep a given currency despite a depreciating trend. In a first stage, monetary conditions are tightened. The export sector can, however, react favourably by anticipating the positive impact of the coming depreciation.

even greater increase in foreign debt. In many cases, however, fiscal policies cannot be used to address the source of the imbalance, and an interest rate rise and an exchange rate appreciation are preferable to letting inflation rise. Moreover, in such a situation, targeted controls on capital inflows, such as the by now famous Chilean tax, can be a useful contribution.

An attractive option for emerging countries

Which countries should use the fourth option of adjustable reference parities? We believe that such an option makes sense for many emerging countries in view of the costs of free-floating exchange rates discussed in section 6.2. A system of adjustable reference parities is not in our view a 'one fits all' solution, but for some countries, such as Brazil, it may be considered an attractive compromise between a currency board and a free float. In some ways, this system is a refinement of the target zone framework for emerging countries discussed by Williamson (1998). The main difficulty with traditional crawling bands, however, is that, in general, monetary policy inside the band is not specified.[10] One view is that monetary policy should be used for internal stabilization as long as the currency stays inside the band. This view is fraught with problems. Unless the fluctuation margin is very wide – in which case this can practically be referred to as a flexible exchange rate – margins for manoeuvre in monetary policy should not be overestimated. If monetary authorities in emerging market countries want to use the entire fluctuation margin, without defending the central parity, market players are likely to react in advance and exchange rates could bounce up or down against the margins before authorities are even willing or able to change interest rates. Indeed, most emerging market countries using crawling bands try to stabilize their currency close to the central rate. The adjustable reference parities framework may provide the best way to do so in a credible, but flexible manner.

6.4 LEARNING HOW TO MANAGE FLOATING RATES

The last 25 years have clearly highlighted how unstable free floating rates can be. Excess volatility is a rather prevalent characteristic of asset prices, but the exchange rate market is probably one of the worst offenders in this respect.

---

[10] Svensson (1992) argues that the data available for the EMS, Nordic countries, the Bretton Woods system and the gold standard point to an actual functioning of existing real world target zones very close to managed float with a target exchange rate level defended by frequent mean-reverting intra-marginal monetary policy intervention – that is, a system that relies on the sort of elastic policy described in our text. His results suggest that more work should be devoted to formalizing policy rules in such managed floats. Work on target zones, in particular, should focus on specifying the behaviour of monetary policy inside the band.

As stressed by Blanchard (1999), there are two conceptually different kinds of bubbles in asset markets. Most real-life bubbles are a combination of these two pure types. First, investors may be grossly wrong, if judged with the benefit of hindsight, on market fundamentals. For example, they may overestimate the trend in firms' profits, as far as the equity market is concerned or, in the foreign exchange (FX) market, the level of exchange rate that is sustainable in a long-term perspective, taking into account all the country's relevant characteristics (labour costs, productivity, savings, etc.). Second, the bubble can be speculative in the sense that investors may be broadly right on the fundamentals, but buy too high or sell too low in expectations that in the short term prices will continue to diverge from the level justified by the economic fundamentals.

The second type of bubble is made possible by the fact that a large part of the investment community does not value financial assets from models based on fundamentals. Indeed, the diversity of the methodologies used by market participants to assess future asset prices and to make decisions about their investments is well documented. In general, the economic literature opposes the chartists and the fundamentalists (see Frankel and Froot (1990)), or the noise traders and the fundamentalists (see Shleifer and Summers (1990)). Noise traders comprise all the irrational investors, including but not only, the chartists.

Obviously, second-type bubbles make it much more likely that first-type bubbles may occur. If people use valuation methodologies that take little account of the economic fundamentals, there are few incentives in the market-place for thorough research efforts since prices tend to be disconnected from these fundamentals. Without such research, views on these fundamentals can become quite naive. On a more general note, one can argue that there is a general coordination problem in financial markets: one has few incentives to find the right model and study the real fundamentals if the other participants in the market do not care. To be successful, a short-term investor has to anticipate his colleagues' moves rather than embark on his own in a thorough research effort.[11]

Overall, public authorities have an important role to play to limit the risks of these two kinds of bubble and ensure the efficient working of the financial markets (see Davanne (1999b) for an extended discussion). First, by being transparent themselves, by requiring the private sector to be transparent as well and by directly or indirectly providing the necessary economic analysis, they may help market participants to have a better grasp of the fundamentals. In other words, they have a mission as information providers. Second, public

---

[11] Obviously, Keynes' (1936) metaphor on financial markets as special beauty contests can be seen as one of the first expressions of this approach to financial markets. See Devenow and Welch (1996) for a survey of the literature on rational herding.

authorities should do their best to avoid speculative bubbles, i.e. they should encourage the use of valuation methodologies based on fundamentals and react if and when destabilizing behaviours drive prices far away from reasonable estimates of equilibrium values. Before discussing precisely what these two general orientations could mean specifically in the FX market, we need first to be more specific about what is behind the concept of economic fundamentals as far as exchange rates are concerned.

Economic fundamentals in the FX market

In the medium to long term, the real economy has the final say, and exchange rates cannot diverge for ever from what is called their long-term equilibrium, i.e. the level consistent with balanced economic growth in the long term. This long-term equilibrium is a key economic fundamental of the FX market and we will address below how it can be estimated. However, one has first to reckon that there is no reason for the exchange rate to stay permanently at its long-term equilibrium.

Two factors may justify normal fluctuations of current, actual exchange rates around the sustainable, long-term equilibrium: discrepancies in real interest rates, and risk premiums.

A positive real interest rate differential implies a real appreciation of the exchange rate relative to the long-term average. The reason is that it increases the attractiveness of investment in domestic financial assets. Such a differential can lead to a significant, albeit rational, real exchange rate appreciation. For example, if domestic real interest rates over a ten-year period are more than 1 per cent higher than abroad, the domestic exchange rate could easily be overvalued by about 10 per cent (in real terms). Over a long period the investor would earn in interest (10 x 1 per cent) what he would lose should the currency go back to the long-term exchange rate equilibrium (progressive elimination of the 10 per cent overvaluation).

As a result, monetary policy is a key determinant of the fundamental value of a currency. As forcefully explained by Dornbusch (1976) more than 20 years ago, a loose monetary policy should have a strong negative impact on a currency since, on the one hand, its medium-term equilibrium value falls (in nominal terms, owing to higher domestic prices in the future) and, on the other hand, in the short term it will fall even more (overshooting mechanism owing to lower interest rates). This is because expectations of future appreciation are needed for investors to be willing to hold the currency at lower nominal interest rates. As a result, it is simply impossible to value a currency correctly when monetary policy is erratic and there is a complete lack of visibility on future inflation and real interest rates.

An independent central bank is often a rather useful first step to give more visibility on these key fundamentals. An independent central bank with an inflation target is even better, since the inflation target makes it easier to monitor its performance. Indeed, for countries with floating exchange rates, the lack of an external anchor makes it all the more necessary to have an internal anchor.

The natural link between exchange rates and spreads in different long-term interest rates assumes perfect asset substitutability, and will in general be affected by the existence of risk premiums. These can stem either from specific barriers to capital mobility that prevent assets from being perfectly substitutable, or from different assessments of risk. For example, a nation with a large external debt may have to serve its foreign creditors a return higher than what they can get in their own country. At given interest rates, risk premiums should therefore play a crucial role in exchange rate determination. If a given currency has to serve a positive risk premium, either the interest rates must increase by the size of the premium or the exchange rate must depreciate considerably in relation to the normal rate and reach a level at which investors will anticipate a future appreciation that will compensate them for the risk. For example, if they require an additional 1 per cent return per year, their compensation over a 10-year period should be an initial currency undervaluation of about 10 per cent. Exchange rate overshooting therefore responds to both the differences between domestic and foreign interest rates and relative risk premiums.

This simple analytical framework is useful for understanding the evolution of many currencies in the foreign exchange market over the last 20 years and major shifts in exchange rates can sometimes be fully explained by substantial real interest rate differentials. For example, the long-term real interest rate differential between the United States and West Germany shifted from –6 per cent to +4 per cent between mid-1979 and early 1982, which on the basis of the previous analysis fully justifies the 100 per cent real appreciation of the dollar over that period.

In fact, the most spectacular shifts in the dollar's value, at least relative to the Deutschmark, can clearly be traced back to the reversal in the US economic policy: an over-lax monetary policy in the late 1970s, followed by the Volcker-Reagan policy mix in the early 1980s, featuring a tight, anti-inflationary monetary policy and a dramatic fiscal expansion through tax cuts and an increase in defence spending. The result was a spectacular growth in real interest rates and a brutal real appreciation of the dollar.

Most empirical work thus reveals a fairly close correlation between shifts in exchange rates and long-term real interest rate differentials for certain currencies (see Baxter (1994), Coe and Golub (1986), Davanne (1990), Sachs (1985)). Instability in exchange rates can often be traced back to vagaries in economic

Figure 6.1 Real dollar–Deutschmark exchange rate

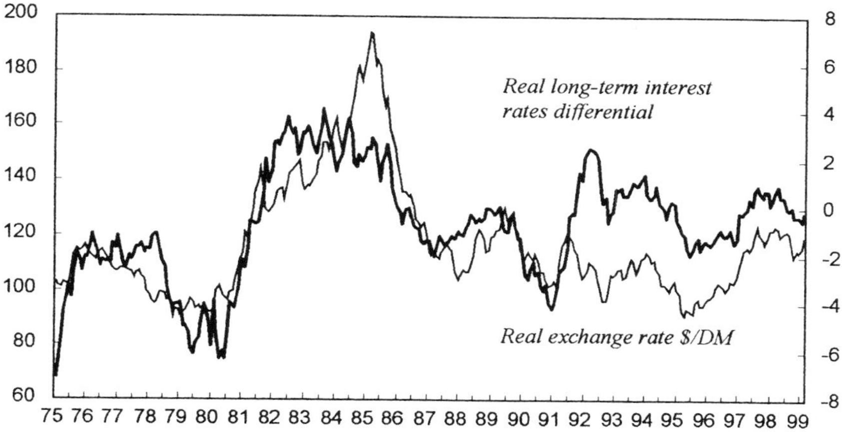

Base 100 in 1980, left-hand scale, and real interest rate differential in %, right-hand scale.

policies: an increase in inflation and an excessive drop in real interest rates (the United States in the late 1970s or France in the mid-1970s), an unbalanced policy mix and a real interest rate hike in response to an over-expansionist fiscal policy (the United States in the early 1980s or Germany in the initial phase of unification at the end of the same decade). Figure 6.1 illustrates the correlation between the dollar–Deutschmark real exchange rate and the long-term real interest rate differential between the United States and Germany (see also Blanchard (1997), Davanne (1990) and Dominguez and Frankel (1993) for similar charts used to interpret 25 years of floating exchange rates).

This correlation sometimes comes as a surprise, such has been the influence of two papers published by Meese and Rogoff (1983 and 1988). They maintained that exchange rates did not obey stable economic logic and followed what is referred to as a random walk. These papers are still quite influential and are among the most quoted in the exchange rate literature (see, for example, Svensson (1992), which quotes Meese and Rogoff (1983) three times), despite the fact that they did not correctly test the existence of a strong relation for some currencies between real long-term interest rates and exchange rates. The 1983 paper relied on short-term interest rates rather than long-term rates and in the 1988 paper real long-term rates were calculated on the basis of the inflation rate of the last three months (annualized), which introduced a lot of noise into the data.[12]

[12] In principle, real long-term interest rates should be estimated using the inflation expected by investors over the forthcoming ten years. As a proxy, the chart uses the observed inflation differential over the last 12 months.

In any case, while the correlation is generally fairly strong, one has to reckon that a rational economic analysis based on interest rate differentials cannot account for all periods of instability. Thus, the sudden surge in the value of the US dollar in terms of European currencies in late 1984 and early 1985 remains somewhat mysterious, as does its drop in late 1987 or its relative weakness in 1993–6 (see Figure 6.1).[13]

The dollar peak from late 1984 to February 1985 resembles a speculative bubble (see Krugman (1989)). As for the recent period, shifts in risk premiums for American assets hardly explain the movements of the US currency: the ever-rising external debt constitutes a weakening trend factor for the dollar. But the 1993–6 dollar weakness was followed by a partial recovery at the end of the decade, despite the fact that the American trade deficit continued to surge.

Figure 6.1 should not be taken as an illustration that markets behave rationally most of the time and that private investors keep their eyes on fundamentals. Not only have excessive hikes or drops been recorded at times, but central banks have often had to intervene in order to stem panic situations. The market's relative apparent rationality is hardly a coincidence: it is in large part due to the vigilance of major industrialized nations. For example, in 1985 the dollar drop was accelerated by the intervention of central banks in the wake of the Plaza Agreement; in 1987 it was stabilized thanks to interventions as part of the Louvre accord; and in 1994 it was once again stabilized as the result of interventions. The role of central banks has been even more important in the case of the dollar–yen rate, where major misalignments have been reduced only after massive foreign exchange interventions (notably over the 1995–8 period).

It is now known that sterilized interventions proved to be very effective when properly orchestrated,[14] especially when they were undertaken jointly. There are a number of episodes where coordinated, sterilized interventions helped stabilize exchange rates in the past, but they often came very late, without a systematic process that could help generate them.[15] Despite some success in the past, there

[13] See also the synthesis by the IMF (1998) on links between the economic cycle, interest rates and exchange rates, in *World Economic Outlook,* May 1998, chapter 3, 'The Business Cycle, International Linkages and Exchange Rates'.

[14] See Dominguez (1990), Catte et al. (1994) and Dominguez and Frankel (1993). Dominguez and Frankel offer some convincing evidence on the efficiency of most past coordinated interventions. They also clearly describe the various channels by which sterilized interventions can play a role: signalling on future monetary policy shifts; portfolio effect if foreign and domestic bonds are imperfect substitutes for each other from an investor perspective; bursting of a speculative bubble.

[15] However, over the last 15 years, interventions were decided only when governments reached the conclusion that the market was not fully reflecting the underlying 'economic fundamentals'. Interventions would probably have proved much less efficient if they had been used in a systematic manner without due considerations for the conditions prevailing in the market. Indeed, the Jurgensen report (1983), submitted to the G-7 summit at

is a clear lack of an international standard defining how the FX market should be monitored and when interventions should be decided. We now discuss some general guidelines before turning our attention, in section 6.5, to institutional issues, i.e. how countries could collaborate together and with the IMF.

Monitoring the FX market

Efficient monitoring of the FX market requires the explicit assessment of the position of various currencies on the basis of the three key fundamental variables we have just highlighted: their long-term equilibrium value, the long-term real interest rate, and risks premium differentials. More specifically, surveillance of the FX market is a two-step process.

(a) Step 1: Assessing how far currencies are from a reasonable estimate of their long-run equilibrium

An abundant literature exists on this subject. The dominant approach used in estimating a long-term exchange rate equilibrium (see IMF (1998), Williamson (1994) and Wren-Lewis and Driver (1998)) is first to define a sustainable trade balance for the medium to long term, and then to identify the level of competitiveness that enables the trade balance to reach its sustainable level.

The definition of a sustainable trade balance over the medium term will depend on the nature of the external financing constraint faced by the country. For a country without external financial constraints, the sustainable value is determined by the level of net savings (domestic savings minus domestic investment) that the country generates on a path of balanced growth (full employment and sustainable public debt).[16] For a country facing an external financial constraint, the sustainable trade (current account) balance is equal to the availability of funds.

Once the sustainable trade balance has been defined, the equilibrium real exchange rate is generally derived using external trade equations that link foreign trade, domestic demand and external competitiveness. Interestingly, however, this process can lead to long-term equilibrium real exchange rate estimates that are rather far from traditional competitiveness indicators such as relative prices (purchasing power parities (PPP) estimated by the Organization for Economic Coordination and Development (OECD), for instance), relative labour costs or

---

Williamsburg in 1983, concluded that the effects of sterilized interventions could at most be minor and transitory, but the working group members were probably at that time influenced by their experience with badly devised interventions.

[16] The central open economy national accounting identity states that net savings equal the current account balance. This can also be seen from the balance-of-payments identity. The current account equals net capital outflows, that is the net acquisition of foreign assets, identically equivalent to net national savings.

average long-term real exchange rates. For example, as far as the euro–dollar rate is concerned, most estimates put the long-term equilibrium between 1.20 and 1.30 dollars per euro, while the OECD puts the PPP rate at 1.06 (1998 figures) and most other traditional indicators on costs and prices put the normal rate at around one dollar per euro (see Borowski and Couharde (1999)).

As far as the currencies of major industrialized countries are concerned, the main explanation for such discrepancy rests in the very low price elasticity of trade volumes typically produced by traditional econometric trade equations. A large adjustment in relative prices is therefore necessary to engineer any required change in the volume of exports and imports. As far as the dollar is concerned, many observers relying on traditional trade equations believe that the dollar will have to become very weak, both relative to the euro and the yen, if the United States is to cut down its external deficit to a sustainable level in the medium to long term.

But the very low price elasticity found in authoritative empirical studies is somewhat puzzling, as thin export margins suggest a high degree of competition in most international markets. Moreover, export price elasticities below 1 for some countries are almost impossible to believe since they mean that on average exporters can raise their foreign sales in value terms simply by increasing their prices to whatever level they want. Common sense seems to point in the direction of much higher price elasticities in a medium- to long-term perspective, and thus the need for less currency depreciation in countries with balance-of-payments problems. This suggests that applied economic research on what determines international trade volumes needs to be further encouraged and developed.[17]

As a result, while real equilibrium exchange rate quantification has made important headway in the recent past, one should probably not completely forget, for the time being, traditional competitiveness indicators based on costs and prices.

(b) Step 2: Discussing whether or not cyclical conditions and interest rates in various countries justify, from an investor perspective, the degree of undervaluation of some currencies

In well-functioning financial markets, countries where economic activity is particularly weak should have lower real long-term interest rates and a relatively weak exchange rate. The consistency between real long-term interest rates and real exchange rates should be closely monitored. This implies an assessment of any risk premium embedded in interest rates differentials: let us recall that a real long-term interest rate differential of 1 per cent (for 10-year maturities) in favour of the foreign country and an adverse risk premium of 1 per cent against

---

[17] Indeed, the power of traditional econometric tests to estimate the long-term price elasticities of exports seems rather weak and other approaches, for example case studies, might be used.

the domestic currency imply a potential, rational real undervaluation of the domestic exchange rate of up to 20 per cent.

Estimating legitimate risk premiums is quite a difficult part of the exercise. As far as G-7 countries are concerned, especially G-3 countries, political risks and inflation risks are absent and the major source of risk premium probably resides in differences in net external positions. A country with a large net foreign debt and deficits may have to pay a premium to receive the foreign finance it needs at given exchange rates. At present, however, there is no easy way to assess whether a country is already in a situation where its foreign debt is becoming too large to be easily financed. This is especially true for the United States. There is very little detailed information on how easily supply and demands of various currencies match. In principle, it would be very useful to get more detailed insights into international investors' portfolios and expectations. There is no doubt a need for a risk premium on a currency issued by an indebted country when, on the basis of high expected returns, the average portfolio is distorted in favour of this currency.

Davanne (1999a) has looked at the way to get insights into investors' asset allocations and the level of risk premium, i.e. the expected excess return over short-term bills. For most categories of investors, there is little that can be done to collect much more information on portfolio structures. However, there is a very important exception.

International banks have developed their own internal systems for measuring market risks. They are capable of studying their exposure on various currencies, notably on the euro–dollar parity since 1 January 1999. Data regarding exposure to the main exchange rates risks could be grouped together by the bank supervisors on a monthly or quarterly basis, integrated by the Bank for International Settlements (BIS) and then circulated. Such a procedure would involve several difficulties, notably that of strictly protecting the confidentiality on individual data, but it would provide the monetary authorities and private investors with a much closer monitoring of the exchange market. Such a process already exists as far as international credit risks are concerned: the BIS and the community of bank supervisors collect data on credit to foreign counterparts and publish the aggregate results on a quarterly basis. An extension to exchange rate exposures might be conceivable.

Whatever the methodology employed, there is a need for a better monitoring of financial portfolios. The birth of the euro makes it even more necessary in order to anticipate diversification strategies and get a better grasp of the factors likely to influence a potential excess demand for euros and supply of dollars – at the level of the agreed long-term real exchange rate equilibrium. This analysis of supply and demand trends in the foreign exchange market should be an integral part of any surveillance process.

The public sphere as an expectations coordinator

We are not suggesting that this monitoring process should be confidential and univocally dedicated to the preparation of interventions in the FX market. On the contrary, we believe that it should be based on a permanent interaction with private investors and that its actual function is to make interventions unnecessary thanks to more stabilizing behaviour in the private sector.

Monitoring authorities, whoever they are (we will come back to the issue of international cooperation), should not only form a view on the three key FX market fundamentals (equilibrium exchange rates, inflation and real long-term interest rates differentials, risk premiums) but also monitor the private sector's consensus on these variables. Ideally, this dialogue will lead monitoring authorities and private investors to share a similar assessment of these fundamentals and the degree of uncertainty that inevitably surrounds any estimate.

Currently, one could argue that pure fundamental analysis does not receive the weight it deserves in the FX market. Discussions among market participants seldom focus on notions such as long-term equilibrium, risk premium or even spreads of real long-term interest rates. Indeed, there is not even a consensus about the right valuation methodology to be used. As far as bonds and equities are concerned, market investors and economists who advise them have a sound notion of the valuation model that should be used in theory (based on future profits, shifts in short-term interest rates, risk premiums). This is not the case in the FX market.

A clear quest for value by the official sector, based on a transparent methodology and a permanent dialogue with the private sector, would help focus the mind of private investors on exchange rate fundamentals. More public guidance can help trigger a virtuous circle in which it pays to look at the fundamental economic variables, and in which the exchange rate ends up being more stable and predictable because everyone in the market agrees on the valuation methodology to be used.

6.5 THE INSTITUTIONAL SETTING: THE ROLE OF THE IMF AND G-7

In the previous sections, we have argued that emerging markets had more options, with respect to exchange rate policies, than is suggested by the current consensus; we have also contended that, for the G-3 countries and countries opting for managed floating, a careful monitoring of fundamentals and of exchange market behaviour is necessary. These suggestions, however, are not directed to national governments alone. G-3 exchange rate movements and policies clearly are crucial determinants of international interdependence and relate to the wider issue of the international coordination of economic policies. Emerging markets' exchange rate policies mainly matter because the interaction between these policies and international capital mobility can lead to severe misalignments and costly crises that have implications for the banking systems worldwide and that may call for foreign financial involvement, notably through the IMF and the G-7. There are negative externalities on the rest of the world, as well as an element of moral hazard that may yet compound the costs of misdirected policies.

This discussion suggests that, as far as large countries are concerned, exchange rate management should have a multilateral dimension. The more important the currency, the bigger the multilateral concern. This section looks tentatively at ways to organize multilateral surveillance. There are a number of possible routes. Here, we build on the existing institutions already involved in surveillance and on past experience with managing exchange rates. In these tasks, the IMF and the G-7 have played prominent roles. We therefore concentrate on how they might jointly contribute to strengthening the current surveillance of exchange rates.

Our discussion does not directly address the issue of exchange rate management in the poorest developing countries. They may have a wider menu of options, as they may at less cost resort to capital controls and maintain some autonomy in domestic policy-making. They face, however, a crucial need to strengthen their economic policy institutions, and may resort to some nominal exchange rate targeting to import credibility and help build local institutions. While exchange rate mistakes in these countries (as opposed to larger, emerging markets) will have a much smaller impact on the world economy, they still can carry high costs for domestic economies. The latter should benefit from some of the principles of multilateral surveillance highlighted below. The quasi-universal nature of the IMF and of the World Bank suggests that the principles that we introduce should also be extended to the surveillance of exchange rate policies in the poorer countries.

Multilateral surveillance of emerging markets' exchange rate policies

The role of inappropriate exchange rate policies in the dynamics and severity of the recent financial crises suggests that the emerging markets' exchange rate policies are a matter for multilateral surveillance, both in normal circumstances to contribute to crisis prevention, and during balance-of-payments crises to help with crisis management. Crisis prevention calls for the international community to find ways to deter countries from following risky exchange rates policies. On the other hand, in times of crisis, it must be much more resolute in stabilizing disorderly markets and in avoiding blatant exchange rate overshooting. A currency free fall generates risks of serious contagion and of creating a vicious circle of heavier debt burden, further loss of confidence and further depreciation.

These two objectives assigned to multilateral surveillance are somewhat contradictory. A country has few incentives to follow cautious policies if it knows that it can rely on foreign support in case of trouble. Monitoring of exchange rate policies and peer pressure, however necessary, are not enough. The international community must attach some form of conditionality to its intervention as lender of last resort in order to limit moral hazard.

Monitoring

There are several reasons why the IMF should play a central role in exchange rate monitoring. First, it already has a mandate to do so and this comes naturally as part of article IV yearly consultations with individual countries. Second, the IMF has become a reservoir of economic and financial expertise. Such expertise could still be improved, but it must now be mobilized – not to dictate what countries should do, but to assess the sustainability of current exchange rate and financial variables. Third, the IMF is on the frontline to help bail out countries when there is a crisis and should therefore be very active in identifying pre-crisis situations, both in order to help prevent crises and to mitigate any moral hazard associated with the expectation that, one way or another, bail-out will occur.

As mentioned in section 6.2, a central issue in the recent crises was related to the difficulty of commenting officially on exchange rates when hinting at misalignment could precipitate an investor panic and a crisis. But this difficulty rested precisely on the excessive rigidity of exchange rate policies. When a lot of political capital has been invested in maintaining a fixed exchange rate, it is indeed hard to comment officially on that exchange rate being overvalued. Governments cannot afford any doubt in the market about their commitment to the current rate, and the IMF cannot afford to comment on sustainability. Conversely, when some exchange rate flexibility becomes a general prescription, open dialogue on the level of the exchange rate becomes possible and desirable. Hence, surveillance demands flexibility. The post-Asian crisis period is conducive to improving the efficiency of the surveillance process, not least because the costs of excessive exchange rate rigidity in emerging markets have now been blatantly exposed. A consensus has now formed on the need to preserve and manage exchange rate flexibility.[18]

---

[18] An alternative, discussed in section 6.2, is to formally 'abandon' the exchange rate, forgo national monetary policy and create a currency board. For various reasons alluded to above, however, we believe that this course is not without dangers. It should be restricted to countries looking for useful, intermediate steps to build credibility before formally entering a monetary union or before full 'dollarization', if and when an appropriate judgment has been formed about the cost/benefit trade-offs of such dramatic steps.

Crisis management

As a by-product of more flexible exchange rate policies, the international community must be much more concerned and determined to avoid exchange rate overshooting. In this context, the function of lender of last resort deserves discussion. The international community, through the IMF or the G-7, should be ready to commit a very large amount of money to avoid the panics and free falls in the exchange rate market. Panics should be interpreted as the sort of market failure that requires the intervention of the international community. There should be no confusion, however, over the role of the international community as a lender of last resort. Bringing some calm to disorderly markets may be a necessity, but lending massively to defend a rigid exchange rate is more often than not a waste of time and money. Indeed, one of the lessons of the recent exchange rate crises in emerging markets is that IMF financial assistance should not be used to artificially maintain ultimately unsustainable exchange rate policies. In general, countries should meet a number of conditions for eligibility to IMF and other international community money: (a) they should reach an agreement with the IMF on what is an appropriate level for the exchange rate in a medium-term perspective; (b) they should agree to use flexible response to defend the jointly agreed reference level;[19] (c) they should respect a number of more traditional elements of conditionality.

Conditions (a) and (b) mean that the country facing a currency crisis relies on the adjustable reference parities framework introduced in section 6.3, at least temporarily, to stabilize its currency and regain the market's confidence with the help of the international community. Overall, much progress is needed in terms of crisis management. Having learnt that defending a rigid exchange rate may be a rather futile exercise, the IMF now has to learn that free floats are not the only option for countries in the midst of a balance-of-payments crisis. Indeed, Brazil paid a huge price in terms of interest rates, and thus high interest payments on the public debt, for having first tried to defend an unsustainable exchange rate and then allowing its currency to float without enough public guidance.

Other forms of conditionality

Conditionality applies when members call on IMF resources. This is, therefore, *ex post* conditionality, attached to financial resources granted by the IMF once the problem has materialized. Traditional conditionality rests on principles of

---

[19] Like all rules, this one could suffer a few exceptions, for example when a country is faced with hyperinflation, has lost all monetary credibility and needs, at least temporarily, a very rigid external anchor. Moreover, low-income developing countries. which have generally strong capital controls and are less vulnerable to speculative pressures, are better positioned to defend strictly the jointly agreed parity.

good economic governance, as developed through theoretical understanding and experience. These include best practices of fiscal and monetary policy-making (price stability and long-term fiscal sustainability) and, since the Asian crisis, financial transparency and liberalization. This is not the place to discuss such conditionality; the IMF has developed considerable expertise, and occasional timing mistakes are part of a necessary learning process about ways of implementing unquestionable principles in practice and over time. The key remaining issue also lies outside the scope of this paper: how to find the best way to involve private-sector investors in sharing the costs of rescue when the crisis is not a pure liquidity crisis, but comes partly from solvency problems in the public or the banking sector.

The conditionality imposed on a country in crisis substantially reduces the moral hazard created by the readiness of the international community to help. Whether or not bail-out is finally forthcoming, the costs of crises are substantial for the countries in which they occur. Even when external finance is available, it comes with delay and with unpopular strings attached through IMF conditionality. One could even argue that the cost is generally too high when the crisis is related to contagion and contains an element of market failure.

Indeed, one of the current challenges may be to define a new, *ex ante* conditionality. Respecting different codes for good conduct in the phase leading up to the crisis could give an implicit right to much more favourable treatment and less stringent conditionality in the event of crisis. Of prime importance for any such *ex ante* conditionality are questions related to exchange rate policy and banking supervision. Much more work is needed on the forms such *ex ante* conditionality might take. One of the weaknesses of the current surveillance system is that it is solely based on persuasion and discretion. *Ex ante* conditionality might help substantially with implementation.

G-7 exchange rate monitoring

Large industrialized countries are a separate case. First, their expertise in managing exchange rates is comparable to that of the IMF. Second, they have the financial resources to intervene in the market and, except for rare occasions, do not really need foreign help to fight the worst case of bubbles. Third, for large countries, cooperation is necessary because of the n-1 problem: for example, the dollar–euro rate is a matter of concern for the United States and for euro countries. In theory, one could imagine an independent monitoring of this exchange rate by the United States and euro countries, and independent interventions in the event of market turmoil, but such a decentralized process would clearly be much less efficient than joint monitoring as part of the G-7 general process of economic cooperation.

While the G-7 should be the highest monitoring authority, it would make sense to charge the IMF with a secretariat responsibility, given its present role and accumulated expertise. For each regular G-7 meeting, the IMF could be asked to prepare a report presenting and discussing reasonable estimates of long-run exchange rate equilibrium, and assessing how far major currencies diverge from these estimates. In the same report, or in a separate one, the IMF would also discuss whether observed departures from long-run equilibrium can be explained by cyclical conditions and interest rates, including risk premiums. The IMF report would present staff analyses, but also discuss other estimates and analyses available in the market-place. Indeed, it would be extremely useful for the staff to establish a regular and open dialogue with both the academic world and private-sector investors on the issue of the measurement of long-run exchange rate equilibrium. In the current state of knowledge, competitive estimates are more likely than single estimates to convey the relevant information and act as a strong signal possibly anchoring expectations. We strongly advise the IMF to maintain an up-to-date database on the world major financial institutions' estimates of long-term exchange rate equilibrium. Many international bank research departments do not produce such estimates. Our expectation is that an officially sanctioned focus on such estimates would at least provide some incentive for them to do more work on this key issue. We also hope that a practice of dialogue and interaction between the private sector and the IMF staff might help expectations to converge towards reasonable estimates of normal exchange rates.

We fully recognize that knowledge of exchange rate equilibrium is imperfect and limited (see section 6.4). This is why the process we recommend is based on dialogue and interaction, rather than top-down communication. This is inevitably messier, but it is nevertheless necessary and more effective than simply relying on in-house estimates that would lack credibility. Moreover, we insist that both the IMF and the international community strongly back research on producing reliable estimates of exchange rate equilibrium and of their time-path as a central input in the monitoring mechanism.

We do not expect such a process to produce true calculations. Its major contribution would be to help forge a consensus among policy-makers about what is going on in the foreign exchange market. In normal times, attention would be limited to G-7 currencies (the US dollar, euro, yen, pound and the Canadian dollar).

We have already stressed some key advantages of such an enhanced monitoring process, notably in terms of its potential impact on private-sector behaviour and as a practice likely to facilitate interventions in the market in case of clear exchange rate overshooting. Moreover, we expect that the successful implementation of the monitoring process in the G-7 countries could help emerging markets as well, both directly, owing to reduced volatility between world major currencies, but also indirectly if it helps the development, among private investors, of more fundamentally based valuation methodologies. In addition, emerging countries would certainly benefit from the experience gained by G-7 practitioners in their enhanced surveillance process. We strongly recommend that the more advanced emerging countries that decide to pursue the demanding option of managed floating be invited periodically to meet with G-7 representatives to consult on modalities of surveillance and of mutual support. The markets would surely look favourably on such collaboration, which they might even interpret as a stabilizing, implicit endorsement. This spillover effect would considerably strengthen the effectiveness of the surveillance mechanisms reviewed above for emerging markets' exchange rate policies.

Beyond monitoring

Clearly, simply monitoring exchange rate markets does not by itself solve the coordination problem and suppress all instability in exchange rates. When sharply diverging fiscal and monetary policies push interest rates far away in different countries, monitoring should not be expected to stop exchange rates from moving away from reasonable estimates of their long-term equilibrium. In other words, monitoring could suppress part of the volatility due to the inefficiency of the FX market, but it would not stop overshooting, as envisaged by Dornbusch. This approach has the merit of requiring a discussion of policies and of their interaction, which is the very first step of any coordination exercise. Coordination should be understood as a process, rather than a jump towards optimally coordinated policies that internalize economic interdependence. The experience of European integration serves to illustrate that, even in a favourable political context, the process of coordination requires much learning and much time.

Monitoring is an essential and realistic first step towards a deepening of international economic policy coordination. As such, it is both modest and realistic. It demands a substantial effort, but does not infringe much on national sovereignty while presenting clear benefits relative to the current functioning of the international monetary system.

More ambitious schemes share two characteristics. First, authorities do not only discuss plausible values for long-term equilibrium exchange rates, but now agree on a set of reference parities. Second, they decide on acceptable bands of fluctuation around these parities beyond which action is warranted. Such action may involve interventions in the market if the unwelcome movements in the parities have no real justification, or an effort to better coordinate the policy mix if the divergence finds its origin in a lack of economic policy coordination. Bergsten, Davanne and Jacquet (1999) discuss various such schemes, which differ on whether or not the agreement is made public and on the strength of the commitment to the band.

We believe that flexible target zones make a lot of sense. In such a regime, there is no binding commitment to defend the zone, but rather a commitment to cooperate and coordinate economic policies in order to keep a reasonable degree of exchange rate stability. However, such a regime is currently not on the agenda for a variety of good and bad reasons. Many governments are reluctant to commit themselves to cooperate in an active way and prefer to keep maximum freedom despite the costs of large swings in exchange rates. Moreover, the very idea of target zones has a bad reputation owing to the obvious drawbacks of hard bands which are clearly too rigid (see section 6.2). Many officials fail, honestly or not, to see the radical difference between flexible target zones and hard bands: the former is a device to encourage economic policy coordination while the latter may be a dangerous trap which forces countries to defend unsustainable exchange rates. Ministers of finance are not yet ready, maybe rightly so, to put their stamp on the available estimates. However, a few years of successful monitoring can change this situation. Once governments have worked out methods to discuss equilibrium exchange rates, the likelihood that they will agree on some plausible equilibrium value increases.[20]

6.6 CONCLUDING REMARKS

This chapter contains two broad messages. First, exchange rate flexibility is necessary and desirable. Never again should the world economy become hostage to misplaced policies, sanctioned at the highest level, that aim at defending grossly misaligned exchange rates. While we do not rule out 'fixed-fixed' exchange rate systems such as a currency board, we believe that such systems do present dangers, and should be resorted to only in exceptional circumstances and managed very carefully. A currency board, however, may make sense as an intermediate step towards joining a regional monetary union, and this may well be an option for some central and east European countries attracted by EMU.

Second, the current international monetary system blatantly lacks a doctrine of flexibility. As an alternative to fixed but adjustable exchange rate systems (that require capital controls and should appeal to the poorer developing countries), most countries are presented with a choice between losing monetary sovereignty or floating. And, should they chose floating, there is no good practice to follow in order to manage the exchange rate efficiently.

---

[20] The coordination of economic policies can also be improved without waiting for an explicit exchange rate target, as forcefully argued by Coeuré and Pisani-Ferry (1999), who have proposed a coordination process based on the joint endorsement by the G-3 of a core set of broad macroeconomic principles.

Our paper is a first contribution to thinking about what such a doctrine might look like. First, we have argued that the menu of option was too limited. Even with substantial capital mobility, there is a variant of fixed but adjustable exchange rate regimes, which we have called an adjustable reference parity regime, that can help those emerging markets that still wish to anchor domestic policies on an exchange rate target. Such a parity must be based on a basket of currencies, must be readily adjustable in a routine way and must be defended by a flexible feedback-based monetary policy.

Second, we have discussed ways to improve international exchange rate monitoring as a first step towards a practice of regular coordination of economic policies. Monitoring would be based on tracking down the discrepancies between reasonable estimates of long-run exchange rate equilibria and current exchange rates and checking them for valid explanations. We believe that this monitoring effort could help stabilize market expectations and exchange rates, and that it would also help develop methods of exchange rate valuation, in the markets, at last based on assessment of fundamentals.

These proposals are no panaceas to current problems. They require much work, notably on the very notion and calculation of equilibrium exchange rates and risk premiums. But we believe that such work is urgently necessary, and that the modest steps we have highlighted can substantially contribute to exchange rate stability.

References

Bartolini, L. and Prati, A. (1998), *Soft Exchange Rates Bands and Speculative Attacks: Theory and Evidence from the ERM since August 1993*, IMF Working Paper/98/156 (Washington, DC: International Monetary Fund).

Baxter, M. (1994), 'Real Exchange Rates and Real Interest Differentials: Have We Missed the Business-Cycle Relationship?', *Journal of Monetary Economics*, Vol. 33, pp. 5–38.

Bergsten, F., Davanne, O and Jacquet, P. (1999), 'The Case for Joint Management of Exchange Rate Flexibility', Working Paper 99–9 (Washington, DC: Institute for International Economics).

Blanchard, O. (1997), *Macroeconomics* (London: Prentice Hall).

Blanchard, O. (1999), 'Comment on three reports to the French Conseil d'Analyse Economique', Report no.18, Collection des Rapports du Conseil d'Analyse Economique (Paris: La Documentation Française).

Borowski, D. and C. Couharde (1999), 'La Compétitivité Relative des Etats-Unis, du Japon et de la Zone Euro', annexe B, Report no.18, Collection des Rapports du Conseil d'Analyse Economique (Paris: La Documentation Française).

Catte, P., G. Galli and S. Rebecchini (1994), 'Concerted Interventions and the Dollar: An Analysis of Daily Data', in P.Kenen, F. Papadia and F. Saccomani (eds), *The International Monetary System* (Cambridge: Cambridge University Press).

Coe, D. and S. Golub (1986), 'Exchange Rates and Real Long-term Differentials : Evidence for Eighteen OECD Countries', Document de travail de l'OCDE (Paris: OECD).

Coeuré, B. and J. Pisani-Ferry (1999), 'The Case Against Benign Neglect of Exchange Rate Stability', *Finance and Development*, September 1999, Vol. 36, No. 3, pp. 5–8.

Davanne, O. (1990), 'La Dynamique des Taux de Change', *Economie et Statistique*, No. 236, pp. 37–50.

Davanne, O. (1998), *L'instabilité du système financier international*, Report to the French Prime Minister, Collection des Rapports du Conseil d'Analyse Economique (Paris: La Documentation Française).

Davanne, O. (1999a), 'Transparency of Financial Portfolios and Control of Market Risks', prepared for Dominique Strauss-Kahn, French Minister of Finance. Available in French and English on the French finance ministry website (www.finances.gouv.fr/pole_ecofin/politique_financiere).

Davanne, O. (1999b), 'The Role of Transparency for a Better Pricing of Risks', in Graham Ingham (ed.), *World Financial Reform*, Discussion Paper (London: Centre for Economic Performance, LSE).

Devenow, A. and Welch, I. (1996), 'Rational Herding in Financial Economics', *European Economic Review*, Vol. 40, No. 3–5, pp. 603–15.

Dominguez, K. (1990), 'Market responses to coordinated central bank intervention', *Carnegie-Rochester Series on Public Policy*, Vol. 32, pp. 121–64.

Dominguez, K. and Frankel, J. (1993), *Does Foreign Exchange Intervention Work?* (Washington DC: Institute for International Economics).

Dornbusch, R. (1976), 'Expectations and Exchange Rate Dynamics', *Journal of Political Economy*, Vol. 84, pp. 1161–76.

Dornbusch, R. (1999), 'The Euro: Implications for Latin America', paper prepared for a policy research project of the World Bank, available on R. Dornbusch's internet site at web.mit.edu/rudi/www.

Eichengreen, B., Rose, A. and Wyplosz, C. (1994), 'Speculative Attacks on Pegged Exchange Rates: An Empirical Exploration with Special Reference to the European Monetary System', in M. Canzoneri, W. Ethier and V. Grilli (eds), *The New Transatlantic Economy* (New York: Cambridge University Press, 1996).

Frankel, J. and Froot, K. (1990), 'Chartists, Fundamentalists and Trading in the Foreign Exchange Market', *American Economic Review*, Vol. 80, pp. 181–5.

Hausmann, R. (1999), 'Should There Be Five Currencies or One Hundred and Five?' *Foreign Policy*, Fall, pp. 65–79.

IMF (1998), *World Economic Outlook* (Washington DC: International Monetary Fund).

Jurgensen Report (1983), *Report of the Working Group on Exchange Market Intervention* (Washington DC: US Treasury, March).

Keynes, J.M. (1936), *The General Theory of Employment, Interest and Money* (London: Macmillan).

Krugman, P. (1989), 'The Case for Stabilizing the Exchange Rate', *Oxford Review of Economic Policy*, Vol. 5, pp. 61–72.

McKinnon, R. (1998), 'Exchange Rate Coordination for Surmounting the East Asian Currency Crisis', Paper presented at the conference on 'Financial Crises: Facts, Theories, and Policies' (Washington DC: International Monetary Fund, 18 November).

Meese, R. and Rogoff, K. (1983), 'Empirical Exchange Rate Models of the Seventies : Do They Fit Out of Sample?' *Journal of International Economics*, Vol. 14, pp. 3–24.

Meese, R. and Rogoff, K. (1988), 'Was it Real? The Exchange Rate Interest Differential Relationship over the Modern Floating-Rate Period', *The Journal of Finance*, Vol. 43, pp. 933–48.

Mundell, R. (1968), *International Economics* (New York: Macmillan).

Sachs, J. (1985), 'The Dollar and the Policy Mix: 1985', *Brookings Papers on Economic Activity*, 1.

Sachs, J. and F. Larrain (1999), 'Why Dollarization Is More Straitjacket than Salvation', *Foreign Policy*, Fall, pp. 80–93.

Shleifer A. and Summers, L. (1990), 'The Noise Trader Approach to Finance', *Journal of Economic Perspectives*, Vol. 4, No. 2, pp. 19–23.

Svensson, L.E.O. (1992), 'An Interpretation of Recent Research on Exchange Rate Target Zones', *Journal of Economic Perspectives*, Vol. 6, No. 4, pp. 119–44.

Williamson, J. (1994), *Estimating Equilibrium Exchange Rates* (Washington, DC: Institute for International Economics).

Williamson, J. (1998), 'Crawling Bands or Monitoring Bands: How to Manage Exchange Rates in a World of Capital Mobility', *International Finance*, October 1998, Vol. 1, No. 1, pp. 59–79.

Wren-Lewis, S. and Driver, R. (1998), *Real Exchange Rates for the Year 2000* (Washington DC: Institute for International Economics).

7 ASIA IN SEARCH OF A NEW EXCHANGE RATE REGIME

C. H. Kwan

7.1 INTRODUCTION

Led by Thailand, many developing countries in Asia were forced to abandon their traditional dollar-peg system and allow their exchange rates to float in the summer of 1997 amid intense currency attacks by speculators. After a period of sharp depreciation accompanied by high volatility, their exchange rates bottomed out against the US dollar in the autumn of 1998, thanks to the yen's rebound and a return of confidence in the economic prospects of these countries. However, with the notable exception of the Malaysian ringgit,[1] the stability of their currencies against the US dollar has not been restored (Figure 1.1).

The latest financial turmoil has raised a number of important issues in relation to exchange rate management. First, why has the dollar-peg system, which seemed to have served the Asian countries so well in the past, become so vulnerable? Second, is the de-linking of the Asian currencies from the US dollar just an emergency measure that should be reversed when the crisis is over? Finally, if it were better to abandon the dollar-peg system, what are the alternatives available to the Asian countries?

This chapter seeks to answer these questions. Section 7.2 identifies some recent changes in the international environment that have made the dollar-peg system vulnerable. Section 7.3 looks at the wide range of exchange rate regime alternatives. Although it has become fashionable to eliminate intermediate regimes as viable options in favour of either free floating or firm fixing, neither of these polar regimes seems to be appropriate for Asia's developing countries at this stage. A more appropriate strategy, discussed in section 7.4, is to strengthen the institutional framework, both at the national and the international level, so as to reduce the vulnerability of the intermediate regimes to speculative attacks.

---

[1] See Yusof et al. in this volume, Chapter 5.

Figure 7.1: From dollar-peg to managed floating (exchange rates of Asian currencies against the dollar)

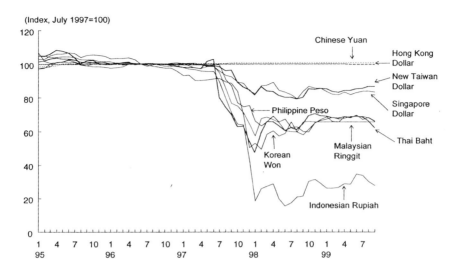

Source: Compiled by the Nomura Research Institute based on Bloomberg data.

7.2   THE VULNERABILITY OF THE DOLLAR-PEG SYSTEM

The latest crisis in Asia has revealed some weaknesses intrinsic to the traditional dollar-peg system adopted by the Asian countries. First, fluctuations of the yen against the US dollar have led to sharp swings in export performance as well as unstable capital flows. Second, the weakening synchronization between Asian and US growth rates, leaving interest rates to be determined in the US (as required to maintain fixed exchange rates against the dollar), has led to macroeconomic instability. Finally, countries committing themselves to fix their exchange rates against the dollar are vulnerable to speculation. These weaknesses, which are to one extent or another common to all fixed exchange rate regimes, have been aggravated by the sharp rise in the scale of capital flows. The dollar-peg system has been further strained by the growing interdependence among the Asian countries (including Japan) at the expense of dependence on the United States, as well as by the sharp deterioration of the US balance-of-payments position.

Figure 7.2: The yen–dollar rate as the major determinant of short-term Asian economic growth

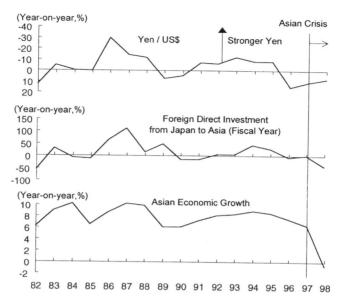

Note: Asia = NIEs + ASEAN + China.
Source: Compiled by the Nomura Research Institute based on official statistics of countries concerned.

A widely fluctuating yen–dollar rate and macroeconomic instability

Led by the yen–dollar rate, exchange rates among the major currencies have become highly volatile since the collapse of the Bretton Woods system in the early 1970s. This has happened against the background of a sharp deterioration in the US balance-of-payments position in general and a growing imbalance between the US and Japan in particular.

Wide fluctuations in the yen–dollar rate have led to macroeconomic instability in Asia's de-veloping countries under the dollar-peg system (Figure 7.2). Every time the yen appreciates against the dollar, the economic growth rate of Asia (the Asian NIEs, the ASEAN countries and China as a group) picks up, as happened between 1986 and 1988 and again between 1991 and 1995. These periods were also accompanied by an expansion of the 'bubble economy', with asset prices rising sharply. The reverse is true when economic growth in these countries decelerates and the asset bubble bursts on the back of a weaker yen, as occurred in 1989–90 and again since mid-1995. The latest downturn in Asian economic growth, apparent since 1996, can be explained largely by the sharp depreciation of the yen against the dollar. The weakening yen also led to a marked deterioration in Asia's export performance and current account balances in 1996, paving the way for the currency crisis. Symmetrically, the rebound of the yen against the US dollar in the autumn of 1998 was followed by rising stock prices, falling interest rates, stabilizing exchange rates and a resumption of economic growth in the Asian countries.

A depreciation of the yen against the dollar (and thus against the Asian currencies under the dollar-peg system) affects the Asian economies mainly in the following five ways.

First, a weaker yen makes Japanese exports less expensive relative to those of the Asian countries, and Asian products become less competitive against Japanese products in international markets as a result. The emergence of a global market implies that it is not so much the regional composition of trade (dependence on the Japanese economy) but the commodity composition of trade (the degree of competition with Japan) that is important in determining the impact of the yen–dollar rate on Asian exports.

Second, with the cost of production in Japan falling relative to the Asian countries, the incentive for Japanese companies to relocate production to Asia is reduced, leading to a decline in the inflow of direct foreign investment from Japan. This hurts Asian economic growth on both the demand side and the supply side.

Third, the capital adequacy ratios of Japanese banks decline as the yen depreciates so that they may need to reduce their overseas lending to meet the minimum capital adequacy ratio set by the Bank for International Settlements (BIS). The capital adequacy ratio is defined as the ratio of risk assets, which is made up of domestic and overseas lending, to capital. For Japanese banks, capital and domestic lending are denominated in yen, but 80 per cent of overseas lending is denominated in dollars. As a result, a weaker yen reduces the capital adequacy ratio by raising the value of risk assets in yen terms. Other things being equal, in order to restore the capital adequacy ratio Japanese banks need to reduce either domestic or overseas lending. According to Koo (1998), every one yen depreciation against the dollar is estimated to reduce Japanese banks' lending capability by one trillion yen.

Fourth, a weaker yen reduces import prices in the Asian countries, as they are heavily dependent on Japan as a source of capital and intermediate goods. Lower import prices, which usually mean lower input prices, in turn boost profit and output for the Asian countries.

Finally, depreciation of the yen reduces the Asian countries' burden of repaying debts denominated in yen terms. Because the bulk of Asia's yen-denominated debt is in the form of official development assistance from the Japanese government, it is the lower-income countries that are more likely to benefit from this factor.

Although the effects of the first three factors on Asian economic growth are negative, they are partly offset (and, in some cases, more than offset) by the positive effects of the last two factors. The net result, which may differ from one country to another, depends on the relative magnitude of these five forces. A weaker yen is more likely to dampen economic growth in higher-income countries with trade structures that are competitive with Japan's (South Korea, for example) than in lower-income countries with trade structures that complement Japan's (Indonesia, for example).[2]

A weaker yen has both negative and positive effects on Asia, but there is strong empirical evidence that its impact on economic growth in the Asian NIEs, ASEAN and China as a group is negative. According to Kwan (1998a), a 10 per cent depreciation (appreciation) of the yen against the dollar tends to drag down (push up) economic growth in Asia's developing countries by one per cent.

Asymmetric shocks and loss of monetary independence

As with all fixed exchange rate systems (the extreme case being a monetary union with a single currency), pegging to the dollar under free capital mobility implies the abandonment of an independent monetary policy. As the host country has to match domestic interest rates to the US level in order to maintain the parity rate, it has little room to use monetary policy to restore stability when the economy is subjected to shocks. For countries whose business cycles synchronize with the ups and downs of the US economy, the costs of giving up an independent monetary policy are relatively small; they are likely to pursue a policy stance similar to that of the United States most of the time anyway. For Asian countries facing shocks that affect the two sides of the Pacific asymmetrically, however, leaving domestic interest rates to be determined in the United States may actually be destabilizing.

The synchronization between Asian and US economic growth has weakened markedly since the Plaza Accord in 1985. The correlation coefficient between Asian and US growth rates fell from 0.731 for the period 1971–84 to –0.193 for the period 1985–98 (Table 7.1). The corresponding figure for 1985–96 was 0.175, indicating that de-synchronization began even before the crisis.[3] This reflects rising intra-regional trade at the expense of exports to the United States

---

[2] Indonesia may actually gain from a weaker yen, as the benefits of lower import prices and a reduced debt burden should be large enough to compensate for the marginal losses in export competitiveness and inflow of foreign direct investment.

[3] Of the ten major East Asian countries (including Japan), all but China and the Philippines have witnessed sharp declines in the correlation between their growth rates and that of the United States. China has become more closely integrated into the global economy, thanks to the open-door policy that started in the late 1970s, while the Philippines has restored stable growth in the post-Marcos period.

Table 7.1: Correlation between Asian and US economic growth rates

Country	1971–84	1985–98	(1985–96)
Asia	0.731	−0.193	0.175
China	0.139	0.161	0.262
South Korea	0.584	−0.298	−0.087
Taiwan	0.857	−0.013	0.090
Hong Kong	0.705	−0.102	0.097
Singapore	0.461	−0.156	−0.074
Indonesia	0.436	−0.321	−0.282
Thailand	0.545	−0.334	−0.068
Malaysia	0.534	−0.343	−0.281
Philippines	−0.189	0.204	0.243
Japan	0.616	−0.163	0.066

Source: Compiled by the Nomura Research Institute, based on official statistics of countries concerned.

(so that US economic growth now has less impact on Asian economic growth than before), on the one hand, and the growing importance of shocks that affect the two sides of the Pacific asymmetrically (or at least to a different extent), such as fluctuations in the yen–dollar rate, on the other (Figure 7.3).

The experience of Hong Kong illustrates how pegging to the dollar can be destabilizing rather than stabilizing in this new environment. Thanks to the close ties through trade and investment with China developed over the last two decades, Hong Kong's growth rate now synchronizes more strongly with China than with the United States. Hong Kong thus no longer meets the conditions for forming an optimum currency area with the United States, as external shocks (the latest crisis in Asia being a typical example) do not usually affect the two economies symmetrically. As Table 7.1 shows, the correlation coefficient between the growth rates of Hong Kong and the US dropped from 0.705 in 1971–84 to 0.097 in 1985–96, and further to −0.102 when the latter period is extended to include the two crisis years.

Hong Kong decided to peg its currency to the US dollar under a currency board system in October 1983, when the Hong Kong dollar fell sharply amid heightening political uncertainty over the return of Hong Kong to China. The Hong Kong dollar has never deviated significantly from its official parity against the US dollar, despite numerous external shocks to the economy (such as Black Monday in October 1987, the Tiananmen incident in June 1989, the contagion effect of the Mexican crisis in early 1995 and the Asian crisis since the summer of 1997).

This stability of the Hong Kong dollar against the US dollar has been achieved, however, at the expense of macroeconomic stability. For example,

Figure 7.3: Rising intra-regional trade

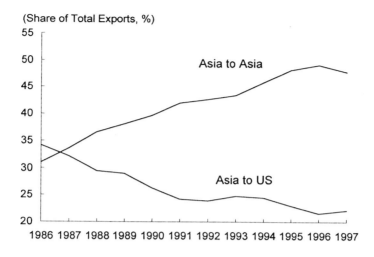

Note: Asia = Japan + China + NIEs + ASEAN.
Source: Compiled by the Nomura Research Institute, based on IMF, *Direction of Trade Statistics.*

Hong Kong's inflation rate has been much higher on average and has fluctuated more widely than the inflation rate in Singapore, which has a more flexible exchange rate regime. Also, the downturn in economic activity during the latest crisis was much sharper for Hong Kong than for Singapore, with Hong Kong's 1998 GDP declining by 5.1 per cent and Singapore's rising by 0.3 per cent.

Under the dollar-peg system, the monetary authorities have lost the flexibility not only to change the exchange rate but also to adjust domestic interest rates when the economy faces shocks. Interest rates in Hong Kong are largely beyond the control of the monetary authorities. In normal times, when exchange rate risks are considered negligible, domestic interest rates closely follow their counterparts in the United States, as the force of arbitrage tends to eliminate any spread between the two markets. When there is downward pressure on the Hong Kong dollar, interest rates in Hong Kong tend to rise above rates in the United States, with the spread reflecting the currency risk premium. Indeed, the overnight interbank rate shot up to an annual rate of nearly 300 per cent on 23 October 1997, when speculators were aggressively short-selling the Hong Kong dollar.[4] The latest economic crisis in Asia has hurt

---

[4] Symmetrically, domestic interest rates can fall below US rates when the Hong Kong dollar is expected to be revalued, as happened in 1988 when the Korean won, the New Taiwan dollar and the Singapore dollar were appreciating under pressure from the United States.

Figure 7.4: Counter-cyclical movement of real interest rates in Hong Kong

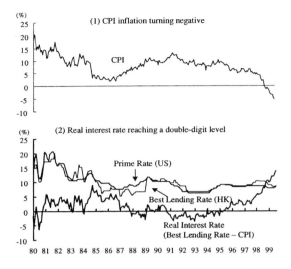

Source: Compiled by the Nomura Research Institute, based on official statistics.

Hong Kong more than the United States, so that following the monetary policy stance adopted by the United States would actually aggravate and prolong the recession in Hong Kong. Indeed, Hong Kong can be said to have fallen into a liquidity trap where monetary policy has become totally ineffective to stimulate demand because interest rates cannot fall below the US level (8.5 per cent in terms of the prime rate as of late 1999, which is far above the 'natural' floor of zero per cent).

Making things worse, real interest rates in Hong Kong have been rising on the back of a falling inflation rate (Figure 7.4). Excluding the possibility of a devaluation, the Hong Kong economy is on the horns of a dilemma: on one hand, a deflation of prices and wages (as has been taking place) is needed to restore export competitiveness; on the other hand, this process pushes up real interest rates, restraining domestic demand. Indeed, the real interest rate stands at the double-digit level of 12.7 per cent (as of late 1999), measured in terms of the difference between the best lending rate (8.5 per cent) and the consumer price index (–4.2 per cent) [that is 8.5%–(–4.2%)=12.7%]. The adverse effect of rising real interest rates on domestic demand has largely offset the positive effect of deflation (through stimulating exports) on economic growth. This situation contrasts sharply with the pre-crisis period when negative real interest rates (reflecting high inflation) fuelled the asset-price bubble. In this way, under Hong Kong's dollar-peg system the counter-cyclical movement in real interest rates (that is, the tendency for real interest rates to decline during a boom and to rise during a recession) has made the economy inherently unstable.

Destabilizing capital flows and speculative attacks

The increasing mobility of capital that has accompanied advances in communications and information technology and the deregulation of financial markets worldwide has increased the vulnerability of fixed exchange rate systems to speculative attacks. Hedge funds now have the leverage to finance very large positions in the foreign exchange market, making it more and more difficult for central banks to defend fixed exchange rates, as the recent experience of the Asian countries has vividly illustrated.

The rising volume of international capital flows is reflected in the rapid expansion of the global foreign exchange market. The Bank for International Settlements (1999) has estimated the daily global turnover of (traditional) foreign exchange activity at US$1,490 billion in April 1998, sharply higher than the US$590 billion in April 1989, when it first conducted the same survey. This figure largely reflects international flows of capital, and dwarfs the volume of global merchandise trade, which averages about US$15 billion a day (based on global export volume, which totalled US$4,458 billion in 1998, according to the IMF).

Furthermore, massive inflows of capital tend to be followed by sharp reversals, and the scale of such shifts seems to have increased. Thailand, for example, experienced a net capital inflow (as approximated by the current account deficit) of 8.1 per cent of GDP in 1996 before the crisis and a net capital outflow equivalent to 12.3 per cent of GDP in 1998 during the crisis, a net swing of over 20 percentage points of GDP. At the same time, South Korea's net capital flows turned from a 4.4 per cent of GDP to −12.5 per cent, a swing of 16.9 per cent. The magnitude of these reversals far exceeded the corresponding figures for Mexico (a swing of 10 percentage points) and Chile (a swing of 9 percentage points) between 1981 and 1983.

For countries under pegged exchange rate regimes, reversals in capital flows have usually taken the form of speculative attacks in the foreign exchange market, when the pegged rate is out of line with economic fundamentals. The reluctance of monetary authorities to alter parity promptly in the face of misalignment tends to offer speculators a one-way bet and to increase their expected return. At the same time, as the latest crisis in Asia has vividly illustrated, countries with pegged exchange rates are also susceptible to the contagion effect of speculation in neighbouring countries.

Defending a pegged exchange rate system is costly in terms of the need to hold a large amount of precautionary foreign exchange reserves and to maintain high interest rates when under speculative attack. In traditional country risk analysis, three months' import coverage is considered a comfortable level for foreign exchange reserves in the absence of capital mobility. Amid the intense speculation of 1997, however, foreign exchange reserves well above this benchmark were not sufficient for the hard-hit Asian countries to avoid having to allow their exchange rates to float.[5]

At the same time, the hikes in short-term interest rates needed to defend the parity rate raise the cost of funding and reduce loan demand, with adverse effects on profitability in the banking sector. In the absence of a well-developed bond market, corporate finance is heavily dependent on short-term bank loans, and higher lending rates bring about rising bad debts, increasing the probability of a banking crisis.

Furthermore, market participants usually interpret a sharp devaluation as an indicator of failed macroeconomic management, which prompts further capital outflows. By raising the debt burden of banks and companies with foreign debts in local currency terms, the devaluation may lead to serious credit crunch problems and falling domestic investment.[6]

The dollar-peg system, coupled with capital account liberalization, has also been blamed for the excessive accumulation of dollar-denominated debt in the Asian countries. The long-standing stability of the Asian currencies against the US dollar before the crisis had prompted both foreign investors and domestic borrowers to underestimate the foreign exchange rate risk associated with borrowing in dollars without hedging, leading to investment in excess of the optimal level and to inefficiency. Borrowers may also have difficulty repaying that debt if local currencies are forced to devalue sharply under speculative pressure, as happened during the Asian crisis.

7.3 EXCHANGE RATE REGIME ALTERNATIVES

The weaknesses of the dollar-peg system come from diverse sources, and the remedies range from moving to more flexible systems to strengthening the dollar-peg. If the widely fluctuating yen–dollar rate is the root of the problem, Asian countries should peg to a basket of currencies in which the yen carries a substantial weight. If loss of monetary independence and excess borrowing are the major sources of instability, allowing the exchange rate to float is

[5] With immense reserves, amounting to over US$140 billion, China succeeded in stabilizing its exchange rate against the dollar, but the opportunity cost of maintaining this level of reserves is great. Being a developing country, China pays much higher interest rates on its overseas borrowings than it receives on its foreign exchange reserves.

[6] Krugman (1999) summarizes this argument elegantly in a simple Mundell-Fleming model that links investment not only to the interest rate but also to the real exchange rate and allows for the possibility of multiple equilibria.

recommended.[7] If unwarranted speculation is blamed, the dollar-peg system should be strengthened, rather than replaced by a more flexible regime. A wide range of exchange rate regimes has been proposed. This section examines each alternative in turn.

Pegging to a basket of currencies

An Asian country can insulate itself from the adverse effect of a widely fluctuating yen–dollar rate by pegging its exchange rate to a basket of currencies in which the yen carries a substantial weight (Box 7.1). As in the case of choosing an appropriate exchange rate regime in general, the optimal composition of the currency basket for a country hinges on (1) the structure of its economy, (2) the nature of the shocks facing it and (3) the objectives of the policy authorities.[8] Studies that estimate the optimal composition of currency baskets for the Asian countries have in common the understanding that the major shock comes from fluctuations in the yen–dollar rate. Accordingly, these studies have focused on determining the optimal weight of the yen in those baskets of currencies with the objective of stabilizing a macroeconomic variable, such as output or the balance of payments.

In a model that focuses on the dual role of Japan as a competitor in international markets and a major source of imports, Kwan (1992, 1994) derives an optimal peg for an Asian country that seeks to stabilize output amidst a widely fluctuating yen–dollar rate. For an Asian country under a dollar-peg system, a stronger yen, on the one hand, boosts demand by enhancing export competitiveness against Japanese products but, on the other hand, suppresses supply by increasing the cost of imports from Japan. The net result depends on the degree of competition (or complementarity) between Japan and the country concerned. Countries having competitive relations with Japan are more likely to benefit from a stronger yen while those having complementary relations with Japan are more likely to be hurt. To stabilize output, the monetary authorities should allow the local currency to follow the yen up when the yen appreciates against the dollar (and to follow the yen down when the yen depreciates against the dollar). Accordingly, the 'optimal' weight assigned to the yen in a currency basket should be high for countries competing with Japan in international markets and low for countries with trade structures complementary to that of Japan. Given the clear tendency for the trade structures of Asian countries to

---

[7] As well as by its exchange rate policy, a country may regain monetary independence and also insulate itself from currency attacks by imposing capital controls, as will be discussed in the section 7.4.

[8] For a survey of the literature on the optimal composition of currency baskets, see Williamson (1982).

Box 7.1: Basket-peg

A currency basket can be considered a currency unit (or composite currency) formed by combining a number of existing currencies. There is no limit to the number of currencies composing a currency basket, although their weights together should add up to 100 per cent. Typical examples of currency baskets are the SDR (Special Drawing Right, created by the IMF) and the ECU (European Currency Unit, created by the European Union to facilitate the transition towards a single currency). The SDR is made up of five major currencies (the US dollar, yen, D-mark, French franc and pound sterling) and the ECU is composed of 12 major European currencies.

A country can stabilize the value of its currency (in terms of purchasing power or export competitiveness) by pegging to a basket of currencies instead of a single currency. For a country pegging its currency to a basket of currencies composing the yen and other currencies, the higher the weight assigned to the yen, the stronger the synchronization between the host country's currency and the yen. For example, if the yen carries a weight of 70% (and the dollar carries the remaining 30%) in Korea's reference basket, the won would be allowed to appreciate by 7% against the dollar when the yen strengthens by 10% against the dollar and to depreciate by 7% when the yen depreciates by 10%, both against the dollar (Figure 7.5). Compared to the dollar-peg system, the won would be more stable against the yen (+/-3% instead of +/-10%, given a +/-10% fluctuation in the yen–dollar rate), although it would become more volatile against the dollar (+/-7% instead of +/-0%). By design, the weighted average of the won rate against the dollar and the yen would remain unchanged (-3% × 70% + 7% × 30% = 0 in the case of a 10% yen appreciation and 3% × 70% − 7% × 30% = 0 in the case of a 10% yen depreciation). A basket-peg should therefore be understood as a fixed exchange rate system, although the value of the currency concerned fluctuates against all other currencies (both the yen and the dollar in this case).

Figure 7.5: Basket-peg versus dollar-peg

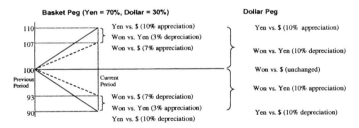

Source: Nomura Research Institute.

The effective exchange rate, which is a widely used measure of export competitiveness of states, can be considered a basket composed of the currencies of a country's major trading partners, with the weight of each currency proportional to that country's share of the host country's total trade. Pegging to a basket of currencies carrying trade weights is therefore equivalent to pursuing an exchange rate policy that seeks to stabilize the effective exchange rate. (The currency basket discussed here is a policy rule determining exchange rates; it should be distinguished from the currency composition of the foreign exchange reserves of central banks.)

approach that of Japan as their economies develop, it follows that higher-income countries such as the Asian NIEs should assign a greater weight to the yen than do lower-income countries such as the ASEAN countries and China.[9] By assigning such an optimal weight to the yen, an Asian country can minimize the ups and downs in their business cycles that result from fluctuations in the yen–dollar rate. As a result, the strong correlation between Asian economic growth and the yen–dollar rate would therefore become a phenomenon of the past.

Ito, Ogawa and Nagataki-Sasaki (1998) estimate the optimal weight of the yen in a currency basket for an Asian country that seeks to stabilize its trade balance amidst a fluctuating yen–dollar rate. They also emphasize the dual role of Japan as a competitor in international markets and as a major source of imports. Their estimation confirms that higher-income countries with competitive relations with Japan should assign higher weights to the yen.

Bénassy-Quéré (1996) estimates the optimal weight of the yen in a basket for a country that seeks to stabilize its balance of payments. Fluctuations in the yen–dollar rate affect the balance of payments not just through the trade account but also by altering the burden of debt service. The debt burden increases as the yen appreciates so that the capital account deteriorates, partly offsetting the improvement in the trade account. The weight of the yen in a currency basket that seeks to stabilize the balance of payments should therefore be inversely proportional to the size of yen-denominated debt. Accordingly, lower-income countries with large yen-denominated debt (such as China and Indonesia) should not peg closely to the yen.

While a system of pegging to a basket of currencies with an appropriately chosen weight for the yen should contribute to macroeconomic stability in Asia, it shares with other fixed exchange rate systems shortcomings such as lack of monetary autonomy and vulnerability to speculative attacks. Compared with a system of pegging to a single currency, a basket-peg system is harder to administer and the commitment to the peg is interpreted as weaker. At the micro-level, the cost of transactions is likely to be higher because all bilateral rates fluctuate.

Floating exchange rates

There is a growing recognition that flexible exchange rates are preferable to pegged exchange rates in terms of reducing a country's vulnerability to currency crises (Box 7.2).

The textbook version of the Mundell-Fleming model provides a theoretical basis for the argument that a country under a floating exchange rate system enjoys

---

[9] This contrasts sharply with a weighting scheme based on the regional composition of trade, in which case the ASEAN countries, rather than the Asian NIEs, should peg closer to the yen.

Box 7.2: To peg or not to peg: general principles

The choice between a fixed exchange rate system and a floating exchange rate system depends on a variety of factors, including economic structures, the nature of shocks and credibility versus flexibility, as has been well documented in Aghevli, Khan and Montiel (1991), IMF (1997) and Cooper (1999).

The major economic structures relevant to the choice between a fixed exchange rate regime and a floating exchange regime are (1) the need to have an independent monetary policy, (2) the effectiveness of monetary policy and (3) the volatility of exchange rates under a flexible regime and its consequences. First, if the market mechanism works smoothly, the cost of abandoning an independent monetary or exchange rate policy is low because there is little need to use these tools for the sake of stabilization. Specifically, if wages and prices are flexible, adjustment in their levels would help to maintain internal and external balances. Second, in very open economies, changes in exchange rates would sooner or later be reflected in offsetting changes in domestic price levels. Flexible exchange rates are therefore not only ineffective in achieving external balance targets but also harmful to price stability. Finally, in developing countries where capital markets are rudimentary, allowing exchange rates to fluctuate involves high volatility and a high cost of hedging through forward market transactions.

The fixed exchange rate system and the floating exchange rate system enjoy different comparative advantages as a built-in stabilizer for various shocks facing the economy. A fixed exchange rate regime, which allows anchoring to a stable price level, is desirable if monetary (money demand) shocks are common. A floating exchange rate regime, which eases adjustment costs in the presence of stickiness of wages and prices, is more desirable for an economy facing real shocks (terms of trade or productivity shocks). When overseas interest rate changes are the major source of disturbance, the choice is less clear-cut. In reality, every economy faces monetary, real and overseas interest rate shocks to one extent or another. The exchange rate regime that promises the highest degree of built-in stability is likely to be neither a purely fixed regime nor a purely floating regime but a managed floating regime that mixes the two (Argy, 1990, and Genberg, 1990).

A major objective of adopting a fixed exchange rate system is to enhance the credibility of economic policy, even at the cost of sacrificing flexibility. The need to maintain exchange rate parity will impose monetary and fiscal discipline on the government, and by providing a clear and transparent nominal anchor, the adoption of a pegged exchange rate may help to establish the credibility of a stabilization programme. However, short of fixing the exchange rate permanently by joining a monetary union, countries adopting some form of fixed exchange rate system may end up losing flexibility without gaining credibility.

A country choosing to adopt a fixed exchange rate system also needs to decide which currency or basket of currencies should serve as the anchor for its monetary policy. For a small economy closely linked to a single country, the obvious choice is to peg to the currency of that major trading partner. At the macro-level the cost of abandoning an independent monetary policy would be small, as the synchronization in the business cycles between the host country and the anchor-currency country is likely to be strong. At the micro-level, the benefit of exchange rate stability in terms of reductions in risk and transaction costs will also be large. An economy with a more diversified trade pattern may not meet the conditions for forming an optimum currency area with any single country. In that case, it is more advisable to join a 'virtual' monetary union by pegging to a basket comprised of the currencies of its major trading partners.

more autonomy in setting monetary policy. Although, under the assumption of perfect capital mobility, domestic interest rates are linked to the overseas level, the monetary authorities maintain control over the money supply, and monetary policy works mainly through its impact on the exchange rate. In the portfolio approach that allows for imperfect substitution between assets denominated in domestic and foreign currencies, changes in the exchange rate risk premium, which allow local interest rates to deviate from the overseas level, provide a further channel through which monetary policy works under a floating exchange rate. In the simple monetary model that assumes purchasing power parity and a stable money demand function, a floating rate regime allows the host country to choose its own level of inflation, which may differ from that of its trading partners.

The daily movement in the exchange rate in a floating rate regime also keeps reminding borrowers of the currency risk involved in incurring liabilities denominated in foreign currencies. By adopting a floating exchange rate, a country can thus discourage the accumulation of foreign-denominated debt, making it less prone to crisis.[10] A given decline in the exchange rate is expected to have a less adverse impact on the real economy under a floating regime than under a pegged regime, as the private sector is likely to have hedged a larger portion of its foreign currency debt. A floating exchange rate regime is also less vulnerable to currency crisis because it allows the exchange rate to absorb market pressure and because it presents less chance of a one-way bet for speculators.

Floating exchange rates are not without problems. The post-Bretton Woods period has witnessed high volatility and misalignment (chronic deviation from equilibrium rates) among major currencies that have been allowed to float. For example, the gyration in the yen–dollar rate from 80 yen to the dollar in the spring of 1995 down to 145 in the autumn of 1998 is difficult to rationalize in terms of major changes in economic fundamentals. Volatility of exchange rates increases the risks from cross-border transactions, with negative effects on international trade and investment. Exchange rate misalignment may aggravate business cycles at the macro-level and lead to a misallocation of social resources (particularly between the tradable and non-tradable sectors) at the micro-level. Freely floating exchange rates are particularly harmful to developing countries with thin and underdeveloped financial and foreign exchange markets and very open economies. Compared with the industrialized countries, their exchange rates would be more volatile, and the availability of financial instruments for hedging against exchange risks would be limited.

Although a floating exchange rate regime acts to cushion the economy from the impact of real shocks, it may actually aggravate the destabilizing effect of

---

[10] If excess borrowing is the problem, however, it should better be coped with by introducing direct measures, rather than exchange volatility, to reduce it.

monetary shocks on domestic output. For example, portfolio shifts by investors (a type of monetary shock) under a floating rate system may lead not only to more volatile exchange rates but also to wider fluctuations in output than under a fixed exchange rate system. Even for shocks arising from changes in overseas interest rates, a floating exchange rate system does a better job than a fixed exchange rate system as a built-in stabilizer for domestic output only under restricted conditions.

Strengthening the dollar peg

Measures proposed to strengthen the dollar-peg system include dollarization, currency boards and commitment to restore traditional parities.

In its purest form, dollarization amounts to replacing the national currency with the dollar or simply forming a (virtual) monetary union with the United States. By eliminating the national currency, there is no longer any need to defend it (by raising interest rates or by intervention in the foreign exchange market), and domestic interest rates should therefore closely follow US rates. This benefit comes at the cost of forgoing once and for all the option(s) to change the exchange rate and/or to pursue an independent monetary policy.

At the same time, dollarization also implies a loss of seigniorage for the host country, as the monetary authority needs to draw down foreign exchange reserves and/or borrow dollars in international markets in order to redeem the local currency in circulation. The central bank also loses its function as the lender of last resort because it can no longer provide liquidity (by printing money) to the banking system in case of a crisis.

Short of eliminating the local currency, some countries have sought to enhance credibility by adopting currency boards, which involve rigidly linking the value of domestic money to that of a foreign currency (the dollar in the case of Hong Kong) and tying the domestic monetary base firmly to the level of foreign exchange reserves through legislation.[11] Unlike complete dollarization, currency boards allow the retention of seigniorage and the option of devaluation in case of emergency.

Because countries with currency boards have not eliminated all possibility of devaluation, they are not fully immune to speculative attacks. The automatic adjustment mechanism under a currency board hinges crucially on interest arbitrage. Under normal conditions, a deterioration in the balance-of-payments

---

[11] For a discussion of the pros and cons of currency boards, see Williamson (1995) and Baliño and Enoch (1997). Ghosh, Gulde and Wolf (1998) argue in favour of currency boards, on the basis of the empirical evidence that countries with currency boards have lower inflation rates and higher economic growth rates on average than countries under pegged exchange rates without them.

position that puts downward pressure on the exchange rate, for example, would shrink the money supply and put upward pressure on domestic interest rates; and this in turn would attract capital inflows to support the exchange rate and keep interest rates from rising. Should confidence in the authorities' ability (and determination) to defend the official parity fade as a result of an external shock, however, containing capital outflow would require maintaining domestic interest rates at an extremely high level, which would have adverse effects on economic growth and the soundness of the financial system. Furthermore, under a currency board system only the monetary base is supposed to be backed up by foreign exchange reserves, but the credit created by the banking sector is many times this amount. Hence, the authorities may possibly run out of reserves amid intense speculation and may have no choice but to abandon the official parity (if not the currency board system itself). Hong Kong's experience suggests that a currency board system is too rigid to allow the pursuit of an independent monetary policy but not rigid enough to convince speculators that the risk of devaluation is zero.

Finally, McKinnon (1999) proposes a gradual restoration of the traditional exchange-rate parities because he sees no fundamental flaws with Asia's dollar-peg system and he views the crisis more as the result of self-fulfilling speculation. Making a firm commitment to exchange rate stability would minimize a country's need to increase interest rates in the short run when the local currency is under attack; it would mitigate the contagion from 'accidental' competitive devaluation in the medium term and keep the domestic price level stable in the long term. The major problem with this proposal is obviously how to make such a commitment credible when there is a total loss of confidence.

7.4 POLAR VERSUS INTERMEDIATE REGIMES

The selection of a country's exchange rate regime involves a spectrum of options including monetary union, currency board, adjustable peg, crawling peg, basket peg, target zone or band, managed floating and free floating (Table 7.2). With various types of pegged exchange rate system becoming more vulnerable to speculative attacks in this age of global financial integration, the debate over the choice of exchange rate regime has shifted from fixed versus floating regimes to polar versus intermediate regimes.

Polar regimes

On the basis of the history of the European Monetary System (EMS) and, more recently, the crisis in Asia, Eichengreen (1994, 1999) argues that the presence of large and liquid international capital markets has made it infinitely difficult for the authorities to support a shaky currency peg, because the resources of the

Table 7.2: Major exchange rate regimes

Fixed corner	1	*Monetary union*: participating members share a common currency as well as a common central bank (e.g. Euroland). This includes the special case of the adoption of a foreign currency as legal tender, such as official dollarization (e.g. Panama).
	2	*Currency board*: rigidly linking the value of domestic money to that of a foreign currency and tying the domestic monetary base firmly to the level of foreign exchange reserves (e.g. Hong Kong).
Intermediate regimes	3	*Adjustable peg*: fixing the exchange rate, but without any open-ended commitment to resist devaluation or revaluation in the presence of a large balance-of-payments deficit or surplus (e.g. European countries under the European Monetary System).
	4	*Crawling peg*: a pre-announced policy of adjusting the exchange rate bit by bit over time (e.g. Indonesia before the 1997 crisis).
	5	*Basket peg*: fixing not to a single currency but to a weighted average of other currencies (e.g. Thailand before the 1997 crisis).
	6	*Target zone or band*: a margin of fluctuation around a central rate (e.g. Israel).
Flexible corner	7	*Managed floating*: allowing the exchange rate to fluctuate subject to intervention but without an explicit exchange rate target (e.g. Japan).
	8	Free floating: no official intervention undertaken in the foreign exchange market; economic policies (especially monetary policy) pursued with benign indifference to the exchange rate (probably does not exist in pure form but the US comes close).

Note: Major exchange rate regimes are arranged along a spectrum from the strongest fixed rate commitment to the most flexible.
Source: Compiled by the Nomura Research Institute, based on Eichengreen (1994) and Frankel (1999).

markets far outstrip the reserves of even the most well-endowed central bank. At the same time, progress in democratization, which reduces the credibility of the government's commitment to maintain exchange rate stability over and above the pursuit of other economic goals, has aggravated this problem.[12] Capital mobility and democratization are thus undermining the viability of contingent rules designed to hit explicit exchange rate targets such as pegged but adjustable rates and narrow target zones, forcing policy-makers to choose between joining a monetary union and allowing exchange rates to float.

[12] The view that fixed but adjustable exchange rates have become more and more difficult to maintain has been supported by Obstfeld and Rogoff (1995), among others.

Although monetary union and free floating occupy the two ends of a spectrum of major exchange rate regimes ranging from the strongest fixed rate commitment to the most flexible, some free-market economists believe that they share the common ground of being the 'market solutions' to the currency conundrum. A floating exchange rate is supposed to be free from official intervention; under an immutably fixed exchange rate the government puts exchange rate policy on autopilot. In contrast, with intermediate arrangements the government uses its discretion to manage the exchange rate.

Eichengreen has been careful in defining a floating regime broadly to include managed floating, which is subject to intervention, although he insists that the authorities should avoid reference to an explicit exchange rate target. Recognizing the need to have a nominal anchor, he suggests that monetary policy should target inflation instead of the exchange rate. However, allowing the government the discretion to intervene would contradict the basic philosophy of letting the market rather than bureaucrats or politicians decide the exchange rate and thereby disqualify it as a market solution. It is also unclear why targeting inflation is superior to targeting the exchange rate in terms of credibility and macroeconomic stability.

When applying his 'going to extremes' principle to Asia, Eichengreen favours floating over monetary union. He doubts the possibility of Asia's developing countries forming a monetary union with the United States, Europe or Japan because their trade and financial flows are diversified and they lack the political will to promote monetary integration. Even Eichengreen, however, would recommend floating only with reservation, cautioning that 'One must hope that the countries of the region succeed in putting in place the institutional and political prerequisites necessary to effectively manage their managed float'.[13] Such prerequisites would be demanding: they would include establishing credibility in monetary policy without using the exchange rate as a nominal anchor, developing liquid and efficient forward and futures currency markets so that corporations can hedge their foreign exchange positions at low costs, and preventing bureaucrats and politicians from abusing their power to influence the exchange rate in order to favour privileged sectors.

Intermediate regimes

If the institutional and political prerequisites for adopting a floating exchange rate regime are lacking and costly to realize, it may be worthwhile for Asia's developing countries to reconsider the alternative of trying to achieve the prerequisites of the intermediate regimes instead. Indeed, the argument in favour of polar

---

[13] Eichengreen (1999), pp. 34–5.

regimes over intermediate regimes has been based on the firm belief that intermediate regimes are not viable rather than that the polar regimes are more desirable.[14] A preferred approach is to improve the intermediate regimes with explicit exchange rate targets so as to make them less vulnerable to currency speculation.

In an attempt to combine the merits of both the fixed and floating rate regimes while minimizing their shortcomings, Williamson (1996) proposes a crawling band wherein a central bank undertakes a public obligation to maintain the exchange rate within a wide, publicly announced band around a parity that is periodically adjusted in relatively small steps in order to keep the band in line with the fundamentals.[15] A band performs the function of guiding the market to where the equilibrium rate lies, and by stabilizing expectations it reduces the risks of volatility and misalignment that characterize floating rates.[16] The exchange rate is free to fluctuate within the band, but the central bank is obliged to intervene at the edges in order to prevent the rate from going outside it.

Consistency between the band and the economic fundamentals is expected to provide the 'first defence' against speculation. The key components of a crawling band system are the parity rate, the rate at which it crawls, and the width of the band. The central parity should be managed so as to track the underlying 'fundamental equilibrium exchange rate' (FEER). The parity rate should be defined in terms of a basket of currencies instead of a single currency, and it should be adjusted not just to offset inflation but also to reflect permanent changes in the fundamentals.[17] Since the FEER can be estimated only with imprecision, the band should be wide enough (say +/-10 per cent) to ensure that the 'true' FEER falls within the band. By increasing the probability that the exchange rate will return to the central rate, it would also increase the risk that speculators face. At the same time, a wide band allows the authorities more room to pursue an independent monetary policy.

Recently, a number of suggestions have been made to improve the crawling band system. In response to the criticism that a crawling band system is just as

[14] As Frankel (1999, p. 5) puts it, 'The rejection of the middle ground is then explained simply as a rejection of where most countries have been, with no reasonable expectation that the sanctuaries of monetary union or free-floating will, in fact, be any better. Therefore, a blanket recommendation to avoid the middle regimes in favor of firm-fixing or free-floating would not be appropriate'.

[15] This band-basket-crawl (BBC) approach has been supported by Dornbusch and Park (1999).

[16] As pointed out by Williamson (1998), the fact that a movement of the spot rate within a band is accompanied by a smaller movement in the forward rate while there is no such tendency with a floating rate is conclusive proof that a crawling band is stabilizing expectations.

[17] Ohno (1999) also favours targeting some real effective exchange rate but suggests that this is consistent with a variety of exchange rate regimes.

vulnerable to speculation as an adjustable peg system, Williamson (1998) proposes a monitoring band that does not involve an obligation to defend the edges of the band, hoping that the modified system would still play a positive role in focusing market expectations on the long-term equilibrium rate. Bergsten, Davanne and Jacquet (1999) insist that even when the exchange rate is well within the band, monetary policy should stabilize the exchange rate so as to enhance credibility. They also propose that the IMF should be involved in determining and supporting the band. The World Bank (1997) adds that, consistent with the insulating properties of the floating and the fixed exchange rate regimes, the band (an indicator of the degree of exchange rate flexibility) should be wide for an economy facing real shocks and narrow for an economy facing nominal shocks. Within the band, nominal shocks should be coped with by intervention, while real shocks call for exchange rate adjustment.

Strengthening the institutional prerequisites to support intermediate regimes

To support the argument that intermediate regimes should be improved rather than abandoned, let us look at some specific measures that may help to reduce the vulnerability of intermediate regimes to currency attacks, including capital controls and international frameworks to stabilize exchange rates among major industrialized countries as well as among the Asian countries.

Capital controls

Although economic theory suggests that it is difficult, if not impossible, for a country to achieve simultaneously fixed exchange rates, free capital mobility, and an independent monetary policy (known as 'the impossible trinity'), a country under a fixed exchange rate system can restore monetary autonomy by imposing capital controls (Figure 7.6).

Capital inflow has played a major role in Asia's economic development, but with imperfect financial markets, perfect capital mobility may lead to market failures. Some form of government intervention should provide a second-best solution.[18] The literature on the sequencing of economic reform, which has identified the prerequisites for a successful opening up of the capital account, provides the strongest theoretical base for a developing country to impose capital controls (McKinnon, 1991). The 1997 crisis in Asia has confirmed that a developing country should not liberalize capital account transactions at too early a stage, when banks' risk appraisal is inadequate and monetary control is difficult. These conditions are more likely to be met by the more advanced countries than by the less developed ones. Premature opening up would not

---

[18] For a discussion of the pros and cons of capital controls, see Eichengreen (1998).

Figure 7.6: Trade-off between the impossible trinity

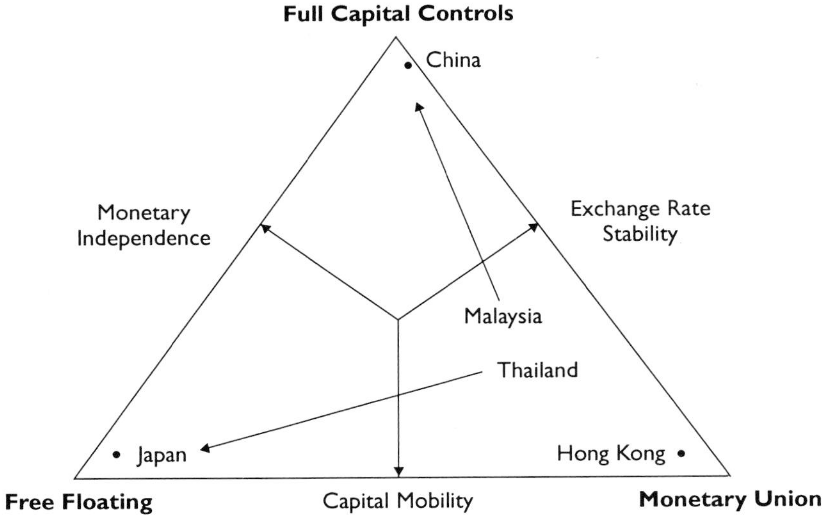

Source: Compiled by the Nomura Research Institute, based on Frankel (1999).

only lead to a misallocation of social resources but also invite speculation. The recent experience of the ASEAN countries has shown that this cost can be very high. In contrast, China is fortunate that it has maintained tight controls on capital flows, which insulate it from speculative attacks, on the one hand, and enhances the flexibility to stimulate domestic demand by pursuing expansionary fiscal and monetary policies, on the other hand.

Capital controls should also be considered as emergency measures to prevent systemic risks when speculation threatens the soundness of the financial system and deprives the government of tools of macroeconomic management. Krugman (1998) recommends capital controls as an alternative to the IMF programme for the Asian countries hard hit by the crisis on the principle that 'extreme situations demand extreme measures'. Indeed, in an attempt to stabilize the exchange rate and to reclaim autonomy over its monetary and fiscal policies, Malaysia imposed drastic capital controls in September 1998.[19] In retrospect, these goals have been broadly achieved, and Malaysia has also been successful in using the breathing space to restructure its financial and corporate sectors.[20]

[19] The key measures included pegging the ringgit to the dollar, imposing a 12-month holding period on repatriations of proceeds from sales of securities, limiting capital outflow by residents, banning the trading of Malaysian shares on Singapore's over-the-counter market and strictly limiting the use of the ringgit in international transactions.
[20] See Yusof et al. in this volume, Chapter 5.

Stabilizing the yen–dollar rate

Given that fluctuations in the yen–dollar rate are destabilizing the Asian economies, it is desirable to stabilize the yen–dollar rate itself. It would then not make much difference whether an Asian country pegged to the dollar, to the yen or to a basket of currencies, and the risk of pegging to a wrong anchor would become minimal. McKinnon and Ohno (1997) propose that the US and Japan jointly announce a target zone of +/-5 per cent for the yen–dollar rate based on purchasing power parity. Concerted intervention should be pursued in order to keep exchange rates within the permissible band, which should narrow over time after confidence in the accord has been established. Coordination of macroeconomic policy would be needed so as to ensure that stabilizing the yen–dollar rate is consistent with other domestic policy objectives. Specifically, monetary policy in the two countries should be assigned to anchor the level of tradable goods in the long run.[21]

Stabilizing exchange rates among Asian currencies

Early in the Asian crisis of 1997, Japan proposed to set up an Asian Monetary Fund to promote financial stability of the region. This proposal was based on the recognition that the amount of speculative capital is much larger than an individual country's foreign reserves for defending against a currency attack and that the IMF's allocation of funds for Asia is inadequate. Although the details of the fund have yet to be worked out, the idea is to pool part of the foreign exchange reserves of the Asian countries and provide participating countries with credit lines to defend their exchange rates and/or to cope with large-scale capital outflows. By exploiting economies of scale, such a facility has the additional advantage of reducing the need for individual Asian countries to hold large foreign exchange reserves. Policy coordination among Asian authorities, including joint intervention in the foreign exchange markets by Asian central banks, should also help to alleviate the contagion effect of currency devaluations.[22]

Asian countries may also seek to stabilize exchange rates among themselves by pursuing some form of monetary integration along the lines of the EMU in Europe. This can be achieved by pegging their currencies to the yen (a yen bloc) or to a common basket of currencies (an Asian Currency Unit, or ACU, analogous to the ECU in Europe), as proposed by Williamson (1999). The diversity of the Asian countries suggests, however, that a 'single currency' for Asia may not be consistent with macroeconomic stability at this stage and is better reserved as a long-term goal (Kwan, 1998b).

---

[21] There have also been many proposals to stabilize exchange rates among major currencies (the dollar, the yen and the euro) based on target zones, including Williamson (1985), Bergsten and Henning (1996), McKinnon (1996), and Bergsten, Davanne and Jacquet (1999).
[22] For the need to establish an Asian Monetary Fund, see Ito (1999), Shinohara (1999), and Wang (1999).

References

Aghevli, B., M.S. Khan, and P. J. Montiel (1991), *Exchange Rate Policy in Developing Countries: Some Analytical Issues*, IMF Occasional Paper No. 78 (Washington, DC: International Monetary Fund).

Argy, V. (1990), 'Choice of Exchange Rate Regime for a Smaller Economy: A Survey of Some Key Issues', in P. De Grauwe, P. and V. Argy (eds), *Choosing an Exchange Rate Regime: The Challenge for Smaller Industrial Countries* (Washington, DC: International Monetary Fund).

Baliño, T. and C. Enoch (1997), *Currency Board Arrangements – Issues and Experience*, IMF Occasional Paper No. 151 (Washington, DC: International Monetary Fund).

Bank for International Settlements (1999), *Central Bank Survey of Foreign Exchange and Derivative Market Activity* (Basle: Bank for International Settlements).

Bénassy-Quéré, A. (1996), 'Exchange Rate Regimes and Policies in Asia', *CEPII Working Paper* No. 96–07.

Bergsten, C. F., O. Davanne and P. Jacquet (1999), 'The Case of Joint Management of Exchange Rate Flexibility', *Working Paper* 99–9 (Washington, DC: Institute for International Economics).

Bergsten, C. F. and R. Henning (1996), *Global Economic Leadership and the Group of Seven* (Washington, DC: Institute for International Economics).

Cooper, R. N. (1999), 'Exchange Rate Choices', *http://www.economics.harvard.edu/faculty/cooper/papers/frbb_full.pdf*.

Dornbusch, R. and Y. C. Park (1999), 'Flexibility or Nominal Anchors', in Collignon, S., J. Pisani-Ferry and Y. C. Park (eds), *Exchange Rate Policies in Emerging Asian Countries* (London and New York: Routledge).

Eichengreen, B. (1994), *International Monetary Arrangements for the 21st Century*, (Washington, DC: Brookings Institution).

Eichengreen, B. (1998), 'Capital Controls: Capital Idea or Capital Folly?', *http://elsa.berkeley.edu/users/eichengr/capcontrols.pdf*

Eichengreen, B. (1999), 'Solving the Currency Conundrum', paper prepared for the Council on Foreign Relations Study Group on Economic and Financial Development, *http://elsa.berkeley.edu/users/eichengr/waltermead.pdf*.

Frankel, J. (1999), 'The International Financial Architecture', Policy Brief No. 51 (Washington, DC: Brookings Institution).

Genberg, H. (1990), 'Exchange Rate Management and Macroeconomic Policy: A National Perspective', in Honkapohja, S. (ed.), *The State of Macroeconomics* (Oxford and Cambridge, MA: Basil Blackwell).

Ghosh, A. R., A. M. Gulde and H. C. Wolf (1998), 'Currency Boards: The Ultimate Fix?' *IMF Working Paper* (Washington, DC: International Monetary Fund).

International Monetary Fund (1997), 'Exchange Rate Arrangements and Economic Performance in Developing Countries', in *World Economic Outlook* (October), (Washington, DC: International Monetary Fund).

Ito, T. (1999), 'New Financial Architecture and its Regional Implications', paper prepared for the First International Seminar on 'Financial Cooperation between China, Japan, and Korea: Issues and Prospects', Cheju Island, South Korea.

Ito, T., E. Ogawa and Y. Nagataki-Sasaki (1998), 'How Did the Dollar Peg Fail in Asia?' *Working Paper Series*, No. 6729, National Bureau of Economic Research.

Koo, R. (1998), 'The Weakening Yen and Japan's Credit Crunch Problem', mimeo (Tokyo: Nomura Research Institute).

Krugman, P. (1998), 'Saving Asia: It's Time to Get Radical', *Fortune*, 7 September.

Krugman, P. (1999), 'Analytical Afterthoughts on the Asian Crisis', *http://web.mit.edu/krugman/www/MINICRIS.htm.*

Kwan, C. H. (1992), 'Formation of a Yen Bloc – An Asian Perspective', *NRI Quarterly*, Winter (Tokyo: Nomura Research Institute).

Kwan, C.H. (1994), *Economic Interdependence in the Asia-Pacific Region – Towards a Yen Bloc* (London and New York: Routledge).

Kwan, C.H. (1998a), 'A Japanese Perspective of Asia's Currency Crisis', *Journal of the Asia Pacific Economy*, Vol. 3, No. 3.

Kwan, C.H. (1998b), 'The Theory of Optimum Currency Areas and the Possibility of Forming a Yen Bloc in Asia', *Journal of Asian Economics*, Vol. 9, No. 4 (Winter).

McKinnon, R. I. (1991), *The Order of Economic Liberalization – Financial Control in the Transition to a Market Economy* (Baltimore, MD and London: Johns Hopkins University Press).

McKinnon, R.I. (1996), *The Rules of the Game: International Money and Exchange Rates* (Cambridge, MA: MIT Press).

McKinnon, R.I. (1999), 'The East Asian Dollar Standard, Life After Death?', *Working Paper* 44, Stanford Institute for Economic Policy Research, Stanford University.

McKinnon, R.I. and K. Ohno (1997), *Dollar and Yen – Resolving Economic Conflict between the United States and Japan* (Cambridge, MA: MIT Press).

Obstfeld, M. and K. Rogoff (1995), 'The Mirage of Fixed Exchange Rates', *Journal of Economic Perspectives*, Fall.

Ohno, K. (1999), 'Exchange Rate Management in Developing Asia – Reassessment of the Pre-crisis Soft Dollar Zone', *ADBI Working Paper Series*, No. 1 (Tokyo: Asian Development Bank Institute).

Shinohara, H. (1999), 'On the Asian Monetary Fund', *Newsletter*, No. 4 (Tokyo: Institute for International Monetary Affairs).

Wang, Y. (1999), 'The Asian Crisis and the Need for Regional Financial Arrangements', paper prepared for the First International Seminar on 'Financial Cooperation between China, Japan, and Korea: Issues and Prospects', Cheju Island, South Korea.

Williamson, J. (1982), 'A Survey of the Literature on the Optimal Peg', *Journal of Development Economics*, Vol. 11, No. 1.

Williamson, J. (1985), 'The Exchange Rate System', second edition, *Policy Analyses in International Economics*, No. 5 (Washington, DC: Institute for International Economics).

Williamson, J. (1995), 'What Role for Currency Boards?', *Policy Analyses in International Economics*, No. 40 (Washington, DC: Institute for International Economics).

Williamson, J. (1996), *The Crawling Band as an Exchange Rate Regime – Lessons from Chile, Colombia, and Israel* (Washington, DC: Institute for International Economics).

Williamson, J. (1998), 'Crawling Bands: How to Manage Exchange Rates in a World of Capital Mobility', *International Finance*, Vol. 1, No. 1 (October).

Williamson, J. (1999), 'The Case for a Common Basket Peg for East Asia', in Collignon, S.,

J. Pisani-Ferry and Y. C. Park (eds), *Exchange Rate Policies in Emerging Asian Countries* (London and New York: Routledge).

World Bank (1997), *Private Capital Flows to Developing Countries – The Road to Financial Integration* (New York: Oxford University Press).

8 EXCHANGE RATE OPTIONS FOR EU APPLICANT COUNTRIES IN CENTRAL AND EASTERN EUROPE

Rolf H. Dumke and Heidemarie C. Sherman

8.1 INTRODUCTION

Romano Prodi started his tenure as the newly elected President of the European Commission (EC) with the promise that the enlargement of the European Union (EU) would receive top priority and that all six current applicant countries (the Czech Republic, Estonia, Hungary, Poland, Slovenia, and Cyprus) would be asked to the negotiating table at the December 1999 summit of EU leaders in Helsinki. In the aftermath of the Kosovo crisis, the EC proposed on 13 October 1999 that accession negotiations should be opened with all remaining candidate countries (Bulgaria, Latvia, Lithuania, Romania, Slovakia and Malta). However, these negotiations should take a 'differentiated' approach, taking full account of each candidate's progress in meeting the 'Copen-hagen criteria' set by the EU. These are the main elements of an ambitious strategy that the EC, at the initiative of Günter Verheugen, Commissioner for Enlargement, recommended to the Helsinki summit. Verheugen considers 2002 to be the earliest possible accession date but assumes that 2004–6 is more likely. The new commission seems intent on speeding up the process of enlargement, confirming the commitment made in January 1995, at the beginning of his mandate, by President Jacques Santer. In July 1997 Santer presented Agenda 2000 to the European Parliament, the cCommission's detailed strategy for strengthening and enlarging the EU in the early years of the twenty-first century.

Although participation in the European Monetary Union (EMU) is not a formal requirement for EU accession, it is reasonable to assume that, by the time of accession, the candidate countries will be expected to be on a path of convergence to meet the key criteria for EMU participation. In June 1993 the European Council meeting in Copenhagen adopted the criteria for membership. Accordingly, membership requires:

A longer version of this paper, which includes country case studies, will be available as an Ifo Discussion Paper, forthcoming.

- stable institutions guaranteeing democracy, the rule of law, human rights and the protection of minorities;
- the existence of a functioning market economy as well as a capacity to cope with competitive pressure and market forces within the EU;
- an ability to take on the obligations of membership, including adherence to the aims of political, economic and monetary union.

New member states will have to adopt the *acquis communautaire* of Stage 2 of EMU, including adherence to the relevant provisions of the Stability and Growth Pact. Furthermore, they will be expected to have completed the liberalization of capital movements, to participate in the exchange rate mechanism (ERM) and to avoid excessive exchange rate changes.[1]

Non-participant (opt-out and left-out) EU members are required to submit annually medium-term convergence programmes, subject to surveillance by the European Council. In addition they should adhere to the new exchange rate mechanism (ERM2), which requires parity between their currency and the euro with a +/-15 per cent margin, to be maintained for at least two years prior to qualifying for Stage 3 of EMU. From this it can be inferred that a basic, albeit implicit, prerequisite for EU accession would be to demonstrate an ability for operating within the ERM2 regime and for eventually participating in EMU. Presumably, this requirement would have to be met along with credible convergence towards EMU reference values for government deficit and debt and for inflation and interest rates.

This chapter seeks to answer the following questions concerning exchange rate options for the central and east European (CEE) candidates for EU accession. First, is there a case for EMU participation by these countries on the basis of the theory of optimum currency areas? Second, do the accession countries meet the institutional and legal requirements of EMU; are they ready to adopt a hard currency strategy? The major part of the chapter then attempts to answer the central question: what are the exchange rate options for these countries on their way to EMU? This entails a description and analysis of exchange rate regimes in the process of transition and an analysis of their vulnerability to external events. A summary and conclusion end the chapter.

---

[1] The *acquis* implies central bank independence, coordination of macroeconomic policies, prohibition of direct central bank financing of public-sector deficits and privileged access to financial institutions. At the outset, EU membership would be limited to participation in the customs union and the single market, as well as convergence towards, but not participation in, the currency union.

8.2 THE CASE FOR PARTICIPATION IN EMU

The economic case for joining ERM2 and eventually EMU rests primarily on the theory of optimum currency areas, assuming that EMU is indeed an optimal currency area.[2] The relevance of this theory for the accession countries goes far beyond the debate over fixed vs. flexible exchange rates for economies in transition.[3] The argument in favour of fixed rates centres on the view that during transition from central planning to a market economy, a fixed peg can serve as a policy anchor for macroeconomic stabilization while the institutional framework is being developed. Alternatively, a flexible exchange rate is considered useful for maintaining external competitiveness and can serve as a more immediate gauge for macroeconomic discipline without constraining the transformation of the economy.

The potential benefits and costs that would accrue to the applicant countries from joining the EMU currency union must be compared. They go, of course, beyond the welfare effects of becoming a member of the EU as a single market and customs union. The benefits would derive primarily from reduced costs of economic transactions (trade, investment, services) between these countries and the existing currency area. Furthermore, currency risk premiums, including the risk of exchange rate depreciation, would fall and eventually disappear. Reduced transaction and information costs and declining currency risk premiums would boost trade, investment, employment and growth.

A potential cost of joining a currency area consists of the impaired ability of the participant country to absorb asymmetric real shocks in the absence of an independent monetary and exchange rate policy.[4] This loss in macroeconomic stability may be substantial for some countries as they attempt both to finance the costs of meeting the single-market requirements and to converge towards a budget deficit of less than 3 per cent of Gross Domestic Product (GDP). In addition, candidate countries may lack sufficient flexibility in their internal goods and labour markets for them to serve as a shock absorber.

In general, the net benefits from joining an optimum currency area will be larger (a) the smaller the candidate country relative to the union, (b) the closer

---

[2] For a recent review of the basic arguments and qualifications in support of this assumption see the essays in Blejer et al. (1997).

[3] See Sachs (1996).

[4] Bayoumi and Eichengreen (1993), for example, show that EU members in the periphery are likely to suffer destabilizing consequences from demand and supply shocks owing to the loss of the exchange rate as a policy instrument. For a recent review see Calmfors et al. (1997). Canzoneri, Valles and Vinals (1996) find, however, that the past shocks that caused most output variations in the EU do not seem to have resulted in nominal exchange rate fluctuation, while the shocks that explained nominal exchange rate movements are monetary in nature. This implies that EMU will not entail significant cost in stability for participating EU member countries.

Table 8.1: Trade of CEE countries with the EU (%)

	Bulgaria	Czech Republic	Estonia	Hungary	Latvia	Lithuania	Poland	Romania	Slovakia	Slovenia
Share of imports with EU-12 1994	32.5	45.0	23.9	45.3	24.9	26.4	57.5	45.7	26.2	57.1
Share of imports with EU-15 1998	45.0	63.3	60.1	64.1	55.3	50.2	65.9	57.7	50.4	69.4
Share of exports with EU-12 1994	35.4	42.6	19.0	51.0	27.9	25.7	62.7	48.2	28.4	59.2
Share of exports with EU-15 1998	49.7	64.2	55.1	72.9	56.6	38.0	68.3	64.5	55.8	65.5
Average annual growth rate of imports from EU 1994–8	25.3	35.2	51.1	39.4	50.4	52.3	5.6	35.3	41.8	29.3
Average annual growth rate of exports to EU 1994–8	22.9	34.9	46.7	53.1	41.8	38.8	43.9	28.6	34.0	28.1

Source: EU Commission on Enlargement, *Enlarging the EU – 2nd Regular Reports*, 13 October 1999.

its economic and political integration with the union, (c) the greater the similarity in economic structure between the candidate and the union, and (d) the higher the public debt of the candidate country. Characteristics (a), (b) and (c) reduce the likelihood of asymmetric shocks in the enlarged union that must be offset by policy action at the country level. Furthermore, under (d) the country benefits from a reduced currency risk premium.

It is difficult to predict for individual CEE countries the net effect of joining EMU. It may be surmised, however, that all five lead countries stand to gain from (a), (b) and (c) and at least one (Hungary) from (d). Most of these countries are relatively small and – gauged by the share of their trade with the EU – have already reached a considerable degree of integration with it (Table 8.1). They are at least as open to trade as several non-core EU countries and more so than Greece and Italy. They have been less successful in attracting significant amounts of foreign direct investment (with the exception of Hungary and Estonia), and cross-border labour mobility has been limited. Important steps towards political integration (OECD and NATO membership) have been taken by the Czech Republic, Hungary and Poland.

The economic structure of most candidate countries (in terms of value added or employment) is only slightly more biased towards agriculture and industry than that of non-core EU countries, with the exception of Greece. This sectoral breakdown hides the great diversity of the candidates' manufacturing base, lowering further their susceptibility to asymmetric shocks. Kopits (1999) notes that all CEE candidates have a more advanced and diversified economic structure than the Communauté Financière d'Afrique (CFA) franc zone members which automatically participate in Stage 3 of EMU.

Therefore, on the basis of their size, integration and structure, most candidate countries are likely to benefit from participating in EMU. In addition, Hungary and, to a lesser extent, Poland should gain more than the others from the decline in the currency risk premium and the lower interest cost associated with servicing a relatively high public debt. Recent findings of a strong relationship between trade intensity and cross-country correlation of business cycles imply a self-reinforcing process: as trade intensifies, the probability of asymmetric shocks declines. Conversely, participation in a currency area leads to trade expansion and thus to highly synchronized business cycles. This suggests endogeneity of the optimum currency area criteria.[5]

[5] Frankel and Rose (1996).

Table 8.2: Maastricht convergence indicators, 1996–8 (%)

	Consumer price inflation[a]			General government balance/GDP[b]			Gross government debt/GDP[c]			Long-term interest rates		
	1996	1997	1998	1996	1997	1998	1996	1997	1998	1996	1997	1998
Bulgaria	123	1082.2	22	-13.4	-4.4	-2.8	105.8	105.2	n.a.	300.1	209.9	10.1
Czech Rep.	8.8	8.4	11	0.4	-1.2	-2.5	10.2	10.9	10.9	12.5	13.2	12.8
Estonia	16.7	11.3	8	-1.5	2	n.a.	6.9	5.6	n.a.	12.3	19.8	16.7
Hungary	23.6	18	14	-3	-4.9	-4.6	74.1	68	n.a.	28.2	23.1	n.a.
Latvia	17.6	8.4	5	-1.3	1.3	0.1	13.8	10.8	n.a.	26.2	15.3	14.3
Lithuania	24.7	8.8	5	-4.6	-1.9	-0.4	23.7	22.2	22.5	24.1	14.4	12.2
Poland	19.9	15.1	12	-2.8	-3.8	-3.7	49.2	48.2	n.a.	19.6	20.3	21.6
Romania	38.8	155	59	-3.9	-3.5	n.a.	23.4	31.3	n.a.	71.5	107	64
Slovakia	5.8	6.1	7	-1.3	-4.8	n.a.	24.5	26.7	n.a.	13.5	20.9	n.a.
Slovenia	9.7	8	8	-0.1	-1.8	n.a.	23.5	24.1	n.a.	23.7	20	16.1

[a] Consumer price inflation data are based on national statistics and may not be consistent with the harmonized consumer prices constructed by EUROSTAT which will be used in applying the Maastricht criteria.

[b] May not correspond to EUROSTAT definitions and coverage. Excludes privatization revenues.

[c] May not be consistent with the definition agreed in Maastricht. For Estonia, data include public and publicly guaranteed foreign debt.

[d] The Maastricht criterion refers to yields on government bonds of 10-year maturities. Owing to the lack of long-term bonds, with market-based yields, interest rates are mostly bank lending rates, except for Poland where the note refers to that on foreign debt.

Sources: National sources; IMF, *World Economic Outlook* (September 1999), *International Financial Statistics* (September 1999).

8.3 INSTITUTIONAL IMPLICATIONS OF EMU FOR EU CANDIDATE COUNTRIES[6]

EMU is part of the *acquis communautaire,* and the EU has decided against additional opt-out clauses for new countries entering the Union. CEE countries wanting to join the EU in the future will therefore have to prepare themselves to join the euro area.

Although some newcomers could get a transitional period for the monetary part of the *acquis,* there are three reasons why such a period is unlikely:

(1) There is a consensus within the EU that transitional periods should be limited in number, scope and duration.
(2) Most candidate countries seem eager to participate in EMU as soon as possible.
(3) Those newcomers which for macroeconomic reasons will not be able to participate in EMU will also be unlikely to comply with the Maastricht convergence criteria required for joining the euro area.

For countries aiming at EU membership and hence at eventual participation in the euro area, EMU has two types of institutional or policy implication. The first stems from the fact that these countries must satisfy the macroeconomic convergence criteria laid down by the Maastricht Treaty before they can join the euro area. This increases pressure on the candidate countries to design their fiscal, monetary and exchange rate policies in a way that will facilitate the convergence. Secondly, unless they obtain transitional periods, countries joining the EU will have to fulfil from their date of membership all the legal and institutional requirements that apply to EU countries remaining outside the euro area. These requirements include the full independence of their central banks, the prohibition of monetary financing of government deficits and the full liberalization of capital flows, including *vis-à-vis* third countries.

Meeting the convergence criteria

Table 8.2 shows that none of the countries has met all four of the Maastricht criteria.[7] However, the Czech Republic, Estonia, the Slovak Republic, Slovenia and the Baltic countries have comfortably met the two fiscal criteria – Estonia

---

[6] See Temprano-Arroyo, Heliodoro and Feldman (1998).
[7] These criteria specify that: (1) A country's inflation rate is not more than 2% higher than the average observed in the three low-inflation countries (1998: 2.7%); (2) Its government budget deficit is not higher than 3% of its GDP; (3) Its government debt has moved significantly towards the norm of 60% of its GDP; (4) Its long-term interest rate is not more than 2% higher than the average observed in the three low-inflation countries (1998: 6.6%).

Table 8.3: Economic performance and structural reform indicators, 1994–8 averages

	EBRD transition indicators	Per capita GDP 1998 US$ ppp	Average GDP growth (%)	Average export growth (%)	Average rate of inflation (%)	Labour Productivity in manufacturing	FDI per capita[a] (US$)	Average growth of fixed investment	Broad money/ GDP	Private-sector credit/ GDP	External debt US$m (End 1998)	International reserves[b] US$m (End 1998)
Czech Rep.	3.5	12,479	2.2	12.8	9.5	8.5	818	6.2	72	60	11,445	542
Estonia	3.3	7,607	4.2	29.7	23.8	7.9	555	10.1	28	24	1,482	811
Hungary	3.5	10,202	3.1	21.9	20.6	11.0	1113	6.9	43	23	9,895	9,319
Poland	3.4	7,658	6.0	18.6	21.4	9.9	321	14.3	36	15	32,186	432
Slovenia	3.2	14,305	4.3	8.6	11.9	7.1	530	11.2	39	29	1,170	639
Bulgaria	2.6	4,776	-2.1	4.1	277.6	2.0	140	-6.2	32	13	3,640	831
Latvia	2.9	5,557	3.2	15.3	18.3	9.4	646	8.8	27	11	792	728
Lithuania	3.0	6,437	2.1	26.9	30.0	5.4	318	7.8	21	13	1,753	409
Romania	2.6	5,646	0.2	12.1	84.4	5.6	208	1.6	25	11	3,064	867
Slovak Rep.	3.3	9,817	5.9	12.2	8.4	6.5	144	9.1	68	36	2,305	869

[a] Cumulative FDI for the period 1994–8; [b] Excluding gold.

Source: IMF, *Economic Outlook*, May 1999 and September 1999, joint BIS-IMF-OECD-World Bank statistics on external debt.

and Latvia have even run budget surpluses. They have shown (except for the Czech Republic) one-digit inflation rates and have had interest rates in the 10–20 per cent range. Poland and Hungary have been in an intermediate position. Poland has met the debt criterion and exceeded the reference value for the deficit/GDP ratio by a relatively small margin. Its interest rates and its inflation rate have been higher, however, than those of the first group of countries. Lagging somewhat behind Poland has been Hungary, which has failed to meet any of the criteria. Its inflation rate and its debt ratio have declined, however. Most progress has been made by Bulgaria, whose inflation rate and interest rate dropped sharply in 1998 and whose deficit/GDP ratio fell below the 3 per cent reference value.[8] The worst-performing country has been Romania, although its fiscal data look good and its monetary convergence data are moving in the right direction.

In summary, a majority of countries appear to satisfy or come close to satisfying the fiscal criteria: all countries except Bulgaria and Romania have complied with the debt criterion and six countries have satisfied or (in the case of Poland and Romania) have come close to satisfying the government balance criterion. The inflation and interest rate criteria seem to remain elusive for most countries, although progress is being made. The correlation between performance in terms of the Maastricht criteria, on the one hand, and progress made with structural reform and levels of economic development (Table 8.3), on the other hand, does not seem to be strong. In fact, some rather advanced countries, including Hungary and Poland, have fared poorly on the convergence criteria, while some with less developed market economies have fared better.

8.4 MEETING THE INSTITUTIONAL AND LEGAL REQUIREMENTS OF EMU

The most important institutional and legal requirements in the area of monetary union applicable to EU states outside the euro zone, and thus to the new EU members from the CEE countries, are:

- *Participation in ERM2.* At its June 1997 meeting in Amsterdam, the European Council defined the main principles and elements of a new exchange rate mechanism (ERM2) for EU currencies in Stage III of EMU. Once the countries of central and eastern Europe join the EU, they will be expected to join ERM2, although membership is voluntary. Participation in the ERM under the normal fluctuation band remains a criterion for

---

[8] Cf. Gulde (1999).

admission to the euro area.[9] ERM2, as currently envisaged, will have standard fluctuation bands of +/-15 per cent *vis-à-vis* the euro. Timely realignments of central parities will be encouraged. Countries reaching a sufficient degree of convergence with the euro area may enter into closer exchange rate links involving narrower fluctuation bands *vis-à-vis* the euro. Such forms of closer exchange rate require approval by EU bodies and the European System of Central Banks (ESCB).

Its voluntary nature, the wide bands, demands for early realignments and the possibility of closer exchange rate links make ERM2 a flexible system which would seem to accommodate the varying circumstances of the associated CEE countries (and other candidates for EU membership), especially the broad spectrum of exchange rate arrangements, ranging from a managed float (the Czech Republic and Slovenia) to fixed pegs and including currency board arrangements (Estonia, Lithuania, Bulgaria). Table 8.4 lists the current exchange rate regimes of the countries under consideration. A majority of these countries currently peg their currencies (*de jure* or *de facto*) to the DM, the euro or a basket of currencies dominated by the euro. Lithuania pegs to the US dollar and Latvia to the SDR (Special Drawing Rights).

As some of these countries join the EU, they may need to adjust their exchange rate arrangements further to conform with ERM2. Countries with currency board arrangements or other fixed pegs could continue with similar arrangements under ERM2, with the associated advantages in terms of intervention and financing facilities. Countries with floating exchange rates or pre-announced crawling pegs (such as Hungary and Poland) would have to modify their exchange rate regimes substantially, however. All countries, including those which decide to stay out of ERM2 after joining the EU, will be subject to the obligation to treat their exchange rate policy as 'a matter of common interest'.

- *Central bank independence.* The *acquis communautaire* also specifies the independence of the central bank. This presupposes in particular that (1) central bank governors should be elected for terms of not less than five years and should be dismissed only under circumstances of serious misconduct or inability to perform their duties (Art. 14 of Protocol No. 3); (2) the central banks should take no instructions from the government (Art. 107 and 7 of Protocol No. 3); (3) the prime objective of the central banks should be the

---

[9] The admission of Finland and Italy (both of which had been in the ERM for less than two years) suggests, however, that the EU Council is not interpreting this criterion strictly. In justifying its decision, the Council noted that the Italian and Finnish currencies had appreciated or remained stable against the ERM currencies since March 1996. See European Council (1998).

maintenance of price stability (Art. 105 and 2 of Protocol No. 3); and (4) national legislation should prohibit any form of direct credit from the central bank to the government.

When establishing two-tier banking systems at the beginning of the transition process, the CEE countries endowed their newly created central banks with a relatively high degree of independence. The new central bank laws were often patterned after the Bundesbank law or mirrored those for the Austrian central bank. New legislation increasing central bank independence was enacted subsequently, some as recently as 1998 (Albania, Romania). Recent changes and amendments to central bank laws aim at better aligning them to EU standards, anticipating EMU entrance.

Following the recent wave of changes in legislation, many CEE countries satisfy or are close to satisfying the first three central bank statutory requirements of the Maastricht Treaty. The Czech Republic, Lithuania and Poland fully comply with these requirements. All CEE countries appoint their governors for tenures of at least five years. In Hungary and the Slovak Republic, however, some of the other members of the governing board have terms of less than five years. In addition, some countries (Bulgaria, Estonia, Hungary, Latvia, the Slovak Republic and Slovenia) fail to limit the possible reasons for dismissal of board members.

Almost all CEE countries have price or currency stability (or both) as their primary objective. Currency stability may be associated with price stability and thus is consistent with the Maastricht Treaty. In some cases, however, it may be in conflict with price stability. The central bank laws of all transition countries except Romania explicitly embody the principle of independence from the government. Finally, in line with the interpretation of the Maastricht requirements by the European Monetary Institute (EMI), many central bank laws contain incompatibility clauses for high central bank officials in order to prevent conflicts of interest.

Whereas the extent of the statutory independence of central banks is considerable, the actual degree of independence is relatively low. One approach to measuring actual independence is to look at the rate of turnover of central bank governors.[10] A comparison of turnover rates for several transition countries with the average turnover rate for 21 industrial countries shows a much higher rate for the CEE countries considered (ranging from 0.17 for Slovenia to 0.49 for Poland) than for the group of industrialized countries (0.13).[11]

- *Financing of the government.* Regarding fiscal financing by the central bank, only Bulgaria, Estonia and Lithuania comply in full with the Maastricht

---

[10] Cukierman (1992).
[11] See Table 9 in Temprano-Arroyo and Feldman (1998).

requirements. The currency board arrangements of these countries prohibit any type of credit from the central bank to the government, including (except in the case of Lithuania) indirect credit via open market operations. Poland, which adopted a new National Bank Act in January 1998 which explicitly prohibits fiscal financing, now also satisfies the Maastricht limits.[12] The National Bank of Hungary is also almost in full compliance with the Maastricht rules, following the amendments to its law of January 1997 (except for a very short-term overdraft facility).

- *Participation in the European System of Central Banks.* All EU central bank governors will be members of the General Council of the ECB. EU members outside EMU will be obliged to consult the ECB on any draft legislative proposal in its field of competence, and their financial institutions could be subject to prudential supervision by the ECB.
- *Liberalization of capital flows.* Free capital movements are an essential component of monetary union. Countries joining the EU will have to comply with this part of the *acquis communautaire,* although some of them may obtain transitional periods for certain types of flows (especially short-term capital movements), as were granted to Spain, Greece, Portugal and Ireland. Effective as of 1994, liberalization of capital flows must also take place *vis-à-vis* third countries.

Although the CEE countries lifted restrictions on foreign direct investment (FDI) inflows at the beginning of the transition because they were aware of the many benefits from FDI and have applied quite liberal treatment to trade credits in order to promote exports, most other capital movements have remained very restricted. The countries feared the destabilizing effects of an open capital account at a time when they were still trying to get their macroeconomics sorted out. A general pattern has been the existence of much tighter controls on outflows than on inflows and on short-term than on long-term transactions. An exception is the Baltic countries (and in particular Estonia), which opted for a very high degree of capital account openness from the beginning.

The process of gradual liberalization started in 1995, when the Czech Republic, Hungary and Poland made substantial commitments as part of their accession to the OECD in December 1995, May 1996 and November 1996 respectively. These three countries have liberalized FDI outflows, outward trade credits, personal capital movements as well as other outflows (e.g. long-term ones) to varying degrees. The Czech Republic, Hungary and Poland have further committed themselves to abolishing all remaining capital controls within three to four years of their dates of accession, macro-

---

[12] Hochreiter and Kowalski (2000).

economic conditions permitting. The Baltic countries score highest on overall capital account liberalization. These six countries will therefore be in a favourable position regarding compliance with the Maastricht requirements once they join the EU.

- *Policy coordination and surveillance.* From the date of accession, new EU members will have to regard their economic policies as a matter of common concern. They will also have to be part of a number of EU mechanisms for the multilateral coordination and surveillance of the macroeconomic policies of the member states, including the broad economic policy guidelines, the convergence programmes and the excessive deficit procedure. The tight fiscal and monetary policies needed to be part of these initiatives may be difficult to reconcile with the large public investment needs in the transition countries.

- *An efficient market-oriented financial sector.* The prospect of EU membership increases pressure on non-EU candidate countries to make progress towards developing a sound, efficient and market-oriented financial sector. Without considerable improvements in their financial markets, many CEE countries will have difficulty in complying with some of the Maastricht rules. Insufficient competition in the banking sector, for example, can reduce the responsiveness of bank lending rates to changes in monetary policy.

- *A well-functioning payment system.* An essential feature of EMU is the Trans-European Automated Real-time Gross Settlement Express Transfer (TARGET) payment system, which connects national systems through an interlink network. CEE countries which want to become members of EMU have to develop modern national payment systems that are compatible with TARGET. Their status as latecomers permits them to leapfrog by adopting payment systems that are best suited for TARGET. The introduction of the euro and the increase in cross-border transactions between the CEE countries and the EU will reinforce the importance of adopting a TARGET-compatible payment system. The ECB recently published a Blue Book on the status of the payments systems in the nine CEE countries and Cyprus which have applied for membership of the European Union. According to the ECB Blue Book (1999), Poland has the most advanced banking and payment systems, some of the regulations having been implemented in the past two years. Hungary established its current payment system back in the mid-1980s but real-time gross settlement systems for high-value payments and a securities settlement system were only being introduced in 1999. The Czech and Slovak payment systems were replaced by a new interbank payment system and a clearing and settlement centre in 1992. After the division of Czechoslovakia at the beginning of 1993, separate central banks and payment systems were established in the two countries. Progress on a modern payment system in Estonia is quite recent. The central bank started to design a new interbank payment system (which is compatible with EU requirements) in 1998. In Slovenia, the payment system reform programme is to be completed in 2001, at which time payment systems will be based on a real-time gross settlement system for high-value and urgent payments (operational since 1998) and on an integrated small-value payment system for the rest.

8.5   EXCHANGE RATE REGIMES AND THE PROCESS OF TRANSITION

Ten years into transition, the CEE candidate countries for accession to the EU are facing a host of challenges. These countries are adapting to open, market-based international trade, undertaking stabilization programmes to end high inflation and undergoing enormous structural change with large movements in relative prices and productivity. They must implement monetary and financial reforms and deal with fiscal deficits and, in some cases, a large overhang of foreign debt. In addition, these countries are experiencing large inflows and outflows of capital and therefore are subject to shocks emanating from international capital markets. In order better to meet these challenges, they have chosen particular exchange rate regimes, usually upon the advice of the IMF, and established convertibility.

Different exchange rate regimes

Why countries undergoing a similar shock – the transition shock – have adopted such widely different exchange rate regimes remains a puzzle. Country-specific factors, including the political situation and particular economic conditions, have to be a large part of the explanation. Four countries initially chose pegged exchange rates: Czechoslovakia, Estonia, Hungary and Poland. Slovenia, Latvia, Lithuania, Bulgaria and Romania relied on floating exchange rates. After two devaluations, Poland adopted a crawling peg in October 1991 and a crawling band in July 1995. Hungary switched to a crawling peg in March 1995. The Czech Republic moved to a managed float in May 1997. Slovenia and Romania stayed with a managed float, although Slovenia's exchange rate is *de facto* pegged to the euro. In 1994, two of the initial floaters, Latvia and Lithuania, adopted a pegged exchange rate and a currency board arrangement in emulation of Estonia. Bulgaria did the same in July 1997 (Table 8.4). Thus, of the five leading candidates for EU membership, only Estonia and Slovenia have a fixed peg (in terms of the DM or the euro), whereas Poland, Hungary and the Czech Republic have moved towards greater exchange rate flexibility. This seems generally reasonable, as these countries have reduced their inflation rate and remonetized their economy (see Table 8.3).

Table 8.4: Exchange rate regimes

Country	Regime[a]	Previous Regime[a]	Margin (+/-%)	Currency basket	Monetary policy framework
Bulgaria	Fixed peg (July 1997)	Managed float (Feb. 1991)	0		Currency board arrangement
Czech Republic	Managed float (May 1997)	Fixed basket (Dec. 1990)	n.a.	n.a.	Inflation targeting
Estonia	Fixed peg (June 1992)		3	euro[c]	Currency board arrangement
Hungary	Pre-announced crawling peg (March 1995)	Adjustable peg (since before 1989)	2.25	70% euro[c] 30% US$	Implicit inflation targeting
Latvia	Fixed peg (Feb. 1994)	Managed float (July 1992)		SDR	
Lithuania	Fixed peg (April 1994)	Floating (Oct. 1992)	0	US$	Currency board arrangement
Poland	Pre-announced crawling band[b] (October 1991)	Fixed basket (Jan. 1990)	7	40% euro[c] 10% stg 5% SFr 45% US$	Inflation targeting
Romania	Managed float (Aug. 1992)				Various indicators
Slovak Republic	Fixed peg (July 1995)	Fixed basket (Dec. 1990)	7	60% euro[c] 40% US$	
Slovenia	Managed float (October 1991)		n.a.	De facto pegged to euro	M3 combined with real exchange rate rule

[a] Date of adoption shown in parentheses.
[b] Crawling peg prior to May 1995.
[c] Previously D-Mark.

Sources: IMF, *Exchange Arrangements & Exchange Restrictions* (1997); *International Financial Statistics*; Kopits (1999).

There are three basic arguments in favour of pegged exchange rates at the outset of the transformation process,[13] when prices have been liberalized, the official and market exchange rates have been unified, the country has been opened to foreign trade and bringing down the high inflation rate is the key policy objective:

- The pegged rate underpins the government's commitment to the stabilization effort by establishing clear targets and by tying the government's own hands;
- The exchange rate peg helps those on both sides of the product and factor markets to adapt their actions and expectations to a low inflation equilibrium; and
- The pegged exchange rate provides a way for consumers and producers to rebuild their real money balances after a bout of high inflation. By repatriating their offshore capital and converting it into domestic currency, they increase their real money balances while also remonetizing the economy. Under floating rates, there is no automatic mechanism, as the central bank is not committed to purchase repatriated capital for domestic currency and is unlikely to do so. On the other hand, remonetization through credit expansion by the central bank may undermine the credibility of the stabilization programme. Therefore, many central banks refrain from domestic credit expansion, leaving the economy undermonetized and contracting and the exchange rate overvalued. The cost of successful stabilization under floating rates is therefore higher than under pegged rates. And often stabilization under flexible exchange rates simply fails.

Once inflation has been tamed, however, introducing greater flexibility into the exchange rate may be appropriate. Structural weaknesses (rigidities in labour markets and elsewhere, chronic fiscal problems) may be incompatible with a fixed exchange rate. Greater flexibility of the exchange rate combined with strengthened monetary targets and institutions may be better suited to this stage of transition, especially as rising productivity and wages in the tradables sector may lead to an overvaluation of the currency. Capital inflows may be another source of pressure towards currency appreciation. A managed float or a crawling peg will take this pressure off and reduce the risk of a banking crisis.

Max Corden (1993) produces further useful concepts for the choice of an exchange rate regime in developing states or countries in transition:

- In the Keynesian tradition, nominal exchange rate fluctuations affect the real exchange rate, the external competitiveness, because of sticky domestic

[13] Sachs (1996).

prices.[14] If there is concern for external competitiveness, a country will be interested in limiting real exchange rate fluctuations, i.e. in targeting the *real* exchange rate *vis-à-vis* its main trading partners. Given the country's choice of a real target, it will let the nominal exchange rate depreciate to compensate for domestic inflation.

- In the monetarist tradition, a nominal anchor approach argues that nominal exchange rate policy can help to reduce inflation without any *lasting* effect on real variables. Countries which peg their nominal exchange rate wish that their inflation rate will converge towards the inflation rate in the anchor currency. A real appreciation that helps to reduce inflation at the expense of external competitiveness is permitted. During the disinflation process, discretionary or pre-announced devaluations help to reconcile the nominal objective with the real target.

Thus, there is a trade-off between the 'real target approach' and the 'nominal anchor approach' to the choice of an exchange rate regime. The choice of an optimal approach will depend on the policy preferences between external competitiveness and inflation, besides the inflationary consequences of a depreciation and the size of the non-traded goods sector.[15] Most CEE countries tried to solve the trade-off between real and nominal targets by an initially large devaluation, which was succeeded by fixed nominal exchange rates. The initial devaluation left room for real appreciation during the disinflation process. So, from Corden's point of view, one can discern a certain logic to the choice of exchange rate regimes in the transformation countries.

The choice of the exchange rate regime has implications for the stability of the financial sector. Will countries with deep financial markets prefer to float[16] or will they prefer to peg?[17] What is the significance of the strength of the financial sector for the optimality of the exchange rate regime or the implications of the exchange rate arrangement for the stability of the financial sector?

According to the standard textbook, whether fixed or flexible exchange rates are preferable depends on the source of the disturbance. For example, when fluctuations in world interest rates pose a threat to the stability of the banking system, because they make it more difficult for the banks to fund themselves

---

[14] Recall that in Continental European terms: $Q = E(P^*/P)$, where Q is the real exchange rate, E the nominal exchange rate (domestic currency price of foreign currency), P^* and P are foreign and domestic price levels. Given sticky prices, the home country cannot easily adjust to a shock by changing domestic prices, nominal exchange rate flexibility takes up the task. Given P^* and the low flexibility of P, changes in E affect Q, external competitiveness.

[15] For a further discussion of the rationale for exchange rate policies in Asia and in the CEECs, see Agnes Bénassy-Quéré (1996).

[16] McKinnon (1963).

[17] Heller (1976).

offshore, there is a case for exchange rate flexibility to discourage banks from relying excessively on external sources of finance (as in the Asian crisis) and to enhance the capacity of the domestic authorities to act as lenders of last resort. When, on the other hand, the main risks to the stability of the banking system emanate from erratic monetary policies at home, the argument is for a pegged exchange rate in order to discipline domestic policy-makers and to vent shocks via the external sector. But countries adopting pegged rates must tailor their financial systems to accommodate this additional constraint.[18]

Notwithstanding these theoretical arguments for or against fixed exchange rate regimes, the actual economic outcomes (growth, inflation) in the individual transition countries to date appear to bear little or no relation to the type of exchange rate regime chosen (see Tables 8.3 and 8.4).

Equilibrium real exchange rates

Irrespective of the exchange *regime* chosen, the authorities must have a view of the appropriate exchange rate *level*. Determining the appropriate exchange rate is difficult, however, especially for a transition country. The theoretical definition, the rate which delivers a sustainable path for the current account, is of little help in the case of transition countries which combine a short history with rapidly changing domestic conditions. In addition, some of them have started to attract capital inflows of a clearly unsustainable nature. The second difficulty is that transition is synonymous with rapid structural change. Existing theories of the evolution of equilibrium real exchange rates are based on the Balassa-Samuelson view, which emphasizes stronger productivity advances in the traded, compared with the non-traded, goods sector. This characterization of structural change does not describe the transition process to date.

Halpern and Wyplosz (1997) have proposed an alternative approach: compare prices across countries that share similar characterisics. The same approach has been taken by Krajnyák and Zettelmeyer (1998). Usually the first step is to look at the average wage expressed in a common currency, the US dollar. The second step is to identify the variables which may have a long-run effect on the dollar wage. The estimates are then interpreted as equilibrium real exchange rates. Recently Halpern and Wyplosz have updated their attempt to estimate real exchange rates (equilibrium dollar wages) by including more countries, longer time series and more relevant data.[19] Although they counsel that the estimates ought to be viewed with considerable caution, the conclusions are quite significant:

---

[18] Eichengreen (1998).
[19] Halpern and Wyplosz (1993).

Figure 8.1: Historical vs. equilibrium path of the real exchange rate during transition

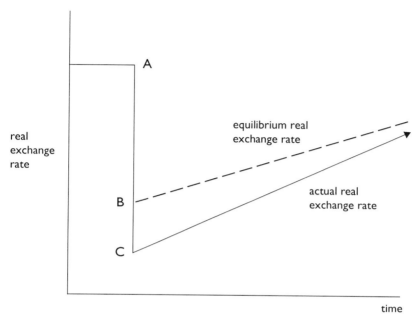

Source: Halpern and Wyplosz (1998).

- The substantial real appreciation observed in most transition countries represents a correction from the initial massive depreciation (from A to C in Figure 8.1) and undervaluation (measured by the distance B-C);
- Most countries have seen their equilibrium real exchange rate appreciate continuously as a result of the transformation process. Exceptions are due mainly to deteriorating indebtedness;
- Thus, there is no guarantee that dollar wages ought to rise continuously. Now that the catch-up phase is over, further gains depend on a deepening of the transition process.

Exchange rate policy remains complicated, as the range of uncertainty regarding the equilibrium exchange rate remains wide. This calls for some flexibility. The case for flexibility is enhanced further by four considerations: first, the general reduction in the rate of inflation means that the need for a nominal anchor recedes. Second, continuous capital account liberalization increases the scope for large and sudden swings in capital movements. Third, idiosyncratic, transformation-induced shocks (structural changes, policy mistakes) are still likely to occur in the accession countries. This would require more flexibility in nominal exchange rates. The combination of weak banks and other financial institutions in transition countries, together with external shocks, are a recipe for currency crises in the future (see Tornell (1999) for the argument). This calls for more flexibility in the exchange rate regime. Fourth, actual real exchange rates may overshoot equilibrium real exchange rates and cause a deterioration in competitiveness and growth in the CEE accession countries. We address below the vulnerability to external events, especially the presence of weak banking systems and the question of current account sustainability. The next section focuses upon the issue of competitiveness.

Competitiveness and the real exchange rate

Recent empirical research by Aaron Tornell (1999) on the probability of events in the exchange rate and financial crises in 1995 and 1997, particularly in Latin America and Asia, finds that investors concentrate their attacks on countries that are very likely to respond with an excessive depreciation. These are countries with very low reserves relative to liquid liabilities, weak banking systems and severe real exchange rate appreciation. This section deals with the question whether the CEE countries have experienced dangerously severe real exchange rate appreciations which have threatened competitiveness and may subsequently lead to unsustainable increases in current account deficits.

Table 8.5 presents estimates by Halpern and Wyplosz of large real exchange rate appreciations in the accession countries since the early 1990s. The dollar wage is used as an indicator of real exchange rates. Halpern and Wyplosz (1997) present an argument as to why the dollar wage is a useful indicator and show its relationship to the usual definitions of the real exchange rate, the doubly (CPI) deflated nominal exchange rate and the relative price of non-tradables to tradables.[20]

The authors present graphs depicting the evolution of these three measures in individual transition countries since the early 1990s. With the exception of Slovenia and Russia, all figures show a parallel movement which suggests the following stylized facts (see also Figure 8.1 above): an initial severe decline of the real exchange rate leads to a substantial undervaluation; then, over time, the real exchange rate appreciates, for two reasons. First, there is a gradual correction of the initial undervaluation. Second, the real exchange

---

[20] The reason why the relative price of nontradables to tradables is equal to the real exchange rate is as follows, p. 211): assume that the price level is a geometric average, with weights n and 1-n of the prices of tradables and nontradables. Take tradables as the numeraire, with a common price of 1 in both countries. Then the home and foreign price indexes are $P = (1)^n p^{1-n} = p^{1-n}$, $P^* = (1)^n (p^*)^{1-n} = (p^*)^{1-n}$. Thus, the home-to-foreign price level ratio is $P/P^* = (p/p^*)^{1-n}$ and home's real exchange rate against foreign depends only on the internal relative prices of nontraded goods.

Table 8.5: Real exchange rate appreciation (% increase in the dollar wage)

Country	Increase from trough or first available data	Year of trough or first available data
Bulgaria	65.1	1991
Czech Republic	90.4	1993
Estonia	225.2	1993
Hungary	42.7	1990
Latvia	75.5	1994
Lithuania	558.3	1992
Poland	175.5	1990
Romania	124.8	1990
Slovak Republic	61.1	1993
Slovenia	64.0	1991

Source: Halpern and Wyplosz (1998).

rate appreciates as a result of the transformation process. The rate of equilibrium appreciation is higher the more complete the market system and the faster the capital accumulation.

The rise of the real exchange rate (an appreciation[21] in Figure 8.1 and Table 8.5) makes it more difficult for a country to sell its goods abroad, and makes it less competitive. On the other hand, an appreciation may reflect productivity increases in the traded sector which enhance competitiveness. This causes rising equilibrium real exchange rates, which do not threaten competitiveness.

Have the dramatic real exchange rate appreciations found in Table 8.5 threatened competitiveness in the accession countries? First, it should be recalled that the short time span of historical data in extraordinary, transformation-shocked times precludes any statement about equilibrium levels of real exchange rates based on this data. Equilibrium exchange rates can be inferred only by finding benchmarks in other countries, e.g. US dollar wages (see below). Secondly, the European Bank for Reconstruction and Development (EBRD) *Transition Report 1997* does not find that the external balance in most transition countries has been negatively effected. Nevertheless, as inflation rates have come down decisively since 1992 in the CEE states, the focus of exchange rate policy has shifted towards sustaining external equilibrium.

Table 8.6 shows that real exchange rate appreciation has been associated with rising unit labour costs in foreign currency terms. Nevertheless, strong productivity growth and lower real wage growth in 1997 have moderated the

[21] In contrast to the Continental definition, the Anglo-American definition of the exchange rate is used here; a rise in the exchange rate is an appreciation.

Table 8.6: Indicators of competitiveness, 1994–7 (% change)

Country	Industrial* (manufacturing) gross output				Productivity in industry* (manufacturing)				Real wage in industry* (manufacturing) (PPI-based)				Real D-Mark exchange rate (CPI-based)				D-Mark unit labour costs			
	1994	1995	1996	1997	1994	1995	1996	1997	1994	1995	1996	1997	1994	1995	1996	1997	1994	1995	1996	1997
Bulgaria*	8.5	4.9	-1.0	-7.0	12.6	7.3	2.1	-3.8	-12.1	3.3	-17.9	-15.9	-5.2	14.2	-12.2	40.9	-32.1	5.4	-23.7	5.3
Czech Republic	0.1	8.2	5.5	6.4	4.9	11.1	9.6	11.1	11.2	9.5	12.0	8.3	6.7	2.6	10.1	5.3	11.3	1.5	10.0	-12.2
Estonia	-3.2	2.9	2.2	16.9	6.7	0.4	3.7	17.8	26.9	14.1	7.8	11.0	44.0	26.6	21.4	9.2	61.7	35.2	19.3	1.1
Hungary	9.3	5.3	3.5	15.0	7.3	11.2	9.1	14.5	9.2	-5.9	-0.2	1.4	-1.6	-6.9	5.5	9.6	-3.6	19.3	-3.5	0.4
Latvia	-12.0	-8.1	0.8	8.1	9.5	-1.0	8.6	28.0	36.6	11.3	-0.1	17.3	57.3	14.8	16.3	16.4	73.0	17.9	5.2	4.2
Lithuania	-29.7	0.9	3.5	5.0	-12.1	12.0	8.5	4.6	13.8	14.0	15.0	19.1	65.7	29.5	29.0	23.2	85.1	23.3	30.5	36.7
Poland	13.6	11.6	10.5	13.9	13.9	7.0	9.9	13.9	5.1	5.4	18.3	8.8	1.4	4.4	11.6	7.1	-6.1	2.9	12.6	1.5
Romania	3.8	12.1	12.5	-11.3	10.1	20.0	12.1	1.0	0.7	16.6	3.6	-23.9	43.9	-5.3	-5.1	23.2	2.2	-4.2	-3.8	-4.9
Slovak Republic*	4.7	8.3	2.5	2.7	6.8	4.0	2.5	4.8	7.0	5.7	10.1	7.2	2.7	3.4	6.2	9.5	2.5	6.2	13.8	12.2
Slovenia*	6.4	2.0	1.0	0.9	11.4	7.2	6.6	5.2	8.1	3.9	7.0	5.3	1.5	7.0	-0.5	4.0	-1.6	4.9	-1.6	3.8

*Industrial gross output, productivity in industry, real wage in industry.

Source: EBRD, Transition Report 1998.

Table 8.7: Competitiveness and US dollar wage levels

Country	U.S. dollar actual gross average monthly wages in manufacturing 1997	Ratio of actual to fitted equilibrium wages[a]
Bulgaria[a]	82	0.28
Czech Republic	332	0.46
Estonia	257	0.68
Hungary	308	0.62
Latvia[b]	219	0.79
Lithuania	207	0.69
Poland	320	0.70
Romania	87	0.27
Slovak Republic[b]	283	0.52

[a] Equilibrium wages were calculated based on coefficients of a cross-country regression of gross US-dollar wages against GDP per capita in purchasing power parities, the share of agriculture in GDP and a measure for the stock of human capital. See Krajnyák and Zettelmeyer (1997) for details.
[b] Wages refer to industry.

Source: EBRD, *Transition Report 1998*.

impact of this appreciation on the competitiveness of manufacturing in the transition countries.

What room is there for further real exchange rate appreciation before competitiveness will be hurt? Studies by Halpern and Wyplosz (1997, 1998) and Krajnyák and Zettelmeyer (1997) have found that US dollar wages in the CEE states in 1995 remained significantly below their equilibrium levels, as determined by productivity measures. Table 8.7 updates the latter authors' estimates to 1997. The update confirms the earlier results, although the wage gaps have been reduced. The EBRD (1997: 66) further states that low dollar wages may also be a reflection of low unit prices for manufactured exports to Western markets, owing to remaining quality differences relative to other exporters. In this case, equilibrium wages might have been *overestimated* by not adjusting measures of relative productivity for such quality differences. Thus, the room for further real exchange rate appreciation would be reduced.

The most probably very large confidence intervals around the point estimates of the equilibrium real exchange rates calculated by Halpern and Wyplosz (1998) and Krajnyák and Zettelmeyer (1997) and also the EBRD critique that quality differences have not been considered in these calculations suggest a cautious interpretation of the room left for further rises in the real exchange rates. For a number of countries – Estonia, Hungary, Latvia, Lithuania and Poland – the ratio of actual to fitted equilibrium wages may already be close to one and thus threaten future competitiveness and growth.

Because of the uncertainty surrounding the CEE accession countries' equilibrium exchange rate levels and because the future path of equilibrium exchange rates in these countries is not well identified, there is a unique difficulty involved in setting the appropriate exchange rate to the euro at the start of ERM2 and EMU. This difficulty would argue for a delay in fixing the euro exchange rate for the majority of the accession countries, with the exception of the currency boards of Estonia, Lithuania and Bulgaria. In these small countries the gains of policy credibility from the currency board arrangement most probably outweigh the potential costs of a loss of competitiveness.

8.6 VULNERABILITY TO EXTERNAL EVENTS

On their way to EU accession and eventual membership of the EU, the countries of central and eastern Europe will have to adopt, for all practical purposes, pegged exchange rates. This will close the circle which for many started with currency pegs (to a single currency or a basket), which were later replaced by managed or adjustable floating exchange rate regimes.

However, two questions remain. How vulnerable are the accession countries to external shocks? Will their present or future system of foreign exchange rate pegs be derailed by future crises? Frankel (1999) points out that the risks of exchange rate and financial crises in a world of increasingly mobile capital flows can be controlled by the choice either of flexible exchange rates or of credibly fixed exchange rate regimes (currency board, euro-ization, monetary union). Intermediately flexible regimes are likely to be vulnerable. Dornbusch and Giavazzi (1998) introduce the argument of the huge costs involved in such crises. Together with the lack of macro policy competence (including monetary policy) in the transition countries to date, this determines the only and optimal exchange rate regime immediately available for these countries: currency boards. Nevertheless, the previous discussion of the notable achievement of a number of the Maastricht convergence requirements by the accession countries suggests that they are not such macro policy basket cases. As we have seen, when disturbances originate abroad, flexible exchange rates are better suited to insulate the financial system (and the economy at large). Under pegged exchange rates, however, the risk to the domestic banking system cannot be ignored.

Research into the characteristics of the East Asian crisis[22] has yielded insights into the fundamental factors determining a country's vulnerability to external

---

[22] The growing body of literature on the empirical evidence on currency crises is surveyed in Kaminsky, Lizondo and Reinhart (1998). For a recent list of references, see Tornell (1999).

events. The repercussions from East Asia also imposed a severe 'stress test' on the market-oriented reforms of the transition countries.[23] The portfolio reallocation of investors revealed that those countries that had large public- or private-sector imbalances and low reserve cover of short-term debt were more vulnerable. These weak fundamentals are, of course, linked to inadequate structural and institutional reforms. Flaws in public finances together with weak enterprises and financial institutions were the key underlying factors.

Fries et al. (1999) have ascertained the vulnerability and resiliency of the transition countries by the impact of the East Asian events on their asset markets from January 1997 to February 1999. The effect on short-term interest rates, the effect on the equity markets and the average increase in the spreads on Euro-bonds were used as indicators. Estonia and Romania were identified as the more vulnerable countries. The group of countries which exhibited greater resiliency included Bulgaria, Croatia, the Czech Republic, Hungary, Poland and the Slovak Republic. Obviously, the exchange rate regime was only one of the elements in this equation, as both groups included floaters and peggers, although only two countries (Bulgaria and the Slovak Republic) in the second group had fixed pegs.

There are a number of fundamentals which should be looked at in this context: the strength of the banking system, current account sustainability, including competitiveness and the real exchange rate (discussed in the previous section) as well as structural reform and the fiscal position. By analysing these factors we should be able to make an assessment of the countries' vulnerability to external shocks and therefore also of their preparedness for European monetary integration.

The strength of the banking system

A functioning market economy requires institutions that lay down foundations and enforce the 'rules of the game'. Properly designed institutions may also speed up the transition by reducing friction and uncertainty. They are also prerequisites for successful stabilization and sustainable growth. In the financial sphere the establishment of a two-tier banking system with an independent central bank whose main tasks are clearly specified is of primary importance. The design and implementation of monetary policy needs appropriate instruments, money markets and politically and functionally independent central banks.

The overriding importance of rapid financial reform for the transition process was not recognized at first. Therefore, the typical sequencing order did not give top priority to financial sector reform. This has been identified as the single most important sequencing error, and it is still causing problems in some of the transition countries. Nonetheless, much has been accomplished in the

---

[23] Fries, Raiser and Stern (1999).

past ten years. The two-tier banking system has been established and – because of liberalized entrance rules – more competing banks, including foreign banks, have emerged. New central bank legislation along Western lines has been adopted and financial markets have been developing.

In the stabilization of the macroeconomy the central bank's monetary policy plays a central role. However, the implementation of monetary policy requires sound banks, a modern payments system and financial markets. A sound banking system is also necessary to withstand external shocks in the form of currency and financial crises. When the central bank decides to raise interest rates drastically in order to fend off a speculative attack on the currency, this must not lead to bank failure owing to too many bad loans on the books. In the past, banks had accumulated a large proportion of bad or non-performing loans because much of their lending was based on political direction rather than commercial decisions. Soft budget constraints on banks, enterprises and governments were a prime cause of financial weakness. When banks bailed out companies and the central bank bailed out banks and provided direct credit to the government, inflation was an unavoidable consequence. In a market economy, entrepreneurs need to convince a commercial bank to lend to them if they do not have sufficient funds of their own. They cannot avoid bankruptcy when none of the banks is prepared to grant them a new loan. Moreover, commercial banks are in competition with one another, and thus require strict supervision and regulation to keep them sound.

How have the transition countries tackled this radical change in their banking systems? Some countries initially adopted a very liberal attitude towards the establishment of new banks. The Baltic states are the main examples of this approach. They have by now all had a banking crisis, and they have seen many of the new banks disappear. Other countries have taken a more gradualist approach, shielding the old banks from competition. Although in this way they might have escaped a major banking crisis, their banking systems still have many problems. Many of the former state banks have continued to lend to large state enterprises incapable of servicing previous loans. This weakens these banks and slows down bank restructuring. The large proportion of non-performing loans also forces the banks to maintain large spreads between credit and deposit rates, thereby discouraging both saving and investment.

Although basic financial reforms have been implemented in the transition economies, strong and sound financial sectors have not emerged yet (see Box 8.1). The reforms to date include the liberalization of deposit and lending rates and the installation of supervisory and regulatory frameworks so that banks can be expected to operate in a market-oriented environment (Table 8.8). Some areas, however, appear to need further reform, such as the enforcement of property rights and the performance of the legal sector. Inadequate accounting

Box 8.1: Recent banking problems in selected CEE countries

Bulgaria (1991–9). About 75 per cent of non-government loans were non-performing in 1995, leaving many banks insolvent. Runs on banks have been reflected in pressure on reserve money and a queue of unsettled interbank payments. The most recent crisis was due to a combination of easy entry, poor supervision, connected lending, failure to implement regulations and outright fraud.

Czech Republic (1991–9). In 1993–4, 38 per cent of bank loans were non-performing. Three small banks were closed in 1993–4, one failed in 1995 and two closed in 1996 while six others, including the biggest private bank, were put into forced administration.

Estonia (1992–5). Banking crisis in 1992. Insolvent banks held 41 per cent of banking system assets. The licences of five banks were revoked, two major banks were merged and nationalized, and two large banks were merged and converted to a loan recovery agency.

Hungary (1987–99). Eight banks accounting for 25 per cent of financial system assets became insolvent. At the end of 1993, 23 per cent of total loans were problematic. There have been two depositor runs.

Latvia (1995–9). Two-thirds of audited banks recorded losses in 1994. Eight bank licences were revoked in 1994 and 15 more during the first seven months of 1995. The subsequent closure of the largest bank (with 30 per cent of deposits) and two other major banks triggered a banking crisis in the spring of 1995.

Lithuania (1995–9). Of 25 banks, 12 small ones are being liquidated, and four larger ones did not meet the capital adequacy requirements. The fourth-largest bank was closed. The operations of two banks, which accounted for 15 per cent of deposits, were supported in 1995. There were large-scale deposit withdrawals at the end of 1995 and the beginning of 1996. A restructuring plan is under implementation.

Poland (1991–9). 16 per cent of loans were classified as losses, 22 per cent as doubtful and 24 per cent as sub-standard in 1991.

Romania (1990–99). Five major state-owned banks had 35 per cent of their accrued interest overdue as of 30 June 1994.

Slovak Republic (1991–5). Loans classified as non-standard were high at the end of August 1995. There were no runs or major bank closures, but all five major state banks required government-sponsored restructuring operations.

Slovenia (1992–4). Three banks, with two-thirds of the banking system's assets, were restructured during this period. The percentage of bad loans is not known. Bank rehabilitation was completed in 1995.

Sources: Lindgren, Garcia and Saal (1996); European Commission, DG II, Economic and Financial Affairs Documentation; *European Economy.* Supplement C, *Economic Reform Monitor* No. 1 – May 1997. Special Topic: 'Bank Restructuring in Central Europe'.

standards and a lack of inspection and intervention by bank supervisors still pose a threat to the financial systems' soundness.

Banks need both new skills in order to be able to assess the creditworthiness of their borrowers and a diversified menu of lending instruments to attract customers. Many banks failed in the early stages of transition because of management weakness, because they were owned or controlled by large loss-making enterprises that continued to receive loans despite being incapable of servicing them and because they were unable to secure a steady inflow of funds. They thus failed to perform their primary function of financial intermediary between savers and investors.

Financial intermediation, which increases the efficiency of the allocation of capital and thus enhances economic growth, remains underdeveloped in the transition countries. Banks play a smaller role in the economy, attracting fewer deposits and providing fewer loans than in developed market economies. A comprehensive analysis of the factors driving financial intermediation identifies the share of bad loans in bank portfolios, the concentration in the banking sector and expected inflation as the most important factors preventing deep financial intermediation.[24]

High levels of non-performing loans impinge on financial developments in two ways. First, they reduce the confidence of potential depositors in the ability of the banks to repay the deposits when due, thus reducing the supply of funds to the banks. Secondly, a large share of bad loans induces banks to widen the spread between borrowing and lending rates so as to accumulate profits against the need to write off non-performing loans.

The structure of the banking market, as measured by the concentration ratio, is an important factor because high concentration enables banks to limit credit expansion, thus inhibiting economic growth. New entrants should be attracted by the provision of a stable legal environment, including modern accounting and supervision standards.

Expected future inflation, finally, impairs financial development because economic agents will be unwilling to enter into long-term financial contracts, which reduces the demand for and supply of financial intermediation. Low inflation and a stable macroeconomic environment, on the other hand, supports financial deepening and economic growth.

A comparison of credit flows to business during the early years of transition, between 1990 and 1995, in five advanced applicant countries shows remarkable differences.[25] Hungary refused to default on inherited financial liabilities; and through a foreign debt write-off or more inflationary financing, it initiated a large-scale disruption in microeconomic discipline without contributing to

[24] Rother (1999).
[25] Sgard (1996).

Table 8.8: EU and CEE countries – main banking prudential regulations

EU/country	Maximum single exposure	Connected exposure limit	Aggregate large exposure limit	Open foreign exchange exposure limit	Investment in enterprises limit
EU	25% of capital	20% of capital for exposures to parent company and subsidiaries	88% of capital	No standard	15% of capital in single firm; 60% for firms in agregate
Czech Republic	25% of capital to nonbanks; 125% of capital for banks in country or OECD	20% of capital	800% of capital	15% of capital	20% of capital
Hungary	25% of capital to one party or group of related parties	15% of adjusted capital	800% of adjusted capital	Net foreign exchange liability limited to 30% of capital	15% of adjusted capital for single non-bank firm (except financial institutions); 100% for all firms combined
Poland	10% of capital for a single entity and 15% for a connected group	15% of capital	Informally expected not to exceed 800% of capital	Aggregate one-way exposure of 40% of capital; net exposure of 30%; max. open exposure in one currency of 15%	25% of capital in single group of non-financial entities, but 50% with approval of supervisor
Slovakia	25% of capital for non-banks; 80% for banks	25% of capital	800% of capital	Total net of foreign exchange liability of 25% of capital; 7–10% limits on individual currencies	25% of capital for non-banks
Slovenia	25% of capital; an exposure of 10% requires approval by Supervisory Council	5% of capital, and exposures require consent of all members of Supervisory Council	800% of capital	As prescribed by supervisor	100% of capital for land, buildings, bus. equity, and shares of non-financial organizations

Source: EU banking directives; national central banks; from Talley et al. (1998).

more confidence in the banking sector. The Czech Republic, in contrast, chose a much softer approach to business financing, made possible by stricter fiscal discipline. The bet was that slower long-term consolidation would not be disrupted by an external shock and would deliver more stability, more savings and more growth eventually. The Polish experience, and to a lesser degree that of Slovenia, lies between these two extremes and came practically to an optimal trade-off between early default on debt and later financial orthodoxy. The short history of the Estonian case provides a counter-example. The currency-board arrangement was accompanied by large-scale financial repression and massive transfers from households to business.

For the period 1994–8, the IMF provides comparative data on the degree of monetization, the relative size of private credit flows and GDP growth (Table 8.3 above). During this period, on average, the Czech Republic enjoyed the highest degree of monetization of all the transition countries and also the largest flows of private credit relative to GDP. During the same period, however, fixed investment, exports and GDP grew faster in Poland, Estonia and the Slovak Republic.

Capital flow reversals and banking stability

Private capital flows have become the main source of external financing for CEE countries, replacing the official flows which dominated in the early years. The increase of private capital flows has been concentrated in a small number of countries, however: Hungary, the Czech Republic and Poland. Reversible capital flows (short-term and portfolio equity flows) have increased rapidly since 1993. By 1997 these types of flow accounted for about one-quarter of total net private capital inflows. International commercial banks are the main suppliers and domestic banking systems are the principal means for absorbing that lending.

A sudden macro economy sharp reversal of these flows, caused, for example, by a currency crisis elsewhere which leads to a loss of investor confidence in emerging countries more generally, would initially bring about a deterioration of the macroeconomy and result in changes in certain key financial market prices. Large-scale capital outflows result in a depreciation of the domestic currency as foreign and domestic investors rush to convert assets denominated in domestic currency into assets denominated in foreign currency. This also causes domestic interest rates to rise and domestic equity prices to decline, often quite dramatically. Currency crises normally lead to a decline in a country's economic growth. This is induced in part by rising interest rates but also by an erosion in public confidence. One factor counteracting the decline in economic activity is exports, reflecting the improved competitive position of the country due to the depreciation of the currency. Depreciation also leads to an increase in import prices, which raise the domestic price level. This does not, as a rule, extend to real estate prices, which tend to decline sharply.

These changes in the macro economy and the financial markets have harmful effects on the financial condition of the banking system. The general slowdown of the economy, the rise in interest rates, which increases the debt burden of borrowers, and currency depreciation, which raises import costs for producers, combine to lower the quality of banks' loan portfolios. In addition, banks will experience a decline in the value of their investment portfolios as the market value of long-term debt instruments and equities held by them falls. The drop in real estate prices tends to affect banks adversely in two ways: first, banks' mortgage loans are supported by collateral whose value is declining. Second, banks frequently own a certain amount of real estate, and these assets are losing value. If the banks incur sizable losses from some of the factors mentioned, they may become subject to significant liquidity pressures.

Many of the effects just described could be considerably amplified in the CEE economies, both at the macroeconomic and banking sector levels, as a disproportionately large part of the region's capital inflows are of the reversible kind and are intermediated by the banks. In addition, key institutions are not yet fully developed in the CEE countries, and some are especially important in terms of the banking sector's vulnerability to external shocks: inadequate accounting and auditing, deficient legal frameworks, poor corporate governance, and weak bank supervision.[26]

Investors are aware of these weaknesses which increase their risks and erode their confidence. The prudential regulation of banks is therefore of critical importance to policy-makers in the CEE countries. As shown in Table 8.8, the CEE countries have rules to contain the various kinds of risk which closely parallel those of the EU directives. There is, however, great variation in the limitations placed on foreign exchange risk exposure, for which no EU standard exists. CEE banks have also adopted the basic Basle framework on capital adequacy requirements. Because of the institutional weaknesses enumerated above and the empirical evidence on banking instability during the transition process (Box 8.1 above), prudential regulation should probably be tighter than in the EU or OECD countries.

Current account sustainability

As evidenced by the recent currency crises in Mexico and Asia, unsustainable current account imbalances may be contributing factors to financial and currency crises. A large number of CEE countries experienced large and growing

[26] See Talley, Giugale and Polastri (1998).

current account deficits in 1996–7 (Table 8.9). Deficits in excess of 5 per cent of GDP (and in some cases around 10 per cent of GDP) were observed in the Czech Republic, the Slovak Republic, Poland, Estonia, Latvia and Lithuania.

Combined with the weak financial systems and the semi-fixed exchange rate systems, will the current account imbalances in the candidate countries be sustainable or are there significant risks of currency crises or exchange rate pressures? Was the currency crisis in the Czech Republic in the spring of 1997 an exceptional event or an early warning sign?

Measuring external vulnerability

One approach to current account sustainability relies on projecting into the future the current policy stance or private-sector behaviour. Sustainability is ensured if the resulting path of the trade balance is consistent with intertemporal solvency. If the unchanged policy stance is eventually going to lead to a drastic shift that reverses the trade balance position or to a balance-of-payments crisis, the current account position is assumed to be unsustainable. The drastic change in policy or crisis situation may be triggered by a domestic or an external shock that causes a shift in domestic and foreign investors' confidence and a reversal of international capital flows.[27] A second approach to current account sustainability relies on a composite set of macroeconomic, financial and external indicators to evaluate the risk of external crises.[28]

Until recently, analyses of external sustainability based on the first approach relied on the standard conditions relating the dynamics of debt accumulation to the trade balance, the economy's growth rate, the real interest rate on the debt and the real exchange rate. Given the change in the composititin of capital flows during the 1990s, however, this approach provides only a partial picture because it ignores the evolution of the net equity position of the country and its impact on future investment income outflows. The approach must therefore be extended in order to account for the effect on non-debt-creating flows, such as foreign direct investment and portfolio equity investment. This raises important measurement problems.

In order to remain solvent, a country must ensure that its external liabilities maintain a favourable ratio to GDP or exports. A simple measure of solvency has therefore been the long-run net resource transfer (trade surplus) that the country must undertake in order to keep the ratio of external liabilities to GDP constant. This says nothing, however, about the appropriateness of the particular ratio. Furthermore, there can be no presumption that in the short and

---

[27] See, for example, Milesi-Ferretti and Razin (1997).
[28] See, for example, Dornbusch, Goldfajn and Valdes (1995); Sachs, Tornell, and Velasco (1996).

Table 8.9 Current account balances (US$)

	1994	1995	1996	1997	1998
Czech Rep.	-745.0	-1362.0	-4292.0	03721.0	-1065.0
Estonia	-165.0	-165.4	-423.1	-561.9	-477.9
Hungary	-3911.0	-2480.0	-1678.0	-982.0	-2304.0
Poland	954.0	854.0	-3264.0	-5744.0	-6900.0
Slovenia	600.1	-23.0	39.0	36.5	-3.8
Bulgaria	-32.0	-26.0	16.0	427.0	-252.0
Latvia	201.0	-16.0	-454.0	-345.0	-714.0
Lithuania	-94.0	-614.4	-722.6	-944.5	-1298.0
Romania	-360.0	-1357.0	-2025.0	1885.0	-2658.0
Slovakia	719.0	390.0	-2090.0	1342.0	-2066.0

Source: EU Commission on Enlargement: Enlargement Reports, 13 October 1999.

medium run a fast-growing country with a low level of external liabilities should aim at stabilizing the ratio of external liabilities to GDP or exports at the current level. Also, the ratio does not take into account the risk that future liquidity constraints may suddenly appear. Because of these shortcomings, a more comprehensive set of financial indicators needs be monitored in addition to the current account so as to correctly evaluate external sustainability. Besides the question of determining this set of indicators, there is also the problem of how to rank them and how to translate them into an overall measure of external sustainability or vulnerability.

There are potentially a large number of variables that might serve as indicators of vulnerability. The choice is determined by one's understanding of the proximate determinants of crises. If the root cause is considered to be fiscal problems, then variables such as the general government deficit and credit to the public sector by the banking system may feature prominently. If weaknesses in the financial sector are perceived to be most important, then private-sector credit growth, the level of foreign short-term indebtedness of the banking system, the ratio of non-performing loans etc. could be used as indicators. Similarly, if foreign sector problems are viewed as the prime weakness, the real exchange rate, the current account balance, changes in the terms of trade etc. may be used.

Determinants of current account sustainability: some general empirical results

The variables identified by ongoing research as affecting current account sustainability include macroeconomic indicators (economic growth, the investment rate, export performance, openness to trade, the real exchange rate and the size of the current account deficit relative to GDP), financial variables (domestic credit expansion, stock market performance and loan quality) as well as external vulnerability indicators (the ratio of broad money (M2) to foreign currency reserves, the size of short-term liabilities relative to total debt and foreign currency reserves). Of course, the degree of currency convertibility within the capital account and external variables such as foreign interest rates and the terms of trade help in assessing resiliency to various shocks. Finally, the degree of political stability and policy-makers' credibility influence foreign and domestic investors' confidence in the economy.

Results so far have shown that large current account deficits relative to GDP do not necessarily imply current account unsustainability. All other things being equal, the current account imbalance is likely to be less sustainable if it is large relative to GDP, if it is due to a decline in savings rather than an increase in investment and if national savings are low. It is also less sustainable the higher the trade deficit. A higher degree of openness enhances current account sustainability, as a country with a relatively open economy has fewer incentives to renege on its external obligations and should have less trouble servicing its debt.

Appreciation of the real exchange rate may mean misalignment relative to inflation or to an equilibrium position. It may also result from a positive differential of labour productivity growth. The composition of capital flows is important. The longer-term the capital inflow is, the less likely a reversal. Large short-term inflows concentrated in time are likely to be highly reversible, and they exert upward pressure on the exchange rate.

The ratio of foreign reserves to imports seems to be more important than the ratio of reserves to M2. A worsening of the terms of trade makes a country more vulnerable to current account reversals, as capital inflows slow in anticipation of a rising trade deficit and imminent devaluation.

High foreign interest rates make deficits less sustainable, as they redirect capital flows away from emerging markets. In addition, a sudden rise in interest rates may lead to problems of debt servicing.

Evaluating the sustainability of the current account in the accession countries: conclusions from country case studies

Several indicators used in the literature were analysed in an attempt to evaluate the sustainability of current account deficits in several transition countries applying for membership in the EU. They were supplemented by information on recent economic developments and structural reform efforts. Generalizations are difficult, however, because the sample is small and the time frame is short.

A number of regularities may be observed. A large current account deficit relative to GDP does not necessarily cause problems with financing or a currency crisis: the Baltic states ran current account deficits larger than the Czech

Republic and did not experience disruptions of their funding. The analysis of sustainability must take other variables into account, which conforms with recent research.[29] The case of the Czech Republic confirms that a balanced government budget is not enough to shield against a currency crisis.

Twin deficits, however, increase vulnerability, as the case of Hungary before 1995 and that of Slovakia since 1996 show. A fall in exports and thus foreign currency reserves featured in both Hungary and the Czech Republic, two of the three countries which experienced difficulties with financing their deficits. Hungary, the Czech Republic and Slovakia also shared another feature: high external indebtedness.

The other stylized facts are the following: trade deficits are the main causes of the current account deficits in this group of countries; exports in dollar terms have grown more slowly than imports in dollar terms. The evidence that real appreciation is a negative factor is rather inconclusive, as gains in labour productivity have tended to offset its impact. The need for modernization and pent-up consumer demand are equally valid explanations. Countries which have made more progress in structural reforms and privatization enjoy greater investor confidence and find it easier to attract private foreign capital to finance the deficit. The soundness of the banking system is an important factor in ensuring investor confidence. Smaller economies in the group tend to run larger current account deficits than the bigger countries because it may be easier to attract the necessary funding out of a world portfolio.

The cyclical aspect of current account deficits must not be ignored. The widening of deficits coincided with a slowdown of growth in the EU and a pick-up of economic activity in central Europe. When growth in the EU accelerated in 1997, many current account deficits expanded more slowly or actually fell relative to GDP.

The Asian crisis did not disrupt the inflow of foreign capital (with the exception of the Czech Republic, where the Asian crisis coincided with the internal political crisis and an overall crisis of confidence). The impact of the Russian crisis was more immediate. The currencies of the Czech Republic, Hungary, Poland and Slovakia, i.e. those which are allowed to fluctuate within certain margins, displayed increased volatility in these periods, while the rigid exchange rate regimes of the Baltic states (and Bulgaria) were never threatened.

Given the weakness of the banking sectors, the strong rise of the real exchange rates and the increases in the current account deficits of the accession countries, it is noteworthy that they weathered both the Asian and Russian currency and financial crises relatively well. Capital flow reversals largely did not take place, except for the Czech Republic, which appears to have been an

---

[29] See Milesi-Feretti and Razin (1997) and (1998).

exceptional event, because of the concomitant political crisis. Thus, the intermediately flexible exchange rate regimes (between the polar cases of full float and currency union/monetary union) in most of the accession countries were not derailed by external shocks. Catastrophic real effects were avoided, contrary to expectations aroused by the arguments of Dornbusch and Giavazzi (1998). The resilience of the currency board arrangements in the Baltic states and Bulgaria *vis-à-vis* external shocks is also noteworthy. However, the asset market test (especially interest rate spreads) by Fries et al. (1999) showed Estonia to be very vulnerable, a finding which shows that currency board arrangements can also be costly.

8.7 SUMMARY AND CONCLUSIONS

Ten countries of central and eastern Europe have signalled their intention to join the European Union. The European Commission has proposed to open accession negotiations with all of them, taking a differentiated approach, however, which gives due consideration to each candidate's progress in meeting the Copenhagen criteria. New member states must not only adopt the *acquis communautaire* of Stage 2 of EMU, but must also demonstrate an ability to operate within the ERM2 regime and eventually to participate in EMU. Questions must be asked about these countries' readiness to follow a hard-currency strategy and to submit to the requirements of ERM2 and eventually EMU and about the exchange rate options they may choose on the way.

A case can certainly be made for these countries joining the common currency area. The potential benefits outweigh the potential costs. Most of these countries have already reached a considerable degree of integration with the EU. They are at least as open to trade as several non-core EU countries and more so than Greece and Italy. Their economic structure is only slightly more biased towards agriculture and industry relative to services, than that of non-core EU countries, and there is great diversity in the manufacturing base, which lowers their susceptibility to asymmetric shocks. In addition, as trade intensifies, the probability of asymmetric shocks seems to decline.

EMU has two types of institutional and policy implication: the candidate countries must satisfy the macroeconomic convergence criteria of the Maastricht Treaty and they will have to fulfil all the legal and institutional requirements that apply to EU countries remaining outside the euro area. Regarding convergence, a majority of countries satisfy or come close to satisfying the fiscal criteria: all countries except Bulgaria and Romania comply with the debt criterion and six countries satisfied or (in the case of Poland and Romania) come close to satisfying the government balance criterion. The inflation and interest rate criteria seem to remain elusive for most countries, although progress is being made.

Fulfilling the legal and institutional requirements is a complex process which requires legal changes that must be agreed by parliament. The Helsinki summit may, however, give the laggard countries new incentives to speed up the process.

The transition countries have adopted quite different currency regimes, which may be explained in part by country-specific factors, including the political situation and particular economic conditions. In almost all currency arrangements, the euro plays the major role. Today there are five countries with more or less fixed exchange rates and five which have chosen greater exchange rate flexibility. There are arguments for both fixed and flexible exchange rate regimes. Pegged exchange rates may be helpful at the outset of the transformation process, when bringing down high inflation is the key policy objective. Once inflation is tamed, introducing greater flexibility may help to overcome structural weaknesses by permitting a correction of an overvaluation of the currency caused, for example by rising wages in the tradables sector and capital inflows.

Irrespective of the exchange rate regime chosen, the authorities must have a view of the appropriate exchange rate level. Determining the appropriate exchange rate is difficult, however, especially for a transition country. One practical approach is that proposed by Halpern and Wyplosz (1997, 1998), who compare the average wage expressed in a common currency (the dollar), an approximation of the real exchange rate. They deduce that because of the uncertainty regarding the equilibrium exchange rate, some flexibility is warranted.

In the end, the CEE countries will have to adopt, for all practical purposes, a pegged exchange rate in order to become members first of ERM2, then of the euro area. The question arises, therefore, of how big these countries' vulnerability to external events is. Fries et al. have tried to ascertain this by looking at the impact of the Asian crisis on the CEE countries' asset markets. Estonia and Romania were identified as the more vulnerable countries, whereas Bulgaria, the Czech Republic, Hungary, Poland and Slovakia were shown as more resilient. Obviously the exchange rate regime was only one of the elements in the equation, as both groups included floaters and peggers.

Among the fundamentals that must be looked at in order to assess a country's external vulnerability are the strength of the banking system and current account sustainability. Regarding the strength of the banking system, there is quite a bit of information on the institutional arrangements, including the independence of the central bank and regulation. The IMF provides comparative data for the period from 1994 to 1998 on the degree of monetization and the relative size of private credit flows. During this period, the Czech Republic did best on both accounts.

Several variables have been identified as affecting current account sustainability. They include macroeconomic indicators, financial variables and external vulnerability indicators. With the help of such a list of variables, those candidate countries which suffered dangerous current account deficits in the 1990s were analysed. This left out Bulgaria and Slovenia, the only countries not beset by external problems.

Although generalizations are difficult, a number of regularities were observed. A large current account deficit relative to GDP does not necessarily cause problems with financing or a currency crisis: the Baltic states ran current account deficits larger than the Czech Republic and did not experience disruptions of their funding. Other variables must be taken into account. The case of the Czech Republic confirms that a balanced government budget is not enough to shield against a currency crisis. Twin deficits, however, increase vulnerability, as the cases of Hungary before 1995 and Slovakia since 1996 show. A fall in exports and thus foreign currency reserves featured in both Hungary and the Czech Republic, two of the three countries which experienced difficulties with financing their deficits. Hungary, the Czech Republic and Slovakia also shared another feature: high external indebtedness. The evidence that real appreciation is a negative factor is rather inconclusive, as gains in labour productivity have tended to offset its impact. Countries which have made more progress in structural reforms and privatization enjoy greater investor confidence and find it easier to attract private foreign capital to finance the deficit. The soundness of the banking system is an important factor. The cyclical aspect of current account deficits must not be ignored. The widening of deficits coincided with a slowdown of growth in the EU and a pick-up of economic activity in central Europe. When growth in the EU accelerated in 1997, many current account deficits expanded more slowly or actually fell relative to GDP.

The CEE countries are to be admitted to the EU in one – differentiated – step. Initially they will become members of ERM2, which, under the present wide fluctuation band, will grant them sufficient flexibility and additional advantages. Subsequently, after meeting the Maastricht criteria, they will be able to join EMU. But which exchange rate route should the candidate countries take before joining the EU?

It is useful to put the choice of an exchange rate regime by the accession countries into a wider perspective. According to Jeffrey Frankel (1999), 'no single currency regime is right for all countries or all times'. This appears to be true for the accession countries. The choice of a regime – either full capital controls and currency board/monetary union or a pure float, which are the polar cases – is determined by the relative benefits and costs associated with desirable policy goals: exchange rate stability, monetary policy autonomy and full financial integration. Exchange rate stability results in lower transaction costs and higher intra-union trade and investment; pegging the exchange rate to a low inflation partner currency as a nominal anchor imports inflation-fighting credibility. Monetary policy autonomy helps in adjusting to external shocks.

Figure 8.2: Policy trilemma for CEE accession economies

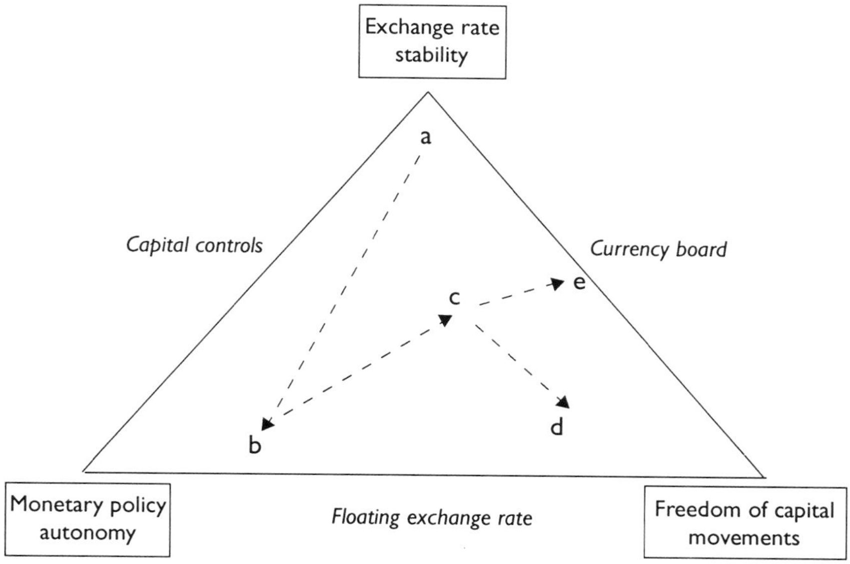

Source of basic diagram: Paul Krugman and Maurice Obstfeld, *International Economics*, 5th edn, 2000 (paths for transition economies added)

Financial integration results in greater investment flows, but it involves costs: the loss of competitiveness in the case of pegged rates with remaining residual inflation, ineffectiveness of monetary policy for small open economies, sharp capital flow reversals and foreign exchange crises.

According to Krugman and Obstfeld (2000) Frankel (1999) and Figure 8.2, one can choose only two of the three policy goals. Given that there is a long-run development towards greater capital mobility – also a goal of the EU's single market, which speeds up the process – this limits the choice to two polar policy regimes: full float or currency union/monetary union. For small, open economies such as the Baltic states, monetary policy autonomy is ineffective and/or undesirable if the central bank has no inflation-fighting credibility. Thus, the regime choice is limited to the currency board. Given the accession countries' long-term political-economic path towards economic and monetary union and their greatly increasing trade flows with the EU, they may quickly gain from monetary union. The argument, for which see Frankel and Rose (1997), is as follows. Monetary and economic union increases members' bilateral trade flows significantly, which in turn increases the correlation of their incomes. This makes a unified monetary policy appropriate for the union. Increased trade flows thus make the optimal currency area criteria endogenous. While *ex ante* the gains from monetary union are not clear, they are *ex post*. This is the basic argument for an early move towards monetary union by all accession countries.

However, there remains the choice of the appropriate exchange rate with the euro. This choice will profoundly affect the competitiveness of the accession countries and should be delayed as long as possible by countries with a degree of monetary policy autonomy and exchange rate flexibility. The argument is that there should be time enough for structural changes in the transformation countries to be worked out and for markets to determine equilibrium exchange rates.

The path of exchange rate regimes for the accession countries is shown diagramatically in Figure 8.2. The movement from a to b is due to the initial internal and external price liberalization at the beginning of transition, when all countries engaged in a massive devaluation of their currencies, searching for an appropriate market exchange rate. Capital transactions on current account were liberalized. The movement from b to c reflects the choice of a pegged exchange rate to a nominal anchor for stabilization purposes, i.e. to get back to greater exchange rate stability. Given the residual inflation, the pegged rates resulted in a real exchange rate appreciation and a loss of competitiveness. Thus, the movement from c to d, via crawling pegs, indicates the increased interest in exchange rate flexibility in order to maintain competitiveness. The timing of the movement from d to e for the majority of the accession countries is the moot question, as discussed above.

An intermediate step towards EMU would be the adoption of currency boards by all accession countries, as argued by Dornbusch and Giavazzi (1998). These authors are concerned with the potentially enormous cost of currency crises. They argue that eastern Europe's demonstrated inability to run a solid macroeconomic policy makes that region liable to financial and exchange rate crises. Thus it is best to take those tools away from the governments of that region. Daniel Gros (2000) argues for the adoption of the euro ('euro-ization') as the national currency for central and eastern Europe. The gain to the region would be the elimination of currency crises and lowered interest risk premiums.

Of the arguments against a rapid adoption of the euro, the problem of choosing the appropriate exchange rate *vis-à-vis* it appears to be the most serious. The example of the German currency union demonstrated that an inappropriate choice of the exchange rate and a massive appreciation of the real exchange rate in the former East Germany destroyed the competitiveness of much of its industry. To the extent that countries in transition are still involved in important structural changes, it may still be too early to fix an irrevocable exchange rate with the euro.

Because this 'equilibrium exchange rate finding time' will mean living with an intermediately flexible exchange rate regime, for example with a crawling peg, and with weak banking structures, it is susceptible to external shocks and crisis contagion problems. However, the noteworthy sustainability of most currency regimes in the accession countries during the recent Asian and Russian crises is an indicator that this risk is manageable. Nevertheless, analysts with different views of the risks at hand will come to different conclusions. The authors of this paper maintain that the potential risks of locking into a misaligned exchange rate *vis-à-vis* the euro is the main problem. The solution is to 'wait and see' and simultaneously to improve banking supervision. Others will see the risks from currency crises as the main problem and will argue for a quick move towards currency boards and/or monetary union, ignoring the problem of misaligned exchange rates.

References

Ambrus-Lakatos, Lorand and Mark E. Schaffer (eds) (1999), *Monetary and Exchange Rate Policies, EMU and Central and Eastern Europe*, Forum Report of the Economic Policy Initiative No. 5, CEPR and East-West Institute.

Bayoumi, T. and B. Eichengreen (1993), 'Shocking Aspects of European Monetary Integration', in F. Torres and F. Giavazzi (eds), *Adjustment and Growth in the European Union* (New York: Cambridge University Press).

Bénassy-Quéré, Agnés (1996), *Potentialities and opportunities of the Euro as an international currency*, Brussels: European Commission, Directorate General for Economic and Financial Affairs.

Bénassy-Quéré, Agnés and Amina Lahreche-Revil (1998), 'Pegging the CEED's Currencies to the Euro', *CEPII, Document de travail* No. 98-04.

Blejer, M., J. Frankel, L. Leiderman and A. Razin (eds) (1997), *Optimum Currency Areas: New Analytical and Policy Developments* (Washington, DC: IMF).

Calmfors, L. et al. [The Calmfors Commission] (1997), *EMU – A Swedish Perspective* (Dordrecht: Kluwer).

Canzoneri, M., J. Valles and J. Vinals (1996), *Do Exchange Rates Move to Address International Macroeconomic Balances?*, CEPR Discussion Paper No. 1498, London, October.

Corden, W.M. (1993), 'Exchange Rate Policy in Developing Countries', in R.C. Barth and C-W. Wong (eds), *Approaches to Exchange Rate Policy* (Washington, DC: IMF Institute).

Cuckierman, Alexander (1992), *Central Bank Strategy, Credibility and Independence: Theory and Evidence* (Cambridge, MA: MIT Press).

Dornbusch, Rudi and Francesco Giavazzi, (1998), 'Hard Currency and Sound Credit: A Financial Agenda for Central Europe', *http://www.mit.edu/rudi*, May.

Dornbusch, Rüdiger, Ilan Goldfajn and Rodrigo Valdes (1995), 'Currency Crises and Collapses', *Brookings Papers on Economic Activity*. 2.

EBRD, *Transition Reports 1997, 1998*.

Eichengreen, Barry J. (1998), *European Monetary Unification: Theory, Practice and Analysis* (Cambridge, MA: MIT Press).

European Central Bank (1999), 'Payment in Countries that have Applied for Membership of the European Union' (Blue Book), August.

European Council (1998), *The Broad Economic Policy Guidelines*, Brussels (July).

European Economy. Supplement C. *Economic Reform Monitor* No. 1 – February 1999. 'Economic situation and economic reform in Central and Eastern Europe'. Special topic: Results of the Commission's Spring 1999 Economic Forecast for the Central European Candidate Countries.

European Economy. Supplement C. *Economic Reform Monitor* No. 2 – May 1999. 'Economic situation and economic reform in Central and Eastern Europe'. Special topic: Bank Restructuring in Central Europe.

European Union Commission (1997), *Agenda 2000: For a Stronger and Wider Union*, Vol. 1, DOC/97/6 (Strasbourg, July 15).

European Union Commission on Enlargement (1999), *Enlarging the EU – 2nd Regular Reports* (13 October).

Frankel, J. (1999), 'No Single Exchange Rate Regime is Right for all Countries or all Times', *NBER Working Paper* No. 7338, September.

Frankel, J. and A. Rose (1996), 'The Endogeneity of the Optimum Currency Area Criteria', *NBER Working Paper* No. 5700, August.

Fries, Steven, Martin Raiser and Nicholas Stern (1999), 'Stress Test for Reforms – Transition and East Asian "Contagion"', *Economics of Transition*, Vol. 7, No. 2.

Gros, Daniel (2000), 'One Euro from the Atlantic to the Urals?' *CESifo Digest*, launch issue, spring.

Gulde, Anne Marie (1999), 'The Role of the Currency Board in Bulgaria's Stabilization', *IMF Policy Discussion Paper* 99/3, April.

Halpern, Lázlo and Charles Wyplosz (1997), 'Equilibrium Exchange Rates in Transition Economies', *IMF Staff Papers*, Vol. 44, No. 4.

Halpern, Láslo and Charles Wyplosz (1998), 'Equilibrium Exchange Rates in Transition Economies: Further Results', paper presented to the Economic Policy Initiative Forum, Brussels, 21–22 November.

Heller, H. Robert (1976), 'International reserves and worldwide inflation', *IMF Staff Papers*, Vol. 23, No. 1.

Hochreiter, Eduard and Tadeusz Kowalski (2000), 'Central Banks in European Emerging Market Economies in the 1990s', *Österreichische Nationalbank Working Papers*, No. 40.

International Monetary Fund (1997), *Exchange Arrangements & Exchange Restrictions*.

International Monetary Fund (1999), *Economic Outlook*, May and September.

International Monetary Fund (1999), *International Financial Statistics*, September.

International Monetary Fund (1999), *World Economic Outlook*, September.

Kaminsky, Graciela and Carmen M. Reinhart (1999), 'The Twin Crises: The Causes of Banking and Balance of Payments Problems', *AER*, Vol. 89, No. 3, June.

Kaminsky, Graciela, Saul Lizondo, and Carmen M. Reinhart (1998), 'Leading Indicators of Currency Crises', *IMF Staff Papers*, Vol. 45, No.1, pp. 1-48.

Kopits, George (1999), 'Implications of EMU for Exchange Rate Policy in Central and Eastern Europe', *IMF Working Paper* WP/99/9, January.

Krajnyák, K. and J. Zettelmeyer (1998), 'Competitiveness in Transition Economies: What Scope for Real Appreciation?', *IMF Staff Papers* Vol.45, No.2 (June).

Krugman, Paul and Maurice Obstfeld (2000), *International Economics* [publisher], 5th edition (Reading, MA: Addison-Wesley).

Lindgren, Carl Johan, Gillian Garcia and Matthew I. Saal (1996), *Bank Soundness and Macroeconomic Policy*, International Monetary Fund.

McKinnon, R.I. (1963), 'Optimum Currency Areas', *American Economic Review*, Vol. 53, No. 4 (September).

Milesi-Ferretti, Gian Maria and Assaf Razin (1997), 'Sharp Reductions in Current Account Deficits: An Empirical Analysis', *IMF Working Papers* 97/168.

Milesi-Ferretti, Gian Maria and Assaf Razin (1998), 'Current Account Reversals and Currency Crisis – Empirical Regularities', IMF Working Paper, No. 98/98.

Nilsen, Jeffrey H. and Riccardo Rovelli, (1996), 'Modeling Financial Fragility in Transition Economies', Phare-ACE Programme Project No. P96-6114-R.

Obstfeld, Maurice and Kenneth Rogoff (1996*), Foundations of International Economics* (Cambridge, MA: MIT Press).

Rother, Philipp C. (1999), 'Explaining the Behavior of Financial Intermediation: Evidence from Transition Economies', *IMF Working Paper* WP/99/36, March.

Sachs, J. (1996), 'Economic Transition and the Exchange Rate Regime', *American Economic Review, Papers and Proceedings* (May).

Sachs, J., Aaron Tornell and Andres Velasco (1996), 'Financial Crises in Emerging Markets: Lessons from 1995', *Brookings Papers on Economic Activity:1*.

Sgard, Jerome (1996), 'Credit Crisis and the Role of Banks During Transition: A Five-Country Comparison', *CEPII Working Paper* No. 96-08.

Talley, Samuel, Marcelo M. Giugale, and Rossana Polastri (1998), 'Capital Inflow Reversals, Banking Stability, and Prudential Regulation in Central and Eastern Europe', *World Bank Policy Research Working Paper* No. 2023, December.

Temprano-Arroyo, Heliodoro and Robert A. Feldman (1998), 'Selected Transition and Mediterranean Countries – An Institutional Primer on EMU and EU Relations', *IMF Working Paper* No. 98/82.

Tornell, Aaron (1999), 'Common Fundamentals in the Tequila and Asian Crises', unpublished paper, May.

9 MORAL HAZARD AND BURDEN-SHARING: THE 1998 RUSSIAN DÉBÂCLE AS A TURNING POINT

Brigitte Granville

9.1 INTRODUCTION

The multiple decisions of the Russian government and the Central Bank of Russia (CBR) on 17 August 1998,[1] which led both to the devaluation of the domestic currency and to default on the internal debt, had unforeseen dramatic repercussions on the global financial market. 'Little' democratic Russia, with 1.5 per cent of world Gross Domestic Product (GDP) and 1.2 per cent of world trade, managed to achieve the Soviet communist dream – to make the capitalist system tremble. The Russian default not only intensified a broad repricing of risks in emerging economies but also challenged the view that the international community, working through the international financial institutions, was able and willing to bail out countries in difficulty. No country from now on could be seen as 'too big to fail'. This episode has led investors and economists to reflect in various ways on the Russian virus,[2] and it has marked a turning point in the debate on changes to the global financial 'architecture'.

The record and remit of the International Monetary Fund became subjects of heated controversy, as if the IMF itself were the cause of the global turmoil. This debate had its origin in the collapse of the par-value system in the 1970s, which forced the IMF to redefine itself. With the liberalization of capital flows and the growing private-sector capital market, the IMF was cast – apparently quite willingly – in the role of international lender of last resort.[3] This universal

---

This paper draws on materials originally contained in 'Bingo or Fiasco?: The Global Financial Situation is Not Guaranteed', *International Affairs*, Vol. 75, No. 4 (October 1999), pp. 713–28.

[1] The decisions of 17 August included the *de facto* devaluation of the rouble: the rouble target band was widened to range from 6 to 9.5 roubles to the dollar for a mean of 7.75 roubles. The internal day-to-day band of 1.5 per cent was abandoned. There was a forced extension of Treasury maturities, a 90-day moratorium on debt servicing of private foreign credits of over 180 days' maturity, as well as margin calls and currency contracts. (See Granville, forthcoming).

[2] Calvo (1998b).

[3] See James (1999) and Obstfeld (1998).

role became fully formed with the collapse of communism, bringing the successor states and former satellites of the Soviet Union into the IMF's already burgeoning client list. However, the IMF staff did not understand the nature and scale of the task they were undertaking. The same could be said of the vast majority of Western officials thrown into the issue of 'transition'; but few others shared the influence, and hence responsibility, of the IMF officials dealing with the former Soviet Union, especially Russia. Nor did the IMF have time to improve its qualifications for the task. Amid the drama of the Soviet collapse, and in particular given the need to get IMF programmes in place as a formal basis for agreeing to restructure Soviet debt, leading Western governments delegated to the IMF the role of arbiter as regards which policies should be supported and by how much.

The 1998 episode challenged the new identity of the IMF as the vanguard and arbiter of Western policy. Despite an emergency IMF programme being in place and on track, Russia was allowed to fail. The question is why. Was it because, from an economic point of view, the rescue could not be justified on economic grounds? But in this case, why was Russia financed in 1996 when very little reform took place but a presidential election did? The Kirienko government was the most reformist government ever seen in Russia, so why were its efforts allowed to collapse if the criterion was purely economics? Or does the reason for letting Russia go lie in the fact that the IMF and its shareholders failed to assess the economic situation properly and to foresee the consequences that the Russian default would have on mature markets and therefore decided that the risk in letting Russia go was minimal? Or was it simply that a smaller country in similar difficulties would have been protected from a similar débâcle, but in the case of Russia the sums required were just too large?

This article aims to answer some of these questions. It argues that the Russian episode introduced enough uncertainty for both international lenders and borrowers to reassess their investment or borrowing strategies in the face of risks rather than on the 'too big to fail' assumption. The IMF has shown, in this episode, that in its present form it cannot act as an international lender of last resort, if only because of the complicated question of moral hazard and the sheer size of the global capital markets. Whether the role of the IMF should be expanded in order to take on the lender of last resort function or be reduced will not be addressed here.[4]

---

[4] The literature on the question of whether or not the IMF should be transformed into an international lender of last resort is extensive. See, for example, Capie (1998), Fischer (1999) and James (1999).

9.2 WHY WAS THE RUSSIAN DEBT DEFAULT SUCH A TURNING POINT?

The Russian crisis

Inflation was very high in Russia during the first years of reform:[5] the average monthly inflation rate reached 41 per cent in 1992 (18 per cent without the price jump of over 200 per cent in January that year following price liberalization), 21 per cent in 1993 and 10 per cent in 1994. In 1995 there was a renewed political drive to control inflation, resulting in the monthly inflation rate falling below 10 per cent for the first time ever. This was achieved by shifting the financing of the budget deficit from central bank credits to treasury bills,[6] and by increasing the central bank's independence.[7] An IMF 'stand-by' programme was signed on 26 March, and in July the rouble was pegged to the dollar. Foreign savings started to flow into the country, filling the gap for the missing domestic savings. Lack of confidence in the government's policies and in the domestic banking system meant that Russian savings were mainly held in cash dollars under the mattress or abroad (Table 9.1).

Given the inadequacy of available Russian domestic savings in the banking system, the budget deficit was being funded to a significant extent by foreign buying of short-term domestic treasury bills. Part of the capital inflows was channelled through the banking sector. As the money supply rose (M2 divided by the exchange rate almost doubled in the period from 1995 to 1997 even though real GDP decreased, except in 1997), the CBR, which implicitly operated as lender of last resort,[8] acquired *de facto* short-term obligations.[9]

The domestic market in rouble-denominated government debt became the main mechanism by which confidence in the exchange rate peg affected interest rates. In 1997, when Asian banks suffered losses on lending at home, they sold their holdings of Russian high-yielding bonds in order to improve their liquidity position, putting pressure on the rouble and on the bond market. The monetary authorities sought to defend the rouble by raising the refinance rate.

---

[5] See Granville (1995).

[6] See the 1995 Federal Budget Law.

[7] See the Central Bank Law, enacted in April 1995.

[8] The CBR established a special supervisory department (OPERU 2) to monitor the largest national banks. Fourteen banks have been made subject to OPERU 2 supervision. They represent 60–65 per cent of Russia's banking assets (excluding the assets of Vnesheconombank) and over 90 per cent of Russia's bank deposits.

[9] Diaz-Alejandro (1985) and Calvo (1998a) show the same effect in the case of Chile and Mexico respectively. The effect is well explained by Obstfeld (1998: 23): 'When market sentiment turns against the exchange rate peg, the government is effectively forced to assume the short foreign-currency positions in some way – or else to allow a cascade of domestic bankruptcies. Since the government at the same time has used its foreign exchange reserves (in a vain attempt to peg the exchange rate) and cannot borrow more in world credit markets, national default becomes imminent'.

Table 9.1: Deposits in the Russian banking system 1993–8 (% of GDP)

Year	Demand deposits	Time and saving deposits	Foreign currency deposits	Total deposits
1993	7.3	2.9	7.0	17.3
1994	5.3	3.9	6.1	15.4
1995	4.4	4.4	3.5	12.2
1996	4.0	4.3	3.2	11.5
1997	5.0	3.9	3.2	12.1
Q3 1998	6.2	4.3	8.7	19.2

Source. Calculated from IMF, *International Financial Statistics*, January 1999.

This rate acted as an effective cap on the treasury bill yield and thus signalled the level at which the CBR would support the price. The refinancing rate was raised first from 21 per cent to 28 per cent in mid-November 1997. In February 1998 it was increased to 42 per cent and in May 1998 to 150 per cent. The calculation was that inflows would be attracted by the huge real returns available from the combination of high nominal yields on rouble-denominated debt and the promise of a stable exchange rate. As things turned out, however, investors were less attracted by this prospect than they were deterred by the present reality of ever higher interest rates in the face of low or zero growth prospects, which created doubts that the government could afford its steeply rising debt service costs: hence the perception of increasing default risk. This perception in turn increased the risk of devaluation: having let interest rates rise in order to defend the exchange rate, the government might be forced into letting the exchange rate go to prevent insolvency. The problem was exacerbated by a fall in oil prices and a rise in imports, which led to the first current account deficit since 1993.

The long-term source of the Russian crisis was the consistent failure to tighten fiscal policy sufficiently. The timing of the financial débâcle, on the other hand, was determined by the peculiarity of the banking system. Pressure on the rouble exchange rate had been intensified by a particular effect of the financial market crisis on leading Russian banks. Unable at any stage to attract large-scale retail deposits, the banks had funded themselves by using their portfolios of dollar-denominated Russian government securities for repurchase operations (repo) with foreign counter-parties. In mid-1998 the progressive collapse of investor confidence in all types of Russian government debt triggered margin calls on those 'repos', that is, instant debt repayment obligations on leveraged positions. To meet these margin calls, the banks raised liquidity by selling their holdings of rouble-denominated short-term treasury bills (GKOs[10])

[10] GKOs, *gosudarstvennye kaznacheiskie obiazatelstva*, mean short-term treasury bills.

and other assets and by buying the necessary foreign exchange with the proceeds. Short-term debt at the end of June 1998 was nearly four times as large as official foreign exchange reserves.

The short maturity of Russia's debt was not the only issue. Thus, far from solving the situation, the move orchestrated by Goldman Sachs in July 1998 (and supported by the IMF) to lengthen the duration of its debt by a voluntary swap of GKOs with new eurobonds precipitated the default. In July 1998, Goldman Sachs arranged for one-tenth of outstanding treasury bills ($6.4 billion) to be exchanged for long-term eurobonds. There was no demand for new Russian debt, and the new eurobonds were a supply shock which drove down all debt prices. Meanwhile, the domestic financial sector now faced large margin calls as debt prices plummeted. The liquidity to meet those margin calls was mobilized by selling more GKOs. Here, then, was the chain reaction which accelerated the crisis to a remarkably rapid climax on 17 August. Completing the vicious circle, the central bank responded by tightening money market lending in order to keep the rouble in its target band. And commercial banks reacted by cutting limits to each other and selling bonds and stocks to sustain liquidity.

The duration of the domestic debt was very short in the first place. That was because it was too expensive or impossible to finance[11] with a longer maturity debt given the risks involved. Foreigners were holding 30 per cent of the domestic debt, but the situation would not have been solved if the debt had been 100 per cent owned by residents:

> to the extent that domestic short-term debt is also an implicit claim on the reserves of the central bank, then such a substitution would not ameliorate the liquidity problems during a SS (Sudden Stop). An exception would be the case where through 'moral suasion' the government and the central bank have greater leverage in 'persuading' the local residents to roll over those debts.[12]

In this environment, all demand, domestic and foreign, for new issues of rouble treasury bills disappeared. That meant that the government could no longer pay debt with debt. Redemption of weekly maturities averaging about Rbs 9 billion ($1 billion) had to be financed from general taxation (emergency eurobond issues, which glutted the last segment of the debt market). Given the impossibility of sufficiently drastic cuts in non-debt-service expenditure, at least a temporary government default became unavoidable, leading to the decisions

---

[11] Further evidence that the short-term duration of the debt is difficult to solve is that creditors use put options to give themselves the option to reduce the contractual maturity of loans of bonds. Debtors accept them because they allow a lower spread. See IMF (1999b: 29).
[12] Calvo and Reinhart (1999: 18). 'Sudden Stop' here means a sudden stop of capital inflows.

of 17 August 1998. The devaluation for its part exposed the insolvency of the banks by leaving them with dollar obligations on forward contracts many times greater than their capital.

Why the central bank chose to defend the exchange rate peg

The CBR's defence of the rouble exchange rate was based on two primary considerations: first, economic fundamentals did not warrant a devaluation; secondly, devaluation would rekindle rapid inflation, because of the high import content of consumption.[13] But other motivations lurked in the background.

The main case for devaluation on the export side was the fiscal one that it would increase export value added in roubles and thereby contribute to improved tax revenues. But the volume of Russian oil exports[14] was limited by internal pipeline and sea port handling capacity and thus could not respond to devaluation in the short term. On the import side devaluation would encourage some switch of expenditure by Russian consumers from imports to domestic products. On the other hand, experience in other emerging markets suggests that devaluation is not a reliable route to lowering real interest rates.

Another strong but unacknowledged disincentive to devaluation was the potentially fatal losses which a devaluation could inflict on the leading banks through their currency forward contracts. This danger was partly due to a supervisory oversight by the CBR, as it gradually withdrew from the system of fixed forwards for foreign investors in the bond market. The banks, for their part, rushed into the currency forward business, apparently tempted by the easy gains in defiance of ordinary prudential principles of risk management. By mid-1998, leading Russian banks had sold several billion 'forward' dollars to foreign counter-parties hedging their GKO investments or other rouble exposures against a possible devaluation. On 2 January 1998 the notional value of outstanding forward foreign exchange (FX) contracts was $365 billion (over 3,000 per cent of the capital of the Russian banking system). To the extent that banks active in this field had troubled to make balancing purchases of 'forward' dollars from domestic counter-parties, the devaluation, when it came, rendered the latter insolvent.[15]

---

[13] This was as high as 60 per cent, according to official estimates.

[14] Exports of oil and oil products in 1997 accounted for 21 per cent of total Russian exports. Russia accounts for about 8 per cent of world crude oil production.

[15] Calvo and Reinhart (1999: 2, fn 2) note also that devaluations have proved to be contractionary in developing countries. Eichengreen (1999c: 10) reinforces this point by noting that 'the Mexican and Asian crises suggest that currency devaluations in developing countries are strongly contractionary. Because developing countries borrow in foreign currency, depreciation increases the burden of debt service and worsens the financial condition of domestic banks and firms. Because those banks and firms don't hedge their foreign exposures, they get smashed when the currency band collapses.'

The exposure to global capital market disciplines was made that much more acute and immediate by the existence of a stock of government debt which was (1) already large by the outbreak of the global financial crisis, (2) growing at an unsustainable rate and, above all, (3) of extremely short duration. Amidst falling investor confidence, this short-maturing debt could not be refinanced at tolerable yields, causing a liquidity crisis which contained within it the threat of insolvency. The vulnerability to this threat could in principle have been reduced, or even eliminated, in three ways. First, the reversal of capital flight, especially of domestic currency substitution (cash dollar savings held 'under the mattress') would have ensured sufficient domestic demand for government debt, thus insulating that market from the vagaries of global capital flows. Secondly, the budget could have been balanced, thereby removing the need for new borrowing and reducing the cost of servicing existing debt. Both those goals call for consistency and perseverance in the application of policies bound to entail pain, and hence political unpopularity, in the short to medium term. The confidence necessary for capital flight repatriation can be built, even with ideal policies, only over several years. The third possible solution, which seems easy by comparison, would have been simply a return to a floating exchange rate, allowing the interest rate to be controlled through domestic monetary policy. In practice, however, the pegging of the exchange rate six months into that programme had a powerful stabilizing effect, which the authorities were afterwards reluctant to forgo. Over the longer term, moreover, exchange-rate stability would assist the repatriation of flight capital by making the rouble more credible as a financial asset worth holding. And until that effect had been achieved, with a normal level of domestic savings available for government and private-sector financing needs, a stable real exchange rate would be essential for attracting into Russia the private voluntary international capital which, apart from the limited funds available from international financial institutions, was the only alternative financing source.

Thus there were compelling reasons, in terms of both short- and long-term priorities and goals, for attempting to defend the rouble exchange rate. Given that the exchange-rate policy was itself an important part of the solution to the constraint of capital flight, the only way to resolve that tension would have been a decisive removal of fiscal imbalances. Unfortunately, it was only in the emergency created by the 'Asian' crisis that the political will crystallized for decisive fiscal action. But by then there was too little time left to overcome all the obstacles, whether external (market confidence) or domestic (political opposition).

The extent of the collapse might have been reduced by having more owner-ship of 'financial institutions, coupled with greater representation in financial sectors of foreign-based intermediaries. These developments would have the side-benefit of reducing the perceived charge of government bailouts.'[16] Unfortunately this move was resisted by the lobby of domestic banks, which was extremely powerful. In 1993, the authorities should have liberalized entry to the banking industry and allowed in foreign banks; but the powerful domestic banking association, supported by the then head of the central bank, Viktor Gerashchenko, strongly opposed this move. If foreign banks had been allowed in, this would have provided the necessary incentive for the soundness of the banking system as well as know-how. In turn the public would have felt more confident and placed some of its savings in these institutions, unstained by the domestic track record of monetary confiscation. As it was, the Russian banking system existed only in name. Banks made profits from 1992 to August 1995 mainly from foreign exchange. Then they turned to borrowing in dollars at relatively low interest rates and investing the proceeds in the high-yield short-term GKOs when the exchange-rate regime was changed. Their involvement with the real sector (mainly with enterprises in natural resources, such as oil companies) was orchestrated for some of them through the so-called financial and industrial groups (FIGs) which had links with the government and business clients. But the FIGs were a figleaf, as government securities dominated banking assets.[17] Private loans represented only a fractional share of their activity. In 1998, private credit as a share of GDP was 10 per cent (of which only 3 per cent had a duration of over six months), compared with over 120 per cent in Japan, for instance. Enforcement of regulations, when they existed, was difficult: seventy years of communism did not provide the CBR with an army of bank experts, and the weakness inherent in this lack of expertise was exposed from October 1997 to August 1998. Given the lack of expertise, and also the intractability of structural problems in the economy, it could be argued that the IMF should not have insisted on financial liberalization[18] to the extent of removing all remaining restrictions on non-residents' access to the GKO market by January 1998. On the other hand, this measure was seen as generating greater demand for the government's short-term bills and therefore allowing yields to decrease, so in principle it could have been an engine of growth. It was unfortunate that the application of this decision came at a time of crisis and consequently led only to yet more debt and yet more capital flight.

The large capital outflows from Russia have been due fundamentally to the large uncertainty and risk that investors associate with keeping money in Russia.

[16] Obstfeld (1998: 25–26).

[17] CBR data show that income on GKOs accounted for 41 per cent of the earnings of the top 100 banks as of September 1997. Thanks to GKOs, Sberbank, which held about 35 per cent of the market, realized pre-tax profits of $2 billion in 1996.

[18] Obstfeld (1998: 27). The IMF is also seeking a proposed amendment to its Articles of Agreement, which would codify the Fund's role in promoting open capital markets, as well as member countries' obligation to work, gradually if need be, towards the same goal.

This uncertainty reflects a number of factors, among them macroeconomic instability, weak enforcement of property rights, an arbitrary and confiscatory tax system (run by a predatory and venal administration) and inadequate supervision and regulation of the banking system. Facilitating tax evasion is another important reason for capital flight. Capital transferred abroad from Russia may represent legal activities such as imports, or flows from illegal sources – whether 'mild', such as non-repatriation of export proceeds, or 'strong', in the sense of pure criminal activity. But it is impossible to determine whether specific capital flows from Russia – legal or illegal – come from a particular inflow, such as IMF loans or export earnings. To put the scale of IMF lending to Russia into perspective, Russia's exports of goods and services have averaged about $80 billion a year in recent years, which is over 25 times the average annual disbursement from the IMF since 1992.

After August 1998, having lost access to international capital markets and seeking to stabilize the situation after the financial débâcle, the Russian monetary authorities introduced a series of new exchange controls. This reversed the course, pursued since 1996 at the IMF's instigation, towards full capital convertibility and culminated in January 1998 in the lifting of all remaining restrictions on flows of foreign capital in and out of the rouble-denominated GKO market. The government's default on its GKO obligations closed off all possible refinancing of the rest of its (mainly external) debt; and at the same time, servicing that debt (and so preventing a yet more calamitous general default) was made even more difficult by the resurgence of capital flight to ever higher levels amidst the shattered confidence caused by the collapse of the rouble exchange rate.

To maintain international reserves at the bare minimum necessary to service the post-1992 external debt ('Russian' debt as opposed to 'Soviet-era' debt, on which payments were halted pending creditor agreement to further relief), the CBR resorted to drastic new administrative measures. Most radical of all was the introduction of split FX trading sessions, with a morning session reserved for exporters selling repatriated foreign exchange proceeds for roubles and a general session in the afternoon for buyers of foreign currency. This system allowed the CBR to profit from spreads between the two sessions. Apart from that, its effects were limited, although in principle it remained a major policy reversal from the unification of the foreign exchange market by the Gaidar government in July 1992. It was no surprise, therefore, to see the CBR forced to reinstate a single trading session as one of the conditions for a revival of IMF lending to Russia in July 1999. The foreign exchange market was reunified on 29 June 1999. The next change, in autumn 1998, was likewise designed to bolster reserves, which were the only source of external debt service (given the prohibitively low dollar value of tax revenues). This was a requirement for exporters to surrender three-quarters of their foreign exchange proceeds for roubles. The effectiveness of this measure was limited, as many exporters failed to repatriate their proceeds in the first place; and these proceeds were increasingly healthy as global commodity prices recovered. A simple comparison of the visible trade surplus and CBR reserves in the first half of 1999 suggests that capital flight from this source was running at about $1.5 billion per month.

Further CBR measures were designed to stifle capital flight from imports. To counter fictive imports, the CBR required importers to deposit an equivalent rouble sum before buying the foreign exchange needed to pay for the imports, and the deposit was returnable only when the importer could prove that the goods had been delivered inside Russia.[19] But this and a raft of related measures met their match in the tireless ingenuity of capital flight artists, for where fundamental confidence is lacking, administrative measures cannot prevail. Besides, some measures had in any case to be repealed at the IMF's behest – for example, a ban on the purchase of foreign currency using rouble balances in the correspondent accounts of foreign banks. But it should be stressed again that IMF conditionality was of minor importance compared with the collapse of confidence. This was reflected above all in the public's lack of demand for roubles and its use of dollar cash as the preferred savings instrument. And it is in this key area – the domestic heart of capital flight – where even the Primakov government baulked at introducing administrative controls. It dared not risk the popular outcry which would have resulted from ending the internal convertibility of the rouble. Here was a little noticed but highly significant indicator of the strength of popular support for an open economy (as opposed to the alternative of systematic Soviet-style confiscation of private wealth).

The Russian financial crisis in the global capital market

Russia's unilateral debt restructuring led to large investment and trading losses and changed market perceptions of default and convertibility risk, which together affected the balance of risks and returns in international portfolios. The

---

[19] Basically two special accounts of type 'S' were introduced: the first for switching currency operations (conversion operations) and the second for operations with securities. All operations with currency and securities should be conducted through these accounts. The funds from an account of type 'S' for switching currency operations cannot be used to buy securities and vice versa. Type 'S' accounts can be opened and maintained only in banks authorized by the CBR. The restrictions on using the funds on these accounts are as follows: to transfer the funds from the second to the first, the authorized bank should first transfer these funds to the transit account with the bank, where the funds stay for 365 days and are then transferred to a type 'S' account for switching currency operations. During this time an equal sum of money should be deposited by the authorized bank with the CBR (for 365 days). The authorized banks are forbidden to conduct switching currency operations on the purchase of foreign currency from non-residents for roubles in order to transfer roubles later to a type 'S' account for switching currency operations.

international financial turmoil which followed the Russian financial crisis is puzzling: was it really due to the situation in Russia or to the nature of the global financial market?

The size of Russia's economy, its trade importance and its global international financial activities really did not justify such turmoil. Russia accounted for little more than 3 per cent of the total international loan commitments and emerging market issuance of international bonds and equities, in the period from 1992 to June 1998. Its external debt on the eve of the August 1998 débâcle amounted to about $160 billion, equivalent to one-third of the combined external debts of the five Asian countries at the end of 1996 and just 8 per cent of the emerging markets' total external debts.[20]

Russia defaulted on $44 billion of domestic debt. Despite several months of visible difficulty, as indicated by the high rates of interest (150 per cent in May) and political instability (a change of government in April 1998), the foreign share in the GKO market was stable at one-third from before the crisis in 1997 right through until the end of August 1998. In the financial markets, the systemic weaknesses of Russia in terms of government management (a high budget deficit) and banking systems (a banking crisis in August 1995) were well known long before the crisis began. Indeed, the resulting risks, and the higher potential returns, constitute the rationale for emerging market securities as an asset in the first place. Acceptance of the risk is often based on authoritative sources of knowledge and expertise. Investors typically refer to reports by the IMF, the Institute of International Finance or the Bank for International Settlements (BIS). Most investment banks spend a substantial amount of money on their own research departments, which are in constant communication with their investing customers. It therefore seems difficult to argue that Russia did not give any signs of potential default before the actual default of 17 August: IMF support was delayed at various points when the Russian government did not honour its commitments; and the Russian IMF programme was the first one to have the conditionality of monthly tranching attached, indicating that the IMF was fully aware that reforms had to be closely monitored. Many investors, however, seem to have taken the decision to stay in the Russian market on the assumption that Russia was too big to fail.

The assumption of no unilateral default seems also to have been present in both the Mexican and the Asian crises, when money continued to flow in, even though widely available statistics made it clear that the stock of *tesobonos* and other short-term debt in the former instance, and the level of short-term international bank lending in the latter, had risen dramatically. These data were widely ignored, although in the Asian case there is also some evidence that non-bank financial institutions did withdraw funds before the crisis struck. These

[20] IMF (1998:28).

observations led the BIS to call urgently for further studies aimed at understanding the mechanisms which led banks to increase their exposure to countries already subject to warning signals, including in some cases warnings emanating from within the banks themselves.[21] In fact, the assumption of no unilateral default seems to have been built into risk management models.

When the Russian default came, the global reassessment of risks which started with the Asian crisis intensified. Russia's default immediately triggered the unwinding of leveraged positions by large international institutions, reflecting the fact that significant holdings of rouble-denominated treasury bills were financed in the mature markets. Some investors bought the Russian bonds on margin, through investment banks. These investment banks secured the deal with short-term repurchase agreements[22] in US markets. Other Russian securities purchases, funded in Japan, were swapped into local currencies or dollars. Foreign investors suffered large losses as a result of the drop of bond prices.[23] This in turn gave rise to margin calls, forcing investors to raise liquidity by selling first their Russian securities and then, when the demand for these dried up, any other high-yield asset they could dump. A number of hedge funds, including Long-Term Capital Management (LTCM),[24] and the proprietary desk of large commercial and investment banks suffered large losses because many investors attempted simultaneously to close out positions and to reduce leverage in the wake of the global market turmoil which followed the collapse of the Russian market. The IMF estimates that 'total credit exposure (including off-balance-sheet positions) of foreign banks to Russia may have been 40 to 65 per cent higher than on-balance-sheet exposure.'[25]

As risks were repriced and positions deleveraged, even the most liquid markets, especially the dollar financial market, were badly affected. The shocks experienced in very liquid mature markets reflected the high degree of leverage and the low margin requirements on over-the-counter derivatives transactions. Derivatives products are meant to transfer or reduce risks against various instruments from which they are derived, such as currency and interest-rate risks, and thereby make investment much more attractive. Their development accelerated in the 1990s in parallel with the spectacular progress in information technology. The 1999 BIS survey of securities market participants indicated

[21] BIS (1998: 169).

[22] IMF (1998: 27): 'repurchase agreements are essentially a short-term loan to the seller, with securities used as collateral. As the value of a security falls, margin calls are triggered.'

[23] IMF (1998: 2): 'Yield premia for emerging market bonds rose sharply to an average of 1,700 basis points in early September from below 600 basis points in most of 1997 and early 1998. Equity prices fell sharply in both emerging and mature markets.'

[24] IMF (1998: 74): 'in early September, LTCM announced that 52 per cent of its capital had been spent on margin calls, only 16 per cent of which were related to emerging market investments.'

[25] IMF (1998: 62).

that the notional value of over-the-counter (OTC) derivative products outstanding was $72 trillion at the end of June 1998 (67 per cent in interest-rate instruments and 31 per cent in foreign exchange instruments) compared with $47.5 trillion (61 per cent in interest-rate instruments and 37 per cent in foreign exchange instruments) at the end of March 1995. Adjusting for differences in exchange rates and the change to consolidated reporting, this represented an increase of about 130 per cent since March 1995.[26] This compares with an equity market capitalization of about $13 trillion, some 40 per cent of the $33.5 trillion total bonds and equities market in 1995. The bond market grew from $2 trillion in 1980 to about $25 trillion at the end of 1997.[27]

When vulnerable economies are hit by financial crises, the extent and nature of hedging techniques mean that contagion effects can be quickly observed in both emerging and mature markets. The sheer relative volume of hedging and speculative transactions, and the growing use of so-called portfolio insurance and dynamic hedging techniques,[28] which replace human judgment with computerized decision-taking analogous to stop-loss orders on the stock exchange, partially explain the global turbulence. Financial engineering, such as dynamic hedging techniques, tends to drive market participants to buy assets when prices have risen and to sell when they have fallen. Such behaviour amplifies price movements. Garber and Spencer indicate how the widespread use of dynamic hedging strategies and their rapidity of implementation interfere with the central bank policy's defence of the exchange rate:

> In an exchange rate attack, a large defensive rise in the interest rates aimed at imposing a squeeze on speculators will instantaneously trigger hedging programmes to order sales of the weak currency ... The existence of such programmes in the market undermines the use of an interest rate defence of a weak currency – the moment that a central [bank] raises interest rates, it might face an avalanche of sales of its currency rather than the purchases of the squeezed shorts that it had anticipated. In effect the hedging programmes make the hedgers insensitive to the added costs of funding their weak currency sales.[29]

[26] BIS (1999: 4). These figures are indicative only. The derivatives market is continuously growing and because the activities take place off balance sheets no reliable information is available. A complete picture would require knowledge of all market participants' positions, which are not easily disclosed.
[27] Warburton (1999: 144).
[28] IMF (1998: 73): 'portfolio insurance [techniques] are techniques that change a portfolio's market exposures systematically in reaction to prior market movements, with the objective of avoiding large losses and securing as much participation as possible in favourable market movements. Dynamic hedging is a position-risk management technique in which option-like return patterns are replicated by adjusting portfolio positions to offset the impact of a price change in the underlying market on the value of an options position (the "delta"). Dynamic hedging relies on liquid, continuous markets with low transaction costs.'
[29] Garber and Spencer (1995: 513). See also IMF (1998).

These techniques therefore seem to have magnified the Russian shock. Russia on its own could not have created such turmoil, but Russia in the global financial market could and did. The turbulence in the mature markets revealed deficiencies in systemic risk management at both the private and the public level. On the private side, investors appear to have been engaged in higher risks than expected; and on the public side, market surveillance and banking supervision were obviously insufficient. But whatever the degree of market surveillance and banking supervision, financial crisis and sovereign default will always occur. The real legacy to the financial market of the August 1998 decisions is the reminder that 'no country is too big to fail' and that there is no international lender of last resort.

9.3 MORAL HAZARD AND BURDEN-SHARING

In the last fifteen years, the rapid growth of markets for all sorts of security has been encouraged by financial liberalization both at the level of foreign exchange controls, which has led to capital crossing borders, and at the level of domestic financial markets, which has led to increased competition within the financial system. Competition between banks and non-banks has encouraged financial innovation and the expansion of off-balance-sheet activities,[30] which fall outside regulatory frameworks. In turn, off-balance-sheet activities, such as derivative products and repurchase agreements ('repos'), have encouraged flows of capital across borders. Thus the 1990s were marked by a dramatic increase in emerging market bond financing and in leveraged funding through derivatives transactions based on those bond issues.

The search for high-return, high-yield instruments with returns enhanced by leveraged funding may explain why debt crises in the 1990s were frequent, rapid and violent. It also explains why capital flows have proved to be so resilient. After the Mexican crisis of 1994–5, 'the total flow to emerging markets rebounded as early as 1995 when it increased by 20 per cent'.[31] The same applied to the Asian countries in 1999 and to some extent to Russia. By contrast, after the 1982 Latin American crisis, capital flows took almost ten years to return, and did so then thanks largely to the Brady plan for write-downs of existing debt. The decline in world interest rates in the early 1990s contributed to redirecting international finance towards high-yield assets in emerging markets (Table 9.2).[32]

Higher returns in emerging markets seem to have been made much more attractive by the perception developed after the 1994–5 Mexican crisis that the

---

[30] Warburton (1999: 271): 'examples of bank assets which do not have to appear on their balance sheet are those acquired by leasing or hire purchase, project finance, letters of credit, financial derivatives and loan assets that have been securitised'.
[31] Giannini (1999: 27).
[32] Calvo, Leiderman and Reinhart (1996).

Table 9.2: Short-term interest rates, 1981–98 (%)

Country	1981–89[a]	1990–95[a]	1996	1997	1998
United States	8.5	4.9	5	5.1	4.8
Japan	6	4.3	0.6	0.6	0.7
European Union	10.5	9	4.7	4.2	3.9
South Korea[b]	n.a	15	12.7	13.4	15.2
Mexico	61.1	24.9	32.9	21.3	26.1

[a] Average.
[b] The average for South Korea is for 1991–5.
Source: OECD (1999), Annex, Table 36, p. 260.

IMF was the new international 'Zorro', riding to the rescue of vulnerable countries, and creditors, always in time to prevent the default.

The perception of high returns at almost no risk was fundamentally altered after the Russian default. Ironically, the débâcle of August 1998 came a mere four weeks after Russia had secured a much-trumpeted IMF-led rescue package worth $22.6 billion. The IMF's $4.8 billion first instalment was disbursed to Russia on 23 July 1998, 25 days before the Russian financial collapse. By average standards of fiscal adjustment in emerging economies with deep structural problems, fiscal reforms under the Kirienko government were achieving commendably rapid results. But progress could never be fast enough, and the bail-out was too little and too slow when about $1 billion worth of maturing treasury bills had to be redeemed every Wednesday as investors flooded out of the market. The CBR's hard currency reserves stood at roughly $13 billion in late July 1998. The IMF-led programme entailed the usual disbursements by tranches over 18 months linked to continuous progress with fiscal adjustment. The markets could see that neither the fiscal adjustment nor the tranched IMF money could relieve the immediate liquidity crisis: default was expected and investor panic intensified. Thus Russia defaulted and devalued while the IMF 'bail-out' programme remained on track.

This event illustrates how badly equipped the IMF is to handle liquidity crises.[33] Assistance is too slow in coming, because agreement has to be reached, and too small in volume, because the amounts granted are usually spread over several months. Indeed, the IMF is not a full-fledged lender of last resort (LLR),[34]

[33] Helleiner (1999) makes the point that the IMF provides exceptional lending but not liquidity.
[34] James (1999:3): 'The classic exposition is in Bagehot (1873), who saw a central bank as preventing the spread of financial crises by lending to illiquid banks on any collateral that would be marketable in the ordinary course of banking, if there is no panic, and charging a rate of interest above the market level. The LLR should lend freely and dearly.'

providing unconditional liquidity under certain *ex ante* criteria.[35] The IMF does not issue international money, and its actual resources are no match for the global capital market.

This discussion is especially complicated because of moral hazard. Moral hazard can be defined as the tendency for economic agents to be less careful when they do not expect to bear the full consequences of their behaviour. The moral hazard issue led Schwartz to see no further role for the IMF and to call for the market to do the job (Schwartz, 1998). Indeed, even if a rescue package is organized and successful, there remains the question of how to make sure that it will not encourage either further risk-taking from investors or even worse management by makers of economic policy in emerging market economies.[36] It seems indeed that the IMF-led and -coordinated bail-outs which preceded the Russian crisis were an important factor in creditors' risk-taking.

The servicing of sovereign debt has always been more difficult to ensure than private debt.[37] The lack of collateral and of an international equivalent of receivership and Chapter 11 bankruptcy proceedings in lending to sovereign states makes enforcing norms of repayment very difficult.[38] 'Bankruptcy law is designed to solve problems of creditor co-ordination in the absence of contracts that might otherwise do the job.'[39] But in its absence contracts should do the job. Unfortunately, as currently designed, they do not.

This has led to the idea that private investors could be asked to share some of the responsibility for the continuing provision of credit to customers to whom they had previously lent.[40] This could involve the development of contingent liquidity facilities in which the private sector would take an important stake,[41] as well as improved arrangements in the case of moratoria on foreign debt. Such provisions could force lenders to be more careful in appraising loans, because they would be hit harder financially if a crisis did occur. This could also limit the volatility of capital flows.

To call on the private sector – banks and bondholders – to prevent the default and to try to design a single model as a basis for this involvement is not

---

[35] In April 1999, the IMF created the Contingency Credit Line (CCL) to provide countries facing contagion. See Griffith-Jones (1999).

[36] See Giannini (1999) for an extensive account of both the literature and the questions raised by this debate.

[37] See Aggarval (1996) for a historical account of sovereign debt default.

[38] See James (1999:5): 'There is no practical mechanism, as yet, for country bankruptcies, although there has been some discussion of the applicability of the U.S. style "Chapter 11" solutions, in which the affected entity remains in operation.'

[39] Miller and Stiglitz (1999: 2).

[40] See Griffith-Jones and Antonio-Ocampo (1999: 59–66) for a good survey of the different proposals.

[41] IMF (1999b: 32): 'Argentina, Mexico and Indonesia have each entered into financing agreements with consortiums of foreign commercial banks with the aim of creating a mechanism to provide liquidity in times of crisis.'

without problems. Private creditors are not homogeneous; and syndicated loans and bond issues have different legal and institutional frameworks. It would be difficult to design a mechanism satisfying both groups, as each class of creditor will tend to seek preferential treatment. Eurobonds, for instance, have historically been assumed to be senior to other claims, but there seems to be no objective reason why they should stay immune from restructuring agreements in the face of repayment and restructuring difficulties, especially as they represent a growing share of claims. New ground was broken by the Paris Club's decision to require that the Pakistani authorities approach their bondholders to seek 'comparable treatment' to the relief offered by it. The same issue of burden-sharing was even stronger in the case of Ecuador. In the case of Russia, burden-sharing was effected by the tough restructuring imposed by the government on foreign holders of GKOs. Also, to bail in hundreds of bondholders is not the same as bailing in bank lenders, as was done in the case of the first Mexican crisis in the 1980s or in the recent South Korean crisis. In both cases there was a clearly identifiable group of overseas creditor banks and a relatively small group of South Korean bank debtors. There was also in the 1980s and the 1990s only a very limited experience with restructuring sovereign bonds.[42]

In emerging markets, most of the sovereign debt is structured in the form of American-style bonds. Under US terms, modifying bond contracts requires unanimous agreement among bondholders. This makes restructuring extremely difficult because any dissenter could sue the issuer of the bonds. Contrary to syndicated loans, American-style bonds do not include any sharing clause requiring individual creditors to split with other bondholders any amounts recovered. This means that nothing can stop an investor from proceeding with legal action. Contracts under English law typically provide for qualified majority voting and are more prone to facilitate debt restructuring.[43] This has led to the suggestion, first proposed by Eichengreen and Portes (1995), of changing the contractual provisions governing sovereign debt. This would encompass measures such as the introduction of qualified majority voting able to modify the terms of a bond contract, including the rescheduling of principal and interest; it would also include collective representation of bondholders and a sharing clause for the proceeds received from the debtor among creditors.

[42] IMF (1999b: 57): 'During the 1980s, there were four examples: the restructuring of bonds by Costa Rica, Guatemala, Panama, and the restructuring of promissory notes by Nigeria. More recently, there have been actual or attempted restructurings by Moldova, Romania, Tatarstan and Ukraine.'

[43] IMF (1999b: 17): 'British-style bonds contain provisions for bondholders to more easily bind in dissident creditors through the modification of terms by qualified majorities. In addition, Trust Deed British-style bonds include prohibitions on the ability of individual bondholders to accelerate bonds and initiate litigation. Instead, litigation must be conducted by the trustee, any resources recovered must be shared with all holders of the issue, thereby imposing a de facto sharing clause.'

However, despite the attractiveness to debtors of British-style bonds, most emerging markets continue to issue American-style bonds. One of the most plausible explanations for this absence of change in bond contracts has been provided by Bryant (See Chapter 10 in this volume). Although the G7 countries strongly support this measure for emerging markets, they are reluctant to 'show leadership in this area by changing their own contracts'.[44] Emerging markets are thus wondering why it will be such a good idea for them but not such a good idea for the G7. But even if more emerging markets were to switch to British-style bonds, or if the G10 states succeeded in imposing their recommendations that bond contracts should be modified accordingly, this change could not be retroactive and would affect only new issues, not the outstanding stock of bonds.

Such schemes are opposed by the private sector because it argues that these contractual revisions may raise funding costs for emerging market borrowers and damage investor confidence and systemic liquidity.[45] This line of argument is rather puzzling. Indeed, if a better chance of debt restructuring in a future crisis can be achieved and if spreads can be increased and access to global finance for uncreditworthy borrowers can be limited, the increased possibility of modifications of bond terms should be seen as a positive step forward. As Wolf (1999) has remarked,

> this is a way of offsetting the subsidy implicit in official rescue packages. ... The risks inherent in foreign currency borrowing – as opposed to equity invest-ment – are very large. They must be priced into contracts, not assumed away. Yet the critics are right to complain that these proposals may raise the cost of borrowing. This is not a compelling objection. It is among their benefits.

Moreover, the IMF (1999b: 19) has stated that 'strengthening incentives for creditors to manage and assess risk, on the one hand, and for debtors to implement policies designed to strengthen their creditworthiness on the other ... could have a beneficial impact on the operation of global capital markets'.

Any form of forced bailing in of the private sector would probably fail to prevent an aggressive holder of defaulted bonds from taking unilateral action, such as seeking to freeze assets of the sovereign country in foreign jurisdictions. The threat of litigation is the key bargaining lever available to bondholders. In terms of facilitating restructurings, and thus extending burden-sharing to private investors, the IMF idea of sharing clauses has the merit of making it unattractive for an individual shareholder to sue a defaulting issuer. The problem with this idea is that some of the bonds may be held by the borrower or by nominees of the borrower (who have bought the bonds at a discount). It would be unjust in the context of a restructuring to force bondholders to

---

[44] Bryant, in this volume, Chapter 10.
[45] See Gray (1999).

effectively share with the borrower.[46]

International organizations such as the IMF have frequently influenced the nature of rescheduling agreements. However, to work out a single model in which both bondholders and banks will be asked to work out debt rescheduling supervised by a third party – the IMF – is complicated by the fact that both creditor governments and international organizations are guided primarily by their own agendas.

The first best solution should be the uncertainty mechanism in a case-by-case model rather than the adoption of a single model. No certainty of a bail-out in any way is the best means of reducing the need for bail-outs in the first place. Uncertainty is the best guarantee that investors will seriously assess the risks involved in high-yield instruments.

9.4 CONCLUSION

The Russian debt crisis episode in 1998 has reinforced conclusions reached after the Asian crisis, such as the fragility and dangers of the exchange rate peg.[47] But more importantly, this episode has shown that the assumption 'too big to fail' does not hold any more and therefore that risk strategy as well as the process of debt restructuring needs to be reassessed.

The Russian crisis will prove to have had a long-term beneficial impact in introducing uncertainty. This is at least as effective a discipline for private investors as the schemes for formal burden-sharing surveyed above, and very much more practicable. After Mexico, investors in emerging markets were led to assume that there would always be bail-outs. After Russia, the assumption is the contrary, even if some investors tend to reassure themselves by treating Russia as a 'special case', that is a basket case. Soon enough, however, there will be a new crisis in which investors consider the IMF powerless to act and disaster to be inevitable. But then, unexpectedly, a group of governments may come to the rescue. The minority of investors who see that possibility will make large profits. From one standpoint, that is a bailout; from another, the investors will have had their reward from taking advantage of a well-judged risk premium. So this hypothetical case does not involve a risk-free bailout. The very uncertainty provides the necessary discipline.

---

[46] See Gray (1999).
[47] See Chapters 6 (by Davanne and Jacquet) and 7 (by Kwan) in this volume.

Table A9.1: The Russian Federation: macroeconomic indicators, 1996–9

	1996	1997	1998	1999
Production and prices[a]				
Real GDP	−3.5	0.9	−4.9	−3.2
Change in consumer prices				
Annual average	47.6	14.6	27.8	85.7
12-month	21.8	11.0	84.4	36.5
Change in GDP deflator	43.9	16.6	11.4	n/a
Public sector[b, c]				
Federal government				
Overall balance	−7.9	−6.8	−4.9	−1.7
Primary balance	−2.2	−2.8	−1.1	1.9
Revenue	11.8	12.6	10.1	13.3
of which: cash	9.2	10.0	9.0	n/a
Expenditure	−19.9	−20.0	−15.1	−15.0
Interest	−5.9	−4.6	−3.9	−3.6
Non-interest	−14.0	−15.4	−11.2	−11.4
External sector[d]				
Total exports f.o.b.	90.6	89	74.8	74.3
Total imports f.o.b.	72.8	77.4	56.8	46.1
External current account (deficit = −)	3.9	−3.0	2.3	11.4
Federal government external debt service due	17.5	15.9	17.4	18.5
As % of exports of goods and services	17.0	15.4	19.8	22.3
Stock of federal government external debt	136.1	134.6	152.4	157.0
As % of GDP	32.6	30.9	48.7	93.1
Gross reserves coverage (months of imports of goods and services)[b]	2	2	2.2	2
Memorandum items				
Nominal GDP (bn roubles)	2,145.7	2,478.6	2,696.4	4,545.5
Exchange rate (Rbl/$ period average)	5.1	5.8	9.9	24.9
Nominal GDP (bn dollars)	420.7	427.3	272.4	182.6

[a] Annual percentage changes
[b] Revenues and expenditures are on a cash basis. Primary balance and overall balance are on a commitment basis.
[c] % of GDP.
[d] $bn unless otherwise noted.
Sources: Russian authorities; IMF staff estimates and projections quoted on the IMF web site.

References

Aggarwal, V. (1996), *Debt Games, Strategic Interaction in International Debt Rescheduling* (Cambridge, MA: Cambridge University Press).

Bank for International Settlements (1998), *68th Annual Report, 15th April 1997–31st March 1998*, Basle, 8 June.

Bank for International Settlements (1999), *Central Bank Survey of Foreign Exchange and Derivatives Market Activity, 1998*, Basle, May.

Calvo, G. (1998a), 'Varieties of Capital-Market Crises', in G. Calvo and M. King (eds), *The Debt Burden and its Consequences for Monetary Policy* (Basingstoke, Hants: Macmillan Press), pp.181–202.

Calvo, G. (1998b), 'Understanding the Russian virus with special reference to Latin America', paper presented at the Deutsche Bank conference on 'Emerging Markets: Can They Be Crisis Free?' Washington, DC, 13 October 1998.

Calvo, G., Leiderman, L. and Reinhart, C. (1996), 'Inflows of Capital to Developing Countries in the 1990s', *Journal of Economic Perspectives*, Vol. 10, No. 2, Spring, pp. 123–9.

Calvo, G. and Reinhart, C. (1999), 'When Capital Inflows Come to a Sudden Stop: Consequences and Policy Options', draft, June 29, on *www.bsos.umd.edu/econ/cievalvo.htm*.

Capie, F. (1998), 'Can there be an International Lender of Last Resort?', *International Finance*, Vo. 1, No. 2, pp. 311–25.

Diaz-Alejandro, C. (1985), 'Goodbye Financial Repression, Hello Financial Crash,' *Journal of Development Economics*, Vol. 19, September/October, 1985, pp. 1–24.

Eichengreen, B. (1999a), 'Strengthening the Common Financial House', remarks delivered at the World Bank/Japanese Ministry of Finance Conference on Global Finance and Development, 2 March 1999, and forthcoming in a booklet edited by the Japanese Ministry of Finance.

Eichengreen, B. (1999b), 'Taming Capital Flows', paper prepared for a special issue of *World Development*, ed. Irma Adelman, August.

Eichengreen, B. (1999c), 'Solving the Currency Conundrum', paper prepared for the Council on Foreign Relations Study Group on Economic and Financial Development, September.

Eichengreen, B. and Portes, R. (1995), *Crisis? What Crisis? Orderly Workouts for Sovereign Debtors*, Centre for Economic Policy Research, London, September.

Fischer, S. (1999), 'On the Need for an International Lender of Last Resort', *Journal of Economic Perspectives*, Vol. 13, No. 4, Fall, pp. 85–104.

Garber, P. and Spencer M. (1995), 'Foreign Exchange Hedging and the Interest Rate Defence', *IMF Staff Papers*, Vol. 42, No. 3, September, pp. 490–515.

Giannini, C. (1999), 'Enemy of None but a Common Friend of All? An International Perspective on the Lender of Last Resort Function', Working Paper/99/10, IMF, January.

Granville, B. (1995), *The Success of Russian Economic Reforms* (London: Royal Institute of International Affairs).

Granville,B. (1999), 'Bingo or Fiasco? The Global Financial Situation is Not Guaranteed', *International Affairs*, Vol. 75, No. 4 (October), pp. 713–28.

Granville, B (forthcoming), 'The Problem of Monetary Stabilization' in Granville, B. and Oppenheimer, P. (eds), *Russia's Post-Communist Economy*, Oxford University Press.

Gray, R. (1999), 'Orderly Debt Work-Outs From a Private Perspective', paper prepared for the SIDA–DANIDA–OXFAM–UNDP workshop on capital flows at the Institute of Development Studies, Sussex University, 13–14 September.

Griffith-Jones, S. (1999), 'Towards a Better Financial Architecture', paper prepared for the SIDA–DANIDA–OXFAM–UNDP workshop on capital flows at the Institute of Development Studies, Sussex University, 13–14 September.

Griffith-Jones, S., Antonio-Ocampo, J. with Jacques Cailloux (1999), 'The Poorest Countries and the Emerging International Financial Architecture', Expert Group on Development Issues, EGDI, distributed by Almqvist and Wiksell International, Stockholm, Sweden.

Helleiner, G. (1999), 'Financial Markets, Crises and Contagion: Issues for Smaller Countries in the FTAA and Post-Lome IV Negotiations', paper prepared for the Caribbean Regional Negotiating Machinery, Kingston, Jamaica, January.

International Monetary Fund (1998), *World Economic Outlook and International Capital Markets*, Interim Assessment, December.

International Monetary Fund (1999a), 'Statement of the Government of the Russian Federation and Central Bank of Russia on Economic Policies', Washington, DC, 13 July.

International Monetary Fund (1999b), 'Involving the Private Sector in Forestalling and Resolving Financial Crisis', paper prepared by the Policy Department and Review Department, Washington, DC.

International Monetary Fund (1999c), 'IMF Policy on Lending into Arrears to Private Creditors', paper prepared by the Policy Development and Review and Legal Departments, Washington, DC.

International Monetary Fund (1999d), *International Financial Statistics*, January.

James, H. (1999), 'The Changing Character of the International Monetary Fund', paper presented at the Monetary Unions conference sponsored by City University Business School and American Express, London, 14 May.

Miller, M. and Stiglitz, J. (1999), 'Bankruptcy Protection against Macroeconomic Shocks: The Case for a Super Chapter 11', paper prepared for the conference on capital flows, financial crises and policies, World Bank, April 15–16.

Mishkin F. (1996), 'Understanding Financial Crises: A Developing Country Perspective', in M. Bruno and B. Pleskovic (eds), *Annual World Bank Conference on Development Economics 1996* (Washington, DC: World Bank), pp. 29–62.

Obstfeld, M. (1998), 'The Global Capital Market: Benefactor or Menace?', NBER Working Paper Series, Working Paper 6559 (Cambridge, MA: National Bureau of Economic Research), May.

Schwartz, A. (1998), 'Time to Terminate the ESF and the IMF', Foreign Policy Briefing No. 48 (Washington, DC: The Cato Institute), 26 August.

Warburton, P. (1999), *Debt and Delusion: Central Bank Follies That Threaten Economic Disaster,* (Harmondsworth: Allen Lane, The Penguin Press).

Wolf, M. (1999), 'How to avoid the debtors' prison', *Financial Times,* 20 October.

10 STANDARDS AND PRUDENTIAL OVERSIGHT FOR AN INTEGRATING WORLD FINANCIAL SYSTEM

Ralph C. Bryant

Ralph C. Bryant

10.1 INTRODUCTORY REMARKS ON REFORMING INTERNATIONAL FINANCIAL ARCHITECTURE

I am dissatisfied with the nuances, sometimes even the main thrust, of most discussions about reforming international financial architecture.[1] I therefore begin by sketching, in very broad strokes, what I believe to be the fundamentals of the subject. I stress some basic political constraints and equally basic economic imperatives.

The political structure of the world is multi-layered, heterogeneous and inherently conflictual. The second half of the 20th century was characterized by increasing political pluralism – a marked expansion in the number of governmental decision-making units and a greater diffusion of power among them. Increasing political pluralism has in turn been accompanied by rising nationalism.

Increasing integration among national economies has been a second pervasive trend in the past half-century. Lending and borrowing, with assets and liabilities denominated in several different national currencies as well as domestic currency, have become progressively internationalized, and at an even faster pace than cross-border trade in goods and services.

Despite the fact that economic and financial interdependence has greatly increased, national borders continue to have immense significance in economic terms. Nations are substantially different – in their social and cultural norms, historical experiences, types of private institutions and jurisdictions of government institutions. Many nations still maintain partial separation fences at their

The paper was prepared in November 1999. It draws on the manuscript of the author's book, *Turbulent Waters: Cross-Border Finance and International Governance*, to be published by the Brookings Institution in 2001. The book will incorporate information about further progress in international cooperation in these areas made during the year 2000.

[1] One used to speak of the international monetary system, or the international financial system, or international financial institutions. In 1998, governmental participants in international discussions agreed to use the term 'architecture' instead of 'system'. I am not especially fond of architectural terminology in this context, but I bow to recent fashion.

borders (though much less so than at mid-century).

It is a basic characteristic of free enterprise capitalism that market extremes can cause market failures. It is a basic characteristic of pluralist politics that government extremes and rigidities can cause government failures. Virtually every nation, therefore, has a mixed economy, some combination of decentralized markets and governance infrastructures. But the particular combination – the specifics of the mixed economy – differs widely. All these cross-nation differences help to explain why national borders still have great economic significance despite the intensification of cross-border integration and the globalization of culture brought about by modern communications technology.

The world polity and economy at the turn of the century are at messy, intermediate stages of evolution. The political structure is so heterogeneous and multi-layered as to seem bewildering. Economic structure is neither fish nor fowl. Any sensible approach to international financial architecture must grapple with this hybrid, intermediate messiness.[2]

In this intermediate world, collective action problems with cross-border dimensions will continue to grow in importance relative to domestic governance. National governments will inevitably be forced to cooperate more among themselves and to ask international institutions to carry out a wider range of functional responsibilities. Reform of the international financial architecture, at its deepest level, is thus about the evolution of international collective governance for the world financial system.

Financial activity, when it functions smoothly, is enormously beneficial in promoting growth and efficient resource allocation. It permits the diversification and sharing of risk. It allows ultimate savers and ultimate investors to make independent localized decisions, yet render the decisions consistent in the aggregate. Completely unconstrained financial activity, however, may not be able to deliver these benefits. Informational asymmetries, adverse selection and moral hazard, informational cascades, herding behaviour, contagion and excessive volatility in asset prices cause financial activity to be inherently vulnerable to instability (see Bryant (2001), Diamond and Dybvig (1983), Bikhchandani, Hirshleifer and Welch (1992), Banerjee (1992), Avery and Zemsky (1998), and Masson (1998, 1999a, 1999b)).

The appropriate societal response to this dilemma is to establish and maintain a collective governance infrastructure for the financial system. Within an individual nation, the critical features of this infrastructure include high

[2] Journalism and popular discussion now assert sweeping but superficial generalizations about 'globalization'. Some, for example Thomas Friedman (1999), view the trends approvingly. Others, such as Greider (1997) and Gray (1999), perceive them as alarming and try to incite antipathy. Much of this popular commentary about globalization is unhelpful in understanding the intermediate messiness of today's actual world. For a cogent overview of how much national borders still matter, see Helliwell (1998).

standards for accounting, auditing and information disclosure; well-designed and competently administered legal procedures for enforcing contracts and adjudicating disputes; skilful prudential supervision and regulation of private financial institutions; an effective but limited potential for crisis management and crisis lending (lender-of-last-resort provisions); and, not least, sound and predictable macroeconomic policies that shape the general environment within which the financial system and the wider economy operate.

If a well-functioning collective governance infrastructure is a precondition for a domestic financial system to operate smoothly, why is no analogous infrastructure needed on a world scale for the smooth operation of the conglomeration of all national financial systems? One's intuition suggests that the same logic does apply at the world level. And the economic aspects of the logic are, indeed, persuasive. If there could exist global, supranational analogues to the functions carried out within domestic financial systems by nations' central banks and supervisors of financial institutions, the global economy and financial system could evolve in a more smooth and stable manner.

If cabbages were horses, all could ride like kings. But cabbages are not horses. And because the political preconditions do not exist in our messy intermediate world, the logic cannot be fully applied to the global financial system. The global polity does not yet contain collective-governance institutions that can effectively carry out the functions of a supranational utilities infrastructure.

The international community has only recently begun to develop recommendations for minimum global standards in the areas of accounting, auditing and data collection and dissemination. There exists no world legal system, no infrastructure of international courts or legal bodies for the resolution of cross-border disputes. Even for private entities, cross-border contract defaults and insolvencies (and hence cross-border procedures for arbitration or bankruptcy) pose serious difficulties. When sovereign governments or entire nations are involved, the difficulties are still more serious. The world has only nascent supranational institutions, with very limited responsibilities, for the prudential oversight of financial activity. The issues of crisis management and crisis lending on a global scale are several times more complicated than the issues faced within a national economy by a national central bank. The world does not have global or regional monetary policies as distinct from the separate monetary policies of individual nations. Similarly, the notion of global or regional fiscal policies is an oxymoron. Procedures for intergovernmental cooperation among the fiscal authorities and the monetary authorities of the largest nations are in their infancy.

Given the need for further evolution of international collective governance – but recognizing the hybrid, intermediate status of the world polity – one has to be practical about how to make progress. In key areas, we should encourage a stretching of intergovernmental cooperation. We ought to support a further strengthening of international institutions. This approach, which I like to label pragmatic incrementalism, does not retreat from the need to strengthen international collective governance gradually. But neither does it unrealistically demand too much, too soon. Positioned in the middle of the road, pragmatic incrementalism is distanced both from the extreme untrammelled markets view and from the sweeping institutional reform view.

The untrammelled markets view sees governance failures as pervasive, at both the national level and the nascent international level. From this perspective, efforts to mount governmental action are more likely to be the problem than a solution. This view thus retreats from collective governance and hopes that markets themselves will cope resiliently with any difficulties that materialize.

In sharp contrast, the sweeping institutional reform view sees market failures as pervasive, internationally as well as domestically. It believes that financial markets periodically go out of control, especially with cross-border transactions, and thus wants either to rebuild the separation fences at national borders or else to delegate greatly enhanced authority to international institutions.

Neither the untrammelled markets view nor the sweeping institutional reform view is based on compelling analysis. Both views, furthermore, are politically unrealistic. Market failures and financial turbulence put great pressure on governments to 'do something'. The untrammelled markets advice to 'Don't do something! Just stand there!' almost invariably buckles under crisis-generated political pressure, usually appropriately so. For evidence on this point, witness the last two years of post-crisis intergovernmental discussions that were preoccupied with reforming financial architecture. Meanwhile, the sweeping institutional reform view badly misjudges political constraints. Over the next decade or two, political considerations are unlikely to permit a radical increase in the authority of existing international institutions. The creation of additional international institutions, *de novo*, will be at least as constrained by political difficulties. The cosmopolitan dream of establishing global federalist governmental institutions – the beginnings of a world government – stands no chance of fulfilment for many decades. Political leaders retain many illusions about the effective degree of their nation's sovereignty. They fail to appreciate adequately the difference between *de jure* and *de facto* sovereignty. National governments therefore encourage international institutions to tiptoe rather than to move briskly towards the establishment of a nascent world utilities infrastructure.

I will now turn to a subset of the institutions constituting a collective-governance infrastructure for financial activity. My focus is the areas of accounting and auditing; data collection and dissemination; legal processes and institutions, especially for insolvency and bankruptcy; and the prudential supervision and regulation of financial institutions (in short, prudential oversight). I will identify basic issues and problems in these areas, and then general principles that should guide international cooperation in formulating standards and prudential oversight at the world level. Significant progress has been made in these areas in recent years, and section 10.6 summarizes that progress. Finally, I will discuss some controversial issues that remain to be resolved: the allocation of responsibilities among international financial institutions, the adoption by individual nations of international accounting standards, the introduction of collective-action clauses into bond contracts and the evolution of capital adequacy requirements for banks.

10.2 ACCOUNTING, AUDIT, DATA AND LEGAL SYSTEMS: THE MAIN ISSUES

Mistakes and accidents occur even within a well-functioning domestic financial system. Particular investments in real capital turn out to be disappointments. Financial transactions associated with those investments, and with other individual financial claims, go sour. Mistakes and accidents – mishaps is a convenient shorthand term – are inevitable in an economy in which the actors are fallible human beings, uncertainties and risks are rife, and asymmetric-information and principal agent complexities abound.

What happens when, because of a mishap, a financial contract cannot be, or is not, fulfilled? Sometimes the lender and borrower can agree to rewrite their contract. Alternatively, the allocation of losses from a defaulted contract and the resolution of disputes may be submitted to arbitration. In still other cases, defaults may trigger recourse to litigation. Bankruptcy proceedings may ensue after a default, leading to one or another method of allocating some or all of the defaulting borrower's assets to its creditors. If the mishap has been severe enough to render a borrower insolvent (that is, causing the value of assets to fall below the value of all liabilities), bankruptcy proceedings of some sort will be inevitable. Defaults, insolvencies, bankruptcies, arbitration mechanisms for dispute resolution – all these are inescapable features of capitalist economies with complex financial systems.[3]

Because of the inevitable mishaps, a smoothly functioning financial system must be supported by procedures for monitoring and enforcing contracts and

---

[3] Such events are unfortunate in many ways. They generate losses for individuals and costs for the economy. However, given the pervasive uncertainties and risks, coupled with periodic innovations in the economy, they also have a silver lining. Mistakes should lead to losses, in part to create incentives that will reduce the chances of mistakes in similar financial contracts made in the future. Accidents are often associated with fundamental changes in the economy, reducing the profitability of some types of economic and financial activity and increasing the profitability of others. Obsolescent products and industries should be phased out.

for working out the consequences when particular financial contracts are not honoured. Standardized and widely accepted procedures for accounting and auditing are necessary accompaniments for successful monitoring and enforcement. The collection, aggregation and widespread dissemination of data about the activities of financial institutions are basic requirements. The legal system must provide a foundation of laws and rules that facilitate the resolution of disputes about contracts and the handling of defaults and insolvencies.

Sound accounting standards, demanding audit practices and the dissemination of accurate data are important because the economy and financial system cannot allocate resources efficiently if the information available about businesses and financial institutions is seriously incomplete or misleading. Full, timely and accurate disclosure of financial results and other information material to investment decisions is a necessary – albeit not sufficient – condition for the appropriate identification and pricing of risks. Standardized norms and rules for presenting information, applied consistently over time, mitigate the difficulties of comparing the financial performances of different businesses and financial institutions. Standardized audit procedures – providing for periodic reviews by outside, independent auditors of internal control mechanisms and financial statements – ensure truthful, timely disclosure and facilitate the legal verification of contracts. Data for individual institutions, and aggregative data for sectors and the entire economy, are an indispensable foundation for the evaluation of risk.

The legal system identifies property rights and their status relative to other rights; establishes procedures for resolving disputes about how financial contracts are written and interpreted (including rules for how and when disputes can be brought into courts of law); governs what practices are appropriate in the monitoring, enforcement and legal verification of contracts; and sets out rules to condition arbitration procedures as an alternative to court proceedings. The default and bankruptcy provisions of the legal system are especially critical for the financial system.[4]

The basic rationale for bankruptcy procedures is again to promote the efficient allocation of resources in the economy. A good bankruptcy procedure should, as much as possible, preserve the *ex post* value of the debtor. By providing the debtor with temporary protection from its creditors and possibly with access to interim finance with some form of *de facto* seniority, bankruptcy procedures enable an enterprise whose value as a going concern exceeds its break-up value to continue to operate. To this end, it may be necessary to

---

[4] Bankruptcy can take a variety of forms, such as liquidation of the defaulting borrower's assets or business, receivership (a third party selected to run the business and work out the consequences), structured bargaining supervised by a third party, or administration of the assets or business by a judge or other court-appointed official.

protect the debtor enterprise from creditors who wish to invoke remedies available to them individually as a result of the non-performance of the debt contract. But a good bankruptcy procedure should also penalize the debtor (in the case of a business enterprise, its management) in order to provide adequate *ex ante* incentives for the debtor to manage its assets well while undergoing bankruptcy. By specifying *ex ante* rules for the distribution of partial or delayed payments on impaired debt claims among different creditors – and more broadly for an appropriate distribution of the debtor's *ex post* value across its creditors (one that respects the priority of claims among the various classes of creditors) – bankruptcy procedures reduce uncertainty and make it easier for markets to price risk.

The legal provisions governing bankruptcy are necessarily complex: they require a subtle balancing of the rights and obligations of debtors and creditors. Hence the objectives of bankruptcy are partly in conflict. The bankruptcy laws must encourage adherence to the *ex ante* provisions of financial contracts. If debtors were not substantially penalized in bankruptcy, future debtors would be tempted to escape from their financial contracts by resorting to bankruptcy. At the same time, the bankruptcy laws seek to prevent an uncoordinated, costly 'grab race' among creditors that could lead to a fire-sale dismantling of the debtor's assets and a collective loss to all parties that is much larger than the losses that would otherwise occur through a cooperative bargaining process. The great difficulty in the design of bankruptcy laws is to strike the best possible balance between the competing objectives.

The preceding summary of basics entirely omits complications stemming from multiple nations, different currencies, exchange rates among currencies and cross-border transactions. For nations with advanced financial institutions, the occurrence of a mishap in domestic finance usually triggers well-developed remedial procedures. For cross-border finance, however, these underpinnings exist in only a rudimentary way. In the case of many developing nations, they are egregiously weak. Cross-border finance is thus plagued by four awkward and highly significant facts: an internationally standardized set of accounting and audit procedures does not exist; data for cross-border, and even domestic, assets and liabilities for many nations' financial systems are often either unavailable or unreliable; international law is much less well developed than nations' internal legal systems; and there exists no 'world' legal system, nor any universally accepted method of resolving differences among national legal systems.

Differences across nations in the norms and standards for business and financial accounts can be large. The substantive content of accounts, perhaps especially for financial statements, varies from one nation to another. National practices are sometimes in direct conflict. Traditions differ about the amount and timing of disclosure and the degree of reliance to place on formal audits. A single example illustrates the point. When a bank's loan becomes non-performing in some nations, only the unpaid instalment of the bad loan is considered past due in the reporting of the bank's condition. In other nations, however, the entire loan – current unpaid instalment and all future instalments – is classified as non-performing if any instalment payment is overdue. The latter accounting standard is obviously much more stringent than the former, and more likely to signal future difficulties.

Deficiencies in accounting practices, audit standards and the availability of accurate data appear to have been a significant underlying contributor to past financial crises (see Bordo, Eichengreen, and Irwin (1999)). They are widely perceived to have contributed to the financial crises in Asia and elsewhere in 1997–8.[5]

During the last few years, cooperative efforts to design an agreed set of global accounting standards have been undertaken through the auspices of the International Accounting Standards Committee (IASC). The standardization of auditing procedures has been discussed through the International Federation of Accountants (IFAC). International discussions about standards for securities firms have taken place under the aegis of the International Organization of Securities Commissions (IOSCO) and for the activities of insurance companies through the International Association of Insurance Supervisors (IAIS). Notable improvements in the collection, aggregation and dissemination of financial data in recent years have been made by the International Monetary Fund (IMF), the Bank for International Settlements (BIS), and the World Bank. I will summarize in later sections the activities of these world institutions and the progress on nascent international standards that they have made.

Consider next the complications for legal system issues stemming from cross-border transactions. Problems have arisen for centuries, of course, in which a plaintiff and a defendant – individuals, firms or organizations – are residents of different nations. Numerous volumes concerned with one or another aspect of international law reside on the bookshelves of courts and some lawyers. Even so, there are few institutional mechanisms for formal arbitration procedures and for reconciling differences among national legal systems.

---

[5] One of the Group of Twenty-Two's reports in the autumn of 1998, for example, summarized the 'damaging consequences' of accounting deficiencies in the following terms: 'In many Asian countries, the absence of consolidated financial statements for related companies and, more generally, poor accounting practices hid serious financial weaknesses – the result of bad lending or investment decisions – in the corporate and banking sectors and contributed to the misallocation of resources that led up to the crisis. Faced with inadequate information about firms' financial performance, investors and creditors appeared to give issuers and borrowers the benefit of the doubt until the crisis broke and then to assume the worst after problems became apparent.' Group of Twenty-Two (October 1998b), p. 5.

The International Court of Justice (ICJ) is, in principle, an exception. The ICJ, located in the Hague in the Netherlands, is the principal judicial organ of the United Nations. It was created in 1946 as the successor institution to the Permanent Court of International Justice (created under the League of Nations in 1922). The ICJ has two functions: 'to settle in accordance with international law the legal disputes submitted to it by states, and to give advisory opinions on legal questions referred to it by duly authorized international organs and agencies' (general information about the International Court of Justice can be obtained from their web site: *www.icj-cij.org*). Opinions differ widely about how much authority the ICJ has, and should have, and how well it performs the functions assigned to it. As its mandate makes clear, however, one significant fact is beyond controversy: non-governmental entities such as private businesses and financial institutions are not able to initiate cases at the ICJ.

The relatively new dispute settlement mechanisms in the World Trade Organization can now help to reconcile trade-policy features of national legal and regulatory systems (see Jackson (1998), Ostry (1999), Petersmann (1998)). The UN Commission on International Trade Law (UNCITRAL) and the International Bar Association have provoked international discussions about model standards for insolvency and bankruptcy (summarized below). Every international institution has its own history of legal precedents and their status *vis-à-vis* national laws (for example, for the International Monetary Fund see Gold (1984, 1990)).

Nonetheless, the overwhelming fact remains: the institutional mechanisms for reconciliation of differences among national legal systems are few in number and limited in scope. The Supreme Court and the subsidiary court systems in the United States have sufficient political authority to be regarded as a third branch of the US government. The legal system and its enforcement in many other nation-states have an analogously strong political standing. None of the international legal institutions or procedures has a comparable political muscle for resolving cross-border legal issues.

Given that bankruptcy procedures require a subtle balancing of competing objectives, one should expect that differing national cultures and social norms will suggest different points along the subtle trade-offs. And that in fact is the case, as observed by a study group of the Group of Thirty (1998, p. 4):

> ... the legal authorities available to deal with a financial insolvency vary greatly from country to country, often based on quite different social preferences, with different priority assigned to protection of creditors, borrowers, employees and shareholders. Some are well tested and provide a fair and effective basis for working out competing claims with the national context; others much less so. In addition, virtually none were written with attention to the cross-border dimensions of an insolvency, offering no

mechanism for dealing with matters outside of home jurisdiction or reconciliation of national differences. There is therefore substantial scope for conflict and miscalculation.

In a situation of domestic insolvency when the national bankruptcy code is implemented, the issue of appropriate legal jurisdiction never arises. The creditors and debtor have no uncertainty about which system of national law applies. But which bankruptcy procedures should apply for a cross-border (and often a cross-currency) contract, those of the debtor's nation or those of the lender's? The design of a contract itself can resolve the most obvious uncertainties by spelling out in advance which nation's law applies as the 'proper law of the contract'. But in real life, complex situations can easily arise where the differences among national legal jurisdictions become important.[6] More generally, just as contracts cannot be complete in all their domestic dimensions, many types of cross-border legal contingencies cannot possibly be foreseen. The incremental uncertainties arising from the cross-border aspects of a contract turn out to be especially problematic. For domestic contracts, there at least exists a single, unambiguous legal jurisdiction for the resolution of disputes about the consequences of unforeseen contingencies. Dispute resolution for the inevitable, unforeseen contingencies of cross-border contracts is troubled by the lack of clarity about whether multiple national legal jurisdictions are relevant and how differences between the jurisdictions are to be reconciled.

Sovereign borrowing, where the debtor is the government of a sovereign nation and incurs liabilities to creditors in different foreign nations denominated in several foreign currencies, can be especially problematic. National governments may default on debt contracts, and have done so fairly often. But there is no simple sense in which an entire nation can be insolvent or undergo bankruptcy proceedings.

10.3 RATIONALES FOR THE PRUDENTIAL OVERSIGHT OF FINANCIAL INSTITUTIONS

Within individual nations, broad agreement exists that the government cannot accept a residual responsibility for the stability of the national financial system – and in particular cannot stand ready to provide lender-of-last-resort support in

---

[6] Consider an example in which a firm in nation A borrows from a lender in nation B with a contract specifying that the law of B applies, but also borrows from a lender in C with a contract written to specify that the law of C applies. If the borrower in A becomes insolvent, an important feature of domestic bankruptcy law will be absent: no court system will have jurisdiction over the totality of the debtor's obligations, and hence be able to compel all dissident creditors to accept an orderly, generally agreed restructuring of the debtor's liabilities and assets.

a crisis – unless it also engages in supervision and regulation of financial institutions to ensure sound practices and prevent excessive risk-taking. The term prudential oversight is a convenient shorthand for these supervision and regulation functions.

Emergency action in financial crises by a lender of last resort, if taken, even if merely anticipated in non-crisis periods, creates a moral hazard dilemma. If private financial institutions can confidently count on a lender of last resort extending assistance on a stormy day, on sunny days they may have insufficient incentives to behave prudently in their own lending decisions. Because the lender of last resort is expected to provide assistance in emergencies, it must encourage potential recipients to behave in a way that reduces – or at the least does not increase – the probability that emergencies will occur, and if emergencies should occur and assistance has to be extended, that reduces the private and social losses incurred. (Stiglitz (1994) provides an overview of the prudential-oversight roles of the government in financial markets.) Prudential oversight is thus analogous to the establishment of minimum-standard building codes that help to minimize the damage from real-life earthquakes and hurricanes. It has similarities to land-use zoning policies that discourage people from living in exposed flood plains, in low-lying coastal areas exposed to hurricanes or on top of geological faults where earthquake risk is unusually high.

The smooth operation of the payments mechanism is important for the stability of a nation's financial system. Most policy-makers and analysts believe that the government, as part of its functions as overseer of the soundness of the financial system, should regulate, and thereby protect the integrity of, a society's payments mechanism.

Deposit insurance for deposits held in financial intermediaries is yet another dimension of prudential oversight. If some agency of government provides deposit insurance, moral hazard considerations are again relevant. Such insurance can play a helpful role in reducing the likelihood of stormy-weather runs on the intermediaries, thereby helping to dampen the spread and intensity of financial distress. But the case against a guarantee of deposits is that by mitigating the threat of withdrawal of deposits, deposit insurance removes a check on imprudent risk-taking and irresponsibility by the management of the intermediaries. If the government does decide to provide deposit insurance, it will also be driven to concomitant supervision and regulation of the intermediaries to reduce the moral hazard problem that would otherwise exist.

The preceding rationales for prudential oversight are macroprudential, driven by a concern for systemic stability of the financial system. Many analysts and policy-makers would also identify a microprudential rationale, driven by concerns with the stability of individual financial institutions and the protection of individual consumers. The goal of microprudential oversight is to avert inappropriate conduct or the failure of particular institutions, thereby protecting individuals with deposits or other claims on the institutions and the local communities who depend on the lending activities of the institutions.

A prudential-protection rationale for the supervision and regulation of financial institutions does not raise issues or problems peculiar to purely financial institutions. Some defenders of the microprudential rationale, however, believe it to be peculiarly applicable to financial intermediaries. The balance between microprudential and macroprudential rationales also depends on which types of intermediaries are the focus of the supervision and regulation. For example, the macroprudential motives are particularly important for banks and the payments system, whereas microprudential motives get relatively greater weight as a justification for the regulation of brokerage firms and institutional investment funds.

Still another family of arguments, a concentration competition rationale, can be advanced to justify the supervision and regulation of financial institutions. The contention is that prudential oversight is required to obviate an undue concentration of economic power. Unlike the macroprudential and even the microprudential rationales for oversight, the concentration competition rationale is not distinctively applicable to financial institutions. Financial intermediaries and financial markets do pose some special regulatory issues because the nature of their business differs from that of non-financial organizations. But the same general issues of concentration and competition arise in connection with virtually all types of economic activity in the private sectors of mixed capitalist economies.

10.4 PRUDENTIAL OVERSIGHT: THE MAIN ISSUES

The government officials responsible for supervising and regulating financial institutions – the supervisors – will formulate and implement a wide range of policies (most of which are driven by the multiple rationales I have summarized). The supervisors can set licensing and authorization procedures for the establishment of new financial institutions. A prospective licensee will have to satisfy minimum criteria; the supervisors can reject applications that do not meet the criteria. The supervisors will also probably have authority to review proposals for the transfer to other parties of ownership or controlling interests in a financial institution, and to deny the transfer if appropriate criteria are not met. The supervisors may set minimum requirements for a financial institution's capital adequacy (net worth), and monitor whether financial institutions satisfy the requirements. The supervisors will establish guidelines to proscribe activities by the financial institutions deemed illegal or undesirable. Alternatively, they will have the authority to evaluate such guidelines developed by the institutions themselves.[7] The supervisors may monitor the procedures that financial institutions use to assess the creditworthiness of borrowers and the quality and riskiness of individual assets. They may evaluate the techniques used for management of the overall riskiness of the institutions' balance sheets. The supervisors may also set guidelines or evaluate own-institution guidelines designed to prevent an undue concentration of assets or excessive exposure to single borrowers or groups of borrowers. Finally, and perhaps most important, the supervisors will try to ensure that a financial institution maintains adequate and transparent accounts, that it has adequate procedures for external audits and that it publicly discloses information, including audited financial statements, that correctly reflect its condition.

The supervisors confront many difficult issues as they exercise prudential oversight. One of the most general is the relative degree of reliance to be placed on market-based incentives versus direct, explicit regulations. Prudential oversight relying on market-based, incentive-based regulations will often be less costly. For example, it would be prohibitively expensive to review all the actions of each financial institution's officers to ensure that no insider misconduct or self-dealing have occurred. Even when direct regulations are feasible, moreover, they may be a poor mechanism for achieving supervisory goals. The supervisory officials implementing direct regulations may fall prey to regulatory forbearance or even regulatory capture (see below). When market-based, incentive-based regulations that operate indirectly rather than directly are possible, they will usually be preferable. Requirements that financial institutions disclose timely and accurate information about their financial condition are a prime example. Disclosure of an institution's financial condition can permit market forces to do a substantial part of the needed enforcing and monitoring. A deterioration in the institution's condition, if transparent to the wider community, will be punished by declines in the market price of the institution's stock (and uninsured debentures, if any). Those declines will in turn put pressure on the institution's management to take corrective action. The pressures also work in reverse: transparent disclosure of information about a safe and well-managed institution's condition will enable it to obtain more favourable terms and conditions in its relations with its investors and creditors than those available to institutions perceived as more risky.

Market-based regulations align the incentives of the supervisors and the

---

[7] Examples of the activities deemed to be undesirable include fraud, the use of an institution for criminal purposes, cornering the market in particular securities, trading abuses (e.g. so-called front running) in securities markets, and insider misconduct and self-dealing. So-called connected lending abuses – when the officers of a financial institution make low-interest loans to themselves, relatives or other officers – are an illustration of insider self-dealing.

regulated institution's owners and managers. Requirements that an institution maintain adequate capital are an important example of a market-based, incentive-based regulation. A capital adequacy requirement gives managers and owners a strong incentive to be prudent. If the institution acts imprudently and goes bankrupt, the owners have a lot to lose. Conversely, if an institution's net worth is allowed to fall below a low threshold, managers and owners will be tempted to take risks rather than avoid them. Consider a bank that gets into trouble. If the bank's managers and owners were to have only a small equity stake in the bank because the capital adequacy requirements were set very low, they could be tempted to go for broke, taking on new highly risky loans such as the financing of an expensive new sports stadium in a distant suburb. If the new stadium does not catch on, bad luck – but the supervisors were going to close you down anyway. If the big bet on the stadium does pay off, the bank will look golden. The owners and managers will enjoy the upside gains – if there are upside gains. But the downside risks to them are small because so little of their own money is at stake. The bank is thus tempted to gamble on an excessively risky, go-for-broke strategy that ought to be rejected out of hand.

The setting of standards for capital adequacy, however, is less straight-forward than it might at first appear. A financial institution's net worth is measured with uncertainty and error. Its portfolio of assets continuously fluc-tuates in value, but many of the assets may not have a current market price. Accounting standards, if lax, may permit the understatement of losses or their transfer to the balance sheet of related institutions. Net worth is calculated only at periodic dates. An institution's managers thus may have significant influence over the measurement of its net worth and an incentive to report to the supervisors an optimistic calculation. If net worth could be monitored accur-ately and consistently, the supervisors could set a relatively low standard for minimum net worth and promptly close down an institution whose net worth fell below the required minimum. But with substantial lags and uncertainties in measurement, the supervisors will be forced to set a higher minimum standard to be sure that the true value of the institution's capital is above a target minimum level. A high minimum standard raises the probability that the super-visors will not have to deal with a negative net worth if they must eventually close an institution. The other side of the coin, however, is that supervisors may inappropriately constrain growth of the financial sector if they set the minimum standard excessively high.

In principle, the supervisors would also like to take into account variability in value of the institution's assets when setting a target minimum standard for capital adequacy. One type of such risk-based capital standards might, for example, treat government treasury bills as less risky than commercial loans or equity claims. With this approach, supervisors have to define the relative risk of broadly defined categories of assets and then set an appropriate minimum standard for the ratio of eligible capital to total assets weighted by their risks. Critics of such risk-based capital standards may take issue with the asset classes chosen by the supervisors or the particular weights the supervisors assign to them. Even more fundamentally, critics argue that the approach itself is misguided because the overall risk of the institution's entire portfolio cannot be adequately captured by the definition of asset classes and relative weights attached to the classes. Alternative approaches to the definition of capital adequacy thus include credit risk modelling of the entire portfolio (done with complex mathematical models, and perhaps undertaken by the supervised institution itself rather than by the supervisors) or a requirement that part of an institution's capital take the form of subordinated debentures actively traded in a financial market.

The details of capital adequacy requirements are messy and controversial. Broad agreement exists that capital adequacy requirements are socially desirable, not least because they take advantage of market incentives that align the objectives of the supervisors and the supervised institution. Yet decisions about the details of the capital standards themselves entail choices between market-based incentives versus direct regulations specified by the supervisors.[8]

Some types of prudential regulation must inevitably take the form of direct restrictions rather than market-based incentives. Restraints on abuse transactions (such as insider misconduct and market cornering) and on inappropriate ownership transactions (excessive lending to a single entity) are examples. The purpose of regulations prohibiting insider misconduct and self-dealing is in part to prevent owners or better informed investors from taking unfair advantage of less informed individuals. Such situations are another example of information asymmetries that lead to market imperfections. Though the supervisors cannot ignore such problems, direct regulations to deal with them are difficult to formulate and may lend themselves to government failure. In a loose sense, consensus exists that rigged markets will have thin trading and will not function well, and are therefore socially undesirable. Because asymmetric information is a core characteristic of financial activity, however, trading in securities is necessarily based on differences in information. How much and what sorts of information supervisors should require to be disclosed will thus inevitably be controversial. Some analysts would argue that detailed government regulations can make matters worse rather than better; in that view, *caveat emptor* should be the primary guiding principle.

---

[8] Capital adequacy requirements have a controversial status in international discussions about standards and prudential oversight, and are discussed later.

Though the design of standards and regulations for prudential oversight is a key part of the supervisors' responsibilities, monitoring and enforcement are equally essential. Without sufficient monitoring – and enforcement if necessary – the best-designed regulations could prove to be merely hortatory rather than actually binding. Issues of market-based incentives versus direct supervision are relevant for monitoring as well as for design. Extensive disclosure requirements facilitate indirect monitoring by private-sector investors. Private agencies that assess creditworthiness and that rate securities can complement the monitoring activities of the supervisors. Private rating agencies and other complementary private-sector organizations, however, cannot deal with all potential externalities or abuses, and thus cannot be a complete substitute for direct monitoring by the supervisors.

Who monitors the monitors? What if the supervisors themselves fail to execute their responsibilities appropriately? Supervisors may succumb to what is known as regulatory capture, that is, excessive affinity between the regulators and the regulated. Bribery and corruption are extreme forms of regulatory capture. Lesser varieties, such as regulatory forbearance, are more subtle but potentially just as serious. Regulatory forbearance occurs when the supervisors inappropriately postpone corrective action against a financial institution that is failing to comply with supervisory requirements (for example, permitting an institution to continue to operate if its capital appears to have fallen below the minimum standard). It is human nature to hope that currently perceived problems will correct themselves with the passage of time. Politicians and government officials may have an added incentive to rely on such hopes since any costs of postponed action may be borne not by themselves but by their successors in office.

One proposed solution to the problem of regulatory forbearance is to require supervisors to follow strict *ex ante* guidelines for intervention in particular situations rather than relying on discretionary judgment. But strict rules are not a magic bullet. Invariably, there is a trade-off between rules and discretion. Simple rules, rigidly enforced, could lead to the closure of healthy institutions that should not be shut down, or to the continued operation of unhealthy institutions that really ought to be closed. Less rigid enforcement of rules, permitting greater discretion to the supervisors, will reduce the likelihood of such mistakes but raise the probability of mistakes from regulatory forbearance.[9]

---

[9] New legislation adopted in the United States in 1991, known by the acronym FDICIA, effected changes in the supervision and regulation of depository institutions that were intended, in part, to reduce the incidence of regulatory forbearance. The new legislation included provisions for 'prompt corrective action', requiring the supervisors to take prompt action if an institution's capital ratio falls below a specified level. See for example Garcia (1995), Dahl and Spivey (1995), and Benston and Kaufman (1997).

Within individual nations, difficult institutional questions about monitoring and enforcement have to be resolved. The broadest question is whether all the collective-governance functions of the financial system's utilities infrastructure (not merely standards and prudential oversight but also monetary policy and lender-of-last-resort crisis management) should be lodged in a single institution or, at the other extreme, be parcelled out to different government agencies. One might at first think that the question can be narrowed by focusing only on the standards and oversight functions and asking whether those functions should be carried out by a single government institution or by multiple agencies. Because prudential oversight is so interrelated with monetary and lender-of-last-resort policy, however, the broader form of the question is often an issue. In particular, should responsibility for general monetary policy and crisis lending be combined with, or separated from, prudential oversight? Neither normative arguments nor practical experience have been sufficient to generate a consensus on the matter.

Advocates for separating prudential oversight from general monetary policy tend to be concerned about a possible conflict of interest between the two functions. In times of troubled conditions, it can be argued, a central bank with supervisory responsibilities may be tempted to maintain interest rates at a lower level than would be warranted by general monetary policy because of a concern about the adverse effects of higher rates on the profitability and solvency of financial institutions under its supervision. (Such behaviour would be a subtle form of regulatory forbearance.) Some tension seems inevitable between the objectives of monetary policy and maintaining systemic stability on the one hand and the microprudential objectives of regulation on the other.

Yet separating the two sets of functions would not necessarily make the resolution of that tension easier. If supervisory and regulatory responsibilities were lodged in a separate agency outside the central bank, occasions might arise in which the officials in charge of monetary policy, fearful of systemic stability, would want to provide emergency lending to particular financial institutions whereas the supervisory officials, fearful of moral hazard precedents and possible losses from insolvencies, would instead recommend no emergency lending and liquidation of the institutions. Such conflicts between objectives will have to be resolved in any case, whether the prudential oversight functions have been given to a separate government agency or whether all the functions are lodged together in the central bank. Advocates of keeping the monetary policy and prudential oversight functions together also observe that the central bank would have to be deeply involved in crisis lending to particular institutions even if the formal authority for supervision were given to a separate agency. According to this view, decision-making would be less balanced and less efficient with a separation.

The institutional allocation of the prudential oversight functions also depends on how the residual costs of liquidating insolvent institutions are borne. If substantial amounts of taxpayer money have been and will in the future be used to cover such costs, closure decisions will have an especially high political content. In such circumstances, it may seem politically more natural to lodge the authority in a part of the government other than the central bank. Central banks themselves may even feel relieved, and feel their reputations may be less subject to tarnish, if prudential oversight is formally located elsewhere.

It is not clear whether prudential oversight and the monitoring of standards is likely to be better handled when under its own roof, or in combination with monetary policy under the roof of the central bank. Nor is it clear whether general monetary policy and crisis lending are better conducted together with, or separated from, prudential oversight. The most careful study of the question observes that the arguments for combination and for separation are both inconclusive. About half of the nations examined separate the functions and the other half combine them (see Goodhart and Schoenmaker (1993, 1995).[10]

The preceding review of the main issues in the prudential oversight of financial institutions has scarcely mentioned multiple nations and cross-border transactions. As with accounting, auditing, data and legal systems, international aspects cause an already complicated set of issues to become that much more complex and difficult. While economic logic argues for an extension of individual nations' collective-governance infrastructures to a global infrastructure for prudential oversight, moreover, political constraints impede dramatic progress.

Nonetheless, intergovernmental cooperation for prudential oversight does have a significant forward momentum. The relevant international institutions are the Basle Committee on Banking Supervision (BCBS), the IMF, the World Bank, the IOSCO, the IAIS and the Committee on Payment and Settlements Systems (CPSS). Other cross-institutional mechanisms have recently been established: the Joint Forum on Financial Conglomerates, the Financial Stability Forum (FSF), and the Committee on the Global Financial System (CGFS). The BCBS, the CPSS and the CGFS operate under the auspices of the BIS. These nascent efforts at international cooperation for prudential oversight are summarized below.

---

[10] A wide range of institutional arrangements prevail among nations with regard to which entity of government bears exclusive or primary responsibility for the supervision, regulation, and oversight of financial activity. A few nations have designated a single agency as responsible for supervising and regulating a wide range of financial institutions (e.g. banks, securities firms, insurance companies) and financial markets (e.g. securities exchanges, derivatives, commodity exchanges). For most nations, however, the oversight responsibilities for financial activity are shared among several government agencies.

10.5 GENERAL PRINCIPLES FOR STANDARDS AND PRUDENTIAL OVERSIGHT AT THE GLOBAL LEVEL

The perspective of pragmatic incrementalism suggests seven general principles as anchors for international cooperation in designing and implementing standards and prudential oversight at the world level:

(1) Responsibility for improved standards and prudential oversight must begin, and end, at home.
(2) Standards and oversight at the world level should take the form of 'core principles' rather than detailed codes or fully specified regulations.
(3) The preferred approach at the world level is an encouragement of agreed minimum standards combined with the presumption of mutual recognition.
(4) When possible, world standards and oversight should rely on market incentives rather than direct restrictions.
(5) World standards and oversight should highlight disclosure and transparency.
(6) Monitoring and enforcement of world standards and oversight will eventually be at least as important as sound design.
(7) Improvements are especially needed in emerging market and developing nations, but the advanced industrial nations need to make improvements too.

The principle that responsibility for improvements must begin and end at home is a pragmatic reminder that, for the foreseeable future, supranational institutions will have little political authority. Yes, there will be continued erosion of the *de facto* sovereignty of nations. But the *de jure* political responsibility for taking actions about standards and prudential oversight will remain exclusively at the level of national or subnational governments. Collective design and collective monitoring at the world level can critically shape a supportive world environment that encourages individual national governments to take appropriate actions. Even so, it is strengthened standards and oversight implemented within individual nations that are the *sine qua non* of improved stability for the world financial system.

My second principle – that cooperatively developed standards and guidelines at the world level should take the form of 'core principles' rather than detailed codes or fully specified regulations – is again derived from political pragmatism. For most, if not all, substantive issues, it is premature to try to obtain worldwide intergovernmental agreement on detailed codes and regulations. National governments may be able to accept core principles and guidelines, but typically they will prefer to adapt the core to the particular indigenous characteristics of their own situations, often with justification.

Political constraints likewise underpin the principle that standards and guidelines for the world as a whole should take the form of agreed minimum standards combined with the presumption of mutual recognition. This preferred approach can be distinguished from the negotiation of harmonized standards applicable to the world as a whole.

Explicit harmonization across nations is a much more ambitious and controversial approach. It would require substantial departures from the existing world political situation in which decisions by national governments are essentially decentralized. It would also require a substantial further strengthening of international institutions. In contrast, mutual recognition presumes a continuation of decentralized decisions by national governments. Mutual recognition does entail some degree of intergovernmental cooperation because it presumes exchanges of information and consultations among governments that will constrain the formation of national regulations and policies. As understood in discussions of economic integration within the European Union, for example, mutual recognition entails an explicit acceptance by each member nation of the regulations, standards and certification procedures of other EU members.[11] Governments may agree on rules that restrict their freedom to set policy or that promote gradual convergence in national policies. As international consultations and monitoring of compliance with such rules become more important, one can describe this situation as monitored mutual recognition.

Many differences among nations in standards, regulations, policies, institutions and even social and cultural norms create economic incentives for a kind of arbitrage that erodes and may ultimately eliminate the differences. Explicit harmonization tries to anticipate the result of such arbitrage pressures for areas for which differences among nations are perceived as inequitable, unstable or ultimately unsustainable. Mutual recognition instead relies on market competition among nations to guide the process of eventual international convergence.

Proposals for harmonized global standards rather than mutual recognition are often driven by a yearning for a worldwide level playing field. Differences across nations in standards or regulations often lead to complaints that the behaviour of some other nation is competitively inequitable, with an associated recommendation that this nation should adjust its policies to moderate or remove the competitive inequities. But such complaints, and the yearning for a level playing field in the world economy, are problematic. Cross-border transactions occur precisely because of differences among nations – in resource endowments, labour skills and consumer tastes. Nations specialize in producing

[11] For example, mutual recognition allows a financial institution licensed in any EU country to operate in all EU countries even when licensing and supervision standards in member countries differ.

goods and services in which they are relatively most efficient. In a fundamental sense, cross-border transactions are valuable because the playing field is not level.

Carried to its logical extreme, the yearning to level the playing field implies that nations should become homogeneous. But a recommendation for homogenization – for sweeping harmonization – is not only unrealistic, it is misguided. Suppose nation X is poor and through its political process decides that its government cannot afford the costs of maintaining a large core of supervisors and regulators to oversee its financial system (thereby, of course, accepting higher risks that the nation may experience financial instability). Or suppose nation X concludes that it cannot afford stringent environmental protections against business practices that pollute local air and water supplies. Nation X will then argue that it is inappropriate for other nations to impute to it the value they themselves place on a clean environment and high-quality prudential oversight of the financial system (just as it would be inappropriate to impute the X valuations to the environment and prudential oversight in the other nations). The core of the idea of political sovereignty is to permit national residents to order their lives and property in accordance with their own preferences. Seen from this perspective, the notion of a level world playing field is unhelpful, a rule of thumb that misleads as often as it conveys a sound objective for equity across nations.

Two perspectives about the differences among nations coexist in situations of this sort. Each has some merit. Nation X can be seen as merely exercising its national preferences in setting national standards, appropriately exploiting its comparative advantage even if that leads to a less stable banking system and production of goods that threaten the environment. But because of cross-border spillovers, a legitimate problem may also exist that justifies pressure from other nations urging X to accept changes in its policies (thus curbing X's national sovereignty). When national governments negotiate resolutions to such questions – trying to agree whether individual nations are legitimately exercising sovereign choices or, alternatively, engaging in behaviour that is unfair or damaging to other nations – the resolutions typically entail compromise between the two competing perspectives.

The approach of agreed minimum standards combined with the presumption of mutual recognition will often result in such compromises. For issues where a minimum standard applied in all nations is likely to be desirable for cosmopolitan world goals (for example, the stability of the world financial system as a whole) and for the goals of each nation individually considered, adoption of world minimum standards will be the preferable outcome. But at the same time, individual nations will be free to adopt standards more stringent than the agreed minimum. The acceptance of mutual recognition permits differences among nations, acknowledging the axiom of different strokes (policies) for different folks (nations).

Existing efforts to achieve intergovernmental agreement on standards and guidelines have for the most part followed the two preceding principles. To the best of my knowledge, detailed codes and full-scale harmonization have not been attempted. The main exceptions have been regional rather than world-wide, in particular certain attempts at harmonized, universally applicable regulations within the EU.[12]

In the long run, the arbitrage pressures eroding differences among nations will probably induce governments to make more and more attempts at explicit harmonization. This conjecture applies to standards for accounting, auditing, data dissemination and bankruptcy. It might apply to aspects of prudential oversight. It seems likely to apply to the taxation of the returns to capital.[13] Thus a future time may come when the cooperative approach preferred today, agreed minimum standards combined with mutual recognition, will have been super-seded. But the distance to that future time is doubtless measured not in years but in decades or half-centuries.

In a domestic context within individual nations, standards and prudential oversight that rely on market incentives will usually, when feasible, prove preferable. Essentially the same principle applies to standards and prudential oversight designed to cover cross-border financial transactions and the world financial system as a whole.

The traditional points about market-based, incentive-based oversight sum-marized in the earlier discussion are especially pertinent for nations facing resource constraints more binding than those in advanced industrial nations. A small, relatively poor developing nation, for example, simply cannot afford a large staff to implement supervision and regulation through detailed direct restrictions. Tight constraints on governance resources are thus a strong argu-ment for relying on incentive-based supervision and regulation for those aspects where such an approach is feasible.

The fifth of my general principles is that standards and oversight designed at the world level should highlight disclosure and transparency. A close link exists between the degree of disclosure about individual financial institutions and the

---

[12] I admit to some uncertainty about my generalization on this point. In the areas of account-ing, auditing and legal standards, it may be that some of the efforts can be characterized as attempted harmonization and detailed code rather than merely core principles for minimum standards.

[13] Differences in the taxation of capital across nations is a major motivation for many types of cross-border capital flows. This fact undermines the case that unfettered capital movements are beneficial for efficient resource allocation. Whereas today we can observe large differences in the taxation of capital across nations, it may become harder and harder over time for nations to maintain such large differences.

ability of supervisors to rely on market-based, incentive-based regulations (as emphasized earlier). Without ample disclosure of institutions' accounts and behaviour, with the information readily available globally, an emphasis on incentive-based oversight instead of direct explicit regulations cannot be successful (see the Group of Twenty-Two (1998b), chaired by Mervyn King and Andrew Sheng).

Significant differences exist across nations in the legal authority that supervisors have to set disclosure standards. The supervisors in some nations have the power to implement disclosure requirements directly through binding regulations. In other nations, the supervisors do not have that power, and thus have to rely on indirect encouragement, such as issuing sound practice recommendations. An emphasis on disclosure and transparency in the design of world standards can, among other things, provide encouragement to individual nations to strengthen the powers of their supervisors to require greater disclosure.

Ample disclosure of accurate and timely information about individual financial institutions is useful because it helps to reward safe and well-managed institutions while exerting market pressures on institutions that are excessively risky and poorly managed. It is worth noting here that analogous arguments apply even to individual nations as a whole. A nation will find itself rewarded in global capital markets with lower borrowing costs and more generous inflows of foreign-generated savings if it can demonstrate that it has strong accounting and auditing standards, well-managed financial institutions, sound macroeconomic policies and reliable and comprehensive aggregated data for its financial system and economy. And the global capital markets tend to punish a nation by denying it capital inflows and depreciating its currency if it has weak standards, weak prudential oversight, unreliable data and unsound macroeconomic policies. From the perspective of the stability of the global financial system, this market disciplining is beneficial on balance.

I say 'on balance' because financial markets are also prone to informational cascades, herding behaviour and contagion – behaviour alluded to in the cliché that financial markets know only two gears, overdrive and reverse. Thus any rewarding or punishing carried out by the markets can be exaggerated, and thereby exacerbate underlying problems or spark undesirable exuberance. Principal agent complexities and their associated information asymmetries are endemic features of financial activity. Ample disclosure of information and the market discipline that results are beneficial features of prudential oversight. But they are not a panacea for financial stability.

Standards and guidelines at the world level must first be designed before they can be used as tools to stimulate improved standards and oversight within individual nations. But – principle six – the international community will eventually have to put even more emphasis on monitoring and enforcement than on design. Self-evidently, sound world standards, even when fully agreed, must be actually implemented before most of the associated benefits can be generated.

Because responsibility for improvements must begin and end at home, the bulk of monitoring and enforcement activity necessarily has to take place within individual nations carried out by each nation's collective-governance infrastructure. This is certainly true for the monitoring of individual private financial institutions. Difficult institutional and substantive issues arise at the purely national level, such as whether to have a single or multiple agencies carry out prudential oversight and how to minimize the risks of regulatory forbearance. Different nations resolve these issues quite differently, which complicates the application of world standards and guidelines and the monitoring of compliance with them.

At the world level, the question of who monitors the monitors takes on additional dimensions. Some sort of assessment of whether individual nations are conforming to the (minimum) world standards will be increasingly desirable. Political pragmatism suggests that in the short run the international community might aim for a combination of self-assessment at the national level with overview assessment by international institutions such as the IMF, the BIS and the World Bank. Such assessments might concentrate initially on a transparent description of a nation's existing standards and practices (see International Monetary Fund (1999b)). As intergovernmental cooperation evolves, a day may eventually come when supranational prudential overseers provide a detailed assessment of the quality of a nation's practices (design and enforcement), thereby explicitly reprimanding or applauding the national supervisors.

For most of the last half-century, discussions of international financial reform neglected problems in emerging market and developing nations. Those nations, however, were integrally involved in the financial turbulence that has characterized recent years – for example, the debt crisis of the 1980s, the Tequila crisis set off by Mexico in 1995, the virulence of Asian financial crises in 1997–8 and the worldwide credit risk scare triggered by the August 1998 Russian devaluation.

Accounting, audit and data standards in emerging market and developing nations tend to be less well developed and often are less strongly enforced than in North America, Europe and Japan. The laws governing defaults and insolvencies are less complete. Bankruptcy and arbitration procedures are less fully worked out. Standards and procedures for prudential oversight of financial institutions in many developing nations are less stringent and often less assertively monitored.

The economies of many developing nations are smaller and more open. Herding behaviour and contagion can be more virulent and there is therefore somewhat greater risk of national financial instability. Portfolio investors and creditors from the advanced industrial nations – the dominant actors in the world capital markets – can be very unforgiving about problems within the developing nations. Many such creditors are potential members of a herd, prepared to exercise a disciplining 'exit option' on slight provocation, especially if through informational cascades they observe other creditors exercising their own exit option.

It is unquestionably appropriate that financial problems in emerging-market and developing nations have moved to the front of the stage and are primary targets for many reform proposals. For their own sakes as well as for the sake of global financial stability, these nations should make improvements in standards and prudential oversight.

Today's conventional wisdom, however, appears to hold that the problems in the international financial system are, if not exclusively then at least pre-dominantly, located in emerging-market and developing nations. This idea, emanating from the advanced industrial nations, tends to be self-satisfied, even self-righteous. The industrial nations are perceived as a splendid first team – the 'varsity', spruced up and washed clean. The emerging-market nations are at best a weak second team ('junior varsity'). And the 'unwashed' of the developing nations are merely amateur ('sandlot') teams. Seen from this unfortunate perspective, the enemy is weak private institutions and weak governance in the emerging-market nations and the developing nations.

I am much more in the frame of mind of the American cartoon character Pogo: we have met the enemy, and the enemy is us, too! It is surely wrong to imply that all is well on the varsity team. The industrial nations have plenty of their own problems about standards and prudential oversight and the conventional wisdom ought to be better aware of the industrial nations' contributions to the architectural problems that need fixing.

It is salutary to remember the protracted savings and loan crisis in the United States in the 1980s. Recall the exchange rate turbulence in Europe in 1992 and again in 1993 and the associated severe banking crises in Scandinavia. Throughout the second half of the 1990s the Japanese financial system struggled with huge amounts of bad debts, many weakened financial institu-tions and fundamental questions about Japan's implementation of prudential supervision and regulation. Within most industrial nations, there remain controversial issues about the appropriate details of deposit-insurance schemes and the implementation of capital adequacy requirements. Issues of regulatory forbearance and moral hazard are pervasive.

Many private and government participants in North American, European and Japanese financial systems, for example, acquiesce in the presumption that some banks (possibly even some nonbank financial institutions) are 'too big to fail'. That presumption creates severe moral hazard difficulties for prudential oversight. In effect, large banks may be said to enjoy the benefits of implicit

deposit insurance without having to bear the costs of it. This issue has important spillover implications for the cross-border lending and borrowing carried
out by the allegedly too-big-to-fail institutions. The international interbank
market, for example, played a major funding role for Asian emerging-market
nations in the 1990s. In effect, large banks based in the advanced industrial
nations carried out a major risk transformation – transferring deposits from
large multinational banks to financial intermediaries in developing nations of
lower credit standing – combined with a major maturity transformation –
turning short-term implicitly insured deposits into long-term loans. When the
Asian crisis broke, of course, the large multinational banks all ran together for
the exit. This example is a reminder that, in a significant sense, moral hazard
begins at home in the advanced industrial countries (see Mervyn King (1999)
and, for a recent analysis of moral hazard issues in the international interbank
market, see Bernard and Bisignano (1999)).

When focusing on the need for improvements in standards and prudential
oversight in all economies, a historical perspective is also instructive. Until well
into the 20th century, the United States, Canada and Australia were emerging-
market nations. London and several other European capitals were the advanced
centre of the financial world and had considerably more sophisticated financial
institutions and practices than those in the United States. The United States
had, to put it politely, an altogether undistinguished record of financial stability.
The phrase 'wildcat banking' stems from flagrant abuses in 19th-century US
banking. Severe financial panics occurred in the United States in 1873, 1893
and again in 1907. The United States in the 19th century certainly failed to
have adequate mechanisms in place for the prudential oversight of private
financial institutions and for the collective provision of emergency liquidity
assistance in times of financial crisis.

Accounting, audit and data standards in the United States and in so-called
newly settled nations such as Canada, Australia and Argentina were less well
developed and less strongly enforced than in Britain. Bankruptcy and arbitration
procedures were less fully worked out. Standards and procedures for prudential
oversight of financial institutions were less well developed, less stringent and less
assertively monitored. Most of the generalizations so readily applied to developing nations today were applicable with at least equal merit to the then-emerging
nations at the beginning of the 20th century. The historical experience of the
United States and the other emerging-market nations of the 19th century also
shows that the transfer of stringent standards from advanced to periphery
nations is a slow-moving learning process. The gradual historical strengthening
of US accounting procedures and prudential oversight, for example, was due in
large part to pressure from British investors and imitation of British standards
(see, for example, Bordo, Eichengreen and Irwin (1999)).

If the international community is to encourage an appropriate evolution of collective governance for the world financial system, the supposed varsity team should be more careful about pointing the finger of blame exclusively at the junior varsity and the sandlot players and telling them that they must pull their socks up.

10.6 THE CURRENT STATUS OF INTERNATIONAL COOPERATION ON STANDARDS AND PRUDENTIAL OVERSIGHT

I now turn to summarize the progress that has been made in international cooperation on standards and prudential oversight for financial institutions and financial activity. The summary is doggedly descriptive. The reader runs no risk of cardiac arrest from over-excitement. Acronym overload, on the other hand, may cause indigestion. Nevertheless, I hope this will be a useful overview for those not trying to follow these areas in detail.

Accounting and auditing standards

IASC, a private-sector body based in the UK, was first established in 1973. In 1999 its membership included some 142 professional accountancy organizations in 103 countries. Its goal is to 'achieve uniformity in the accounting principles that are used by businesses and other organisations for financial reporting around the world'. Membership in IASC does not require that member organizations or their nations adopt the international accounting standards (IASs) that are developed. Whether a nation in fact adopts an IAS depends on the decisions of its national authorities or the nation's self-regulatory organizations.

IASC is the primary institutional mechanism for stimulating cooperation among nations about accounting standards. In 1995, it made a commitment to IOSCO to produce a comprehensive core set of accounting standards that IOSCO could recommend for adoption by its member countries. In March 1999 IASC published for the first time a 'comprehensive standard on accounting for financial instruments (known as IAS 39), which takes several steps toward the goal of global standards (on the origins and history of the IASC, see Cairns (1998); for the March 1999 standards, see IASC (1999)).

Nascent cooperative efforts have been undertaken to promote the standardization of auditing procedures through IFAC. This organization is closely associated with IASC and with similar membership (a member of IFAC is automatically a member of IASC). IFAC has developed international standards on auditing and international audit practice statements through its International Auditing Practices Committee. The standards developed by IFAC and its committee do not have legal force, but member organizations are expected to use their best efforts to see that IFAC and IASC standards are used as a basis for developing their own nations' standards and practices. IFAC is said to encourage its members to review their nations' auditing practices to evaluate how they compare with IFAC's international auditing standards.

The International Organization of Supreme Audit Institutions (INTOSAI) links together national institutions whose responsibilities are to audit government agencies and to promote sound financial management and accountability within governments. INTOSAI was founded in 1953 and adopted a Lima Declaration of Guidelines on Auditing Precepts in 1977. In the 1990s INTOSAI issued international standards for auditing government agencies and guidelines for achieving effective internal accounting controls within government agencies (information about INTOSAI can be found at the web site: *www.intosai.org*).

IFAC, collaborating with the IMF, the World Bank and global private accounting firms, established an International Forum on Accountancy Development in February 1999. Its stated purpose is to support efforts to strengthen international financial architecture through the building of accounting and auditing capacity in developing and transition economies. This forum apparently made a commitment to support the use of IASs as the minimum benchmark worldwide.

Standards for data collection and dissemination

The IMF articles of agreement require member countries to provide data about their economic and financial condition. Since its creation half a century ago, the IMF has encouraged member countries to collect more comprehensive and more accurate data. The interaction between the IMF staff and statistical agencies within member governments has played a sometimes influential role in strengthening the countries' own statistical efforts, including the publication of more and better quality national statistics. The World Bank and the BIS have also been important catalysts for member nations improving their data efforts. The three institutions have provided technical assistance, including manuals for the statistical agencies of national governments to use in collecting, aggregating and publishing their data (see, for example, the IMF's *Balance of Payments Manual* and its *Manual of Government Finance Statistics* or the *Guide to the BIS Statistics on International Banking* (prepared by the BIS staff primarily for the use of the institutions which report the data to the BIS)). The IMF, World Bank and BIS themselves publish numerous statistical volumes and reports. The Organization for Economic Cooperation and Development (OECD) is also active in the compilation and publication of comparative national statistics.

In 1996, partly stimulated by the crisis following the 1994–5 Mexican devaluation, improvement of data for cross-border capital flows assumed a higher visibility and priority. A new emphasis was placed on nations making a wider range of data available to the general public, domestic and foreign citizens alike. (Previously, national governments had made some of the data available to the IMF but had not published it. And the IMF was required to treat as confidential some of the key data it received from member governments.)

The dominant new initiative was the establishment of a Special Data Dissemination Standard (SDDS) at the IMF, beginning in March 1996. Its purpose is to guide nations in the dissemination of economic and financial data to the public. By August 1999, there were 47 subscribing nations – a mixture of industrial market economies, emerging-market economies and transition economies. Participants in the SDDS are countries that have, or that might seek, access to international capital markets. Four dimensions of data dissemination are emphasized in the SDDS: the coverage, periodicity and timeliness of a nation's data; access to the data by the public; the integrity of the disseminated data; and the quality of the disseminated data. The SDDS prescribes 'monitorable elements' for these dimensions – good practices that can be monitored by the users of the statistics. Subscribers to the SDDS are required to submit information about their data and their dissemination practices to the IMF for presentation on the IMF's electronic dissemination standards bulletin board.

At the time the SDDS was initiated, its requirements were recognized as 'very demanding and not necessarily applicable or relevant for the entire membership of the fund'. In December 1997, the IMF's executive board accordingly also established the General Data Dissemination System (GDDS). This is in principle applicable to all IMF members. The primary focus of the GDDS is stated as supporting improvements in data quality over time, in contrast with the SDDS, where the focus is on dissemination in countries that generally already meet high data quality standards. The aspiration is thus for IMF members not yet able to adhere to the SDDS to gradually improve their efforts in data collection and publication, thereby eventually graduating to the SDDS. The GDDS is supposed to move into its 'operational phase' in 2000 (see the IMF's Dissemination Standards Bulletin Board (*http://dsbb.imf.org*) for descriptions of the SDDS and the GDDS and the national data of SDDS subscribers).

In March 1999, agreement was reached to strengthen SDDS prescriptions in the areas of debt and international reserves. SDDS subscribers agreed on a new 'reserves template'; the revised standards for reserves are supposed to be in force in subscribing countries by March 2000.

Despite notable improvements in recent decades, serious weaknesses still exist in data pertinent for national financial systems and the world financial system. Data for the outstanding stocks of real capital assets exist for only a subset of nations, and are often of poor quality when they do exist. Only the wealthiest nations have devoted significant resources to the creation of flows of funds accounts and associated data on the outstanding stocks of financial assets and liabilities. The data are especially weak for outstanding amounts of cross-border assets and liabilities, which makes it difficult or impossible to formulate national balance sheets and international investment positions for many countries (see Lane and Milesi-Ferretti (1999) for a recent discussion).

Standards for insolvency and bankruptcy

UNCITRAL is the core legal body of the UN system in the field of international trade law. It was established in 1966 by the UN General Assembly, with a mandate to 'further the progressive *harmonization and unification* of the law of international trade' [my italics]. The commission is composed of 36 member states elected by the General Assembly, with membership structured so as to be representative of the world's various geographic regions and its principal economic and legal systems. The commission carries out its work through working groups and at annual sessions. In past years it has produced a variety of legal documents. Examples include conventions or model laws on arbitration rules (1976); the carriage of goods by sea (the 'Hamburg Rules' of 1978); contracts for the international sale of goods (1980); international commercial arbitration (1985); international credit transfers (1992); the procurement of goods, construction and services by governments (1994); and electronic commerce (1996).

The UNCITRAL document most relevant for financial standards and prudential oversight is the Model Law on Cross-border Insolvency, adopted in 1997. The purpose of the model law is to promote modern and fair legislation for cases where an insolvent debtor has assets in more than one nation. The law deals with 'conditions under which the person administering a foreign insolvency proceeding has access to the courts of the State that has enacted the Model Law, determines conditions for recognition of a foreign insolvency pro-ceeding and for granting relief to the representative of such foreign proceeding, permits courts and insolvency administrators from different countries to cooperate more effectively, and contains provisions on coordination of insolvency proceedings that place concurrently in different States'. UNCITRAL has also published a *Guide to Enactment* to assist governments in preparing legislation based on the Model Law (see the UNCITRAL website: *www.uncitral.org*).

The International Bar Association's Insolvency and Creditors Rights Com-mittee is currently developing a Model Insolvency Code, which would provide a model for nations that are in the process of reforming and updating their insolvency laws. The World Bank is providing information to governments on good practices for reform of insolvency systems, including the role of specialist bankruptcy courts. The World Bank and the International Bar Association are apparently engaged in discussions on an initiative to develop guidelines for sound insolvency laws and the incentives for debtors and creditors to use insolvency mechanisms. The IMF has prepared a paper on effective and orderly insolvency procedures which the World Bank intends to use in its efforts to formulate guidelines for effective insolvency regimes in developing nations. The IMF and the World Bank are also collaborating with UNCITRAL in this area (see IMF (1999c)).

The supervision and regulation of banks

BCBS was established under the auspices of the BIS in 1975. Concerns generated by the Bankhaus Herstatt and Franklin National Bank crises in 1974 were the catalyst for its foundation. In the ensuing years BCBS has become the most influential forum for prompting intergovernmental consultations and cooperation among banking supervisory authorities.

BCBS's first major achievement was the drafting of a concordat on the supervision of banks' foreign establishments, setting out agreed principles and guidelines covering the division of responsibilities among national authorities for the supervision of banks that operate in more than one national jurisdiction. The first version of the concordat was agreed in 1975; a modified version was prepared in 1983 and a supplement agreed in April 1990. In 1992 certain of the principles of the concordat were reformulated as 'minimum standards'. Other early achievements of BCBS include agreements on the principle that banks' cross-border business should be monitored on a consolidated basis and on the appropriate accounting and supervisory treatment of off-balance-sheet exposures.

At the June 1996 meeting of the G-7 heads of state, BCBS was asked to develop a set of principles for banking supervision that would, among other things, stimulate improvements in supervisory standards in emerging market nations. In 1997, the committee accordingly released a document entitled *Core Principles for Effective Banking Supervision.*

This sets out a total of 25 core principles, grouped as: preconditions for effective banking supervision (principle 1); licensing and structure (2–5); prudential regulations and requirements (6–15); methods of ongoing banking supervision (16–20); information requirements (21); the formal powers of supervisors (22); and cross-border banking (23–25). The BCBS interprets the principles as 'minimum requirements' and as a 'basic reference for supervisory and other public authorities *in all countries and internationally*' (Press Statement of 22 September 1997; the italics are mine). The intended eventual scope for these core principles is worldwide: to apply to all banks in each national jurisdiction.[14]

In 1997, BCBS also released a *Compendium of Documents Produced by the Basle Committee on Banking Supervision*. This collection pulled together all the existing BCBS recommendations, guidelines and standards from the committee's inception through to April 1997. The *Compendium* is cross-referenced to the *Core Principles* and is to be periodically updated.

BCBS has been especially active in releasing further documents in the last year. For example, it issued guidance or published papers on: sound practices for loan accounting, disclosure, and related matters (October 1998, July 1999); sound practices for banks interactions with highly leveraged institutions such as hedge funds (January 1999); credit risk modelling (April 1999); managing settlement risk in foreign exchange transactions (July 1999); and enhancing corporate governance in banking organizations (September 1999) (see the BIS website: *www.bis.org*).

A BCBS working group is currently developing a draft handbook on a methodology for banking supervision. This handbook is to be given final approval by BCBS, probably sometime in 2000.

During the 1980s, BCBS became concerned that the capital positions of the banks engaged in cross-border business were deteriorating simultaneously with an increase in risks, especially *vis-à-vis* heavily indebted developing nations. In response, the committee developed a set of international standards to use in measuring the capital adequacy of banks. The negotiations for these standards, which are known as the Basle Capital Accord, were protracted and difficult. The details of the capital requirements were controversial from their first adoption in July 1988, and have grown more so. This aspect of the work of BCBS is an especially noteworthy illustration of the difficulties that are associated with international cooperation for the development of standards.

Various amendments were made to the capital adequacy standards during the 1990s. One of these, for example, incorporated changes in the treatment of credit risks associated with derivatives and similar off-balance-sheet instruments. In 1996, the capital requirements were extended to cover market risk rather than only credit risk, and the committee accepted, with specified safeguards, banks' own internal models of such market risks (see BIS, BCBS (1997b) for the texts of the accord and amendments up to the end of April 1997).

The BCBS *Core Principles for Effective Banking Supervision* emphasize capital requirements. In particular, the wording of the 6th core principle stresses that:

[14] When developing the core principles, the BCBS consulted with national supervisory authorities that were not members of the committee. The document was prepared in a group containing representatives from the BCBS and also Chile, China, the Czech Republic, Hong Kong, Mexico, Russia and Thailand. Nine other countries (Argentina, Brazil, Hungary, India, Indonesia, Korea, Malaysia, Poland, and Singapore) were described as 'closely associated with the work'.

Banking supervisors must set prudent and appropriate minimum capital adequacy requirements for all banks. Such requirements should reflect the risks that the banks undertake, and must define the components of capital, bearing in mind their ability to absorb losses. At least for internationally active banks, these requirements must not be less than those established in the Basle Capital Accord and its amendments.

Extensive modifications to the BCBS standards for capital adequacy were under study during 1998–9. The committee's proposals for possible changes were issued in a consultative document in June 1999 (see BIS, BCBS (1999a)). Comments on these proposals were solicited from interested parties, to be received by the end of March 2000. The intent is to issue definitive proposals later in the year. The proposals for revisions, like the accord itself, have attracted considerable discussion and criticism (as outlined below).

The supervision and regulation of securities markets

IOSCO is a counterpart on the securities side to the international prudential oversight for banking by the BCBS. IOSCO is an intergovernmental institution, based in Montreal Canada, with approximately 160 ordinary, associate, and affiliate members. It was created in the 1970s to promote cooperation and information exchanges among the national authorities with responsibility for regulating securities markets. It operates primarily through an executive committee, two specialized working committees and annual conferences. Recommendations by IOSCO are advisory, rather than binding, for its members.

The contributions of IOSCO to the development of prudential standards for securities markets are summarized in two documents released in 1998: *Objectives and Principles of Securities Regulation* (a set of core principles for securities supervision) and *International Disclosure for Cross-Border Offerings and Initial Listings by Foreign Issuers* (a set of international standards for non-financial statement disclosure). The technical committee of IOSCO has carried out several projects with the BCBS. For example, in October 1999, IOSCO's technical committee and the BCBS jointly issued a paper on guidance for the public disclosure of trading and derivatives activities.

IOSCO's technical committee is currently evaluating the proposed international accounting standards developed by the IASC to determine whether IOSCO should endorse the IASC core standards for use by foreign issuers in cross-border listings and offerings. It is also considering mechanisms to increase the transparency of dealings of highly leveraged institutions (HLIs) with securities firms, the advisability and feasibility of direct disclosure requirements for HLIs, recommendations that would strengthen risk management processes at securities firms that act as counterparts to HLIs, and measures to improve information flows about HLI activities to regulators, market authorities and the general public (see IMF (1999c)).

The supervision and regulation of insurance

Nascent international cooperation for the supervision and regulation of insurance companies has been encouraged through IAIS, established in June 1994. The members of IAIS are national insurance supervisors from more than 100 nations. The mandate of IAIS is to develop internationally endorsed principles and standards on insurance supervision and to assist insurance supervisors to implement those principles and standards through cooperation programmes and training. As with IOSCO, the recommendations of IAIS are not binding on members but have merely an advisory status.

In 1996 IAIS began work on internationally applicable principles for insurance supervision. A compendium of principles, standards and guidance papers was issued in September 1997. Three additional standards – covering licensing, on-site inspections and supervision of derivatives – were issued in September 1998 (for more information on the IAIS, see its website: *www.iaisweb.org*).

An IAIS task force has been created to prepare a methodology for monitoring the implementation of the principles. The methodology is to be prepared 'in close collaboration' with other international organizations engaged in surveillance activities. IAIS has solicited assistance from the World Bank in distributing the principles, standards and guidance notes to national insurance supervisors and in promoting implementation of the basic standards.[15]

Standards and supervision for payments systems

Under the aegis of the BIS, CPSS has a mandate to monitor and improve the safety and efficiency of payments systems with special emphasis on the global dimensions. Representatives to the committee come from central banks. The committee has constituted several working groups to prepare reports. For example, a steering group on settlement risk in foreign exchange transactions completed *Reducing Foreign Exchange Settlement Risk: A Progress Report*, in July 1998. CPSS released a report by its working group on retail payments systems in September 1999.

CPSS has collaborated with the technical committee of IOSCO on several occasions. Joint reports were produced on a disclosure framework for securities settlements systems (1997) and on securities lending transactions (July 1999).

A task force of the CPSS – composed of representatives from the G-10

---

[15] IMF (1999c), pp. 29–30.

nations, emerging-market economies, the IMF, the World Bank and the European Central Bank – is currently working to develop core principles for the design and supervision of payments systems. The first part of a draft report was tabled in December 1999. Interested parties were given until 17 March 2000 to submit comments.

The Joint Forum on Financial Conglomerates

Coordination among international organizations has become increasingly necessary. This need has given rise to several new institutional mechanisms.

The Joint Forum on Financial Conglomerates was created in early 1996 under the collective auspices of three parent organizations, the BCBS, IOSCO and IAIS. The goal was to inspire a more formal cooperation among the bank, securities and insurance supervisory authorities from the largest nations. (A less formal tripartite group from the three types of supervisors prepared a report released in July 1995.) Thirteen nations were represented in the joint forum in 1999: the G-7 nations plus Australia, Belgium, Netherlands, Spain, Sweden and Switzerland. The EU commission attends in an observer capacity.

In February 1999, the joint forum released a series of papers on the supervision of financial conglomerates. These papers had been drafted and revised during 1998 following a study of 14 major international conglomerates and after 'extensive consultation' with industry and the wider supervisory community. The papers covered techniques for assessing the capital adequacy of conglomerates; tests for the fitness and propriety of managers, directors and major shareholders of conglomerates; facilitation of the exchange of information among the various supervisors; and methods of coordinating the activities of the supervisors in emergency and non-emergency situations. The joint forum released further consultation documents in July 1999 discussing principles for the prudent management and control of intra-conglomerate transactions and exposures, and conglomerate risk concentrations.

The Financial Stability Forum

The creation of the FSF stems from the October 1998 meeting of the G-7 finance ministers and central bank governors. That meeting commissioned Hans Tietmeyer (then president of the Deutsche Bundesbank) to prepare a report with recommendations for 'new structures that may be required for enhancing cooperation among the various national and international supervisory bodies and international financial institutions'. The G-7 nations adopted the recommendations in Tietmeyer's report in February 1999 (see Tietmeyer (1999)). The first meeting of the FSF was convened in April 1999.

The FSF is designed to be an institutional mechanism for 'enhancing cooperation among the various national and international supervisory bodies and international financial institutions so as to promote stability in the international financial system'. It brings together, usually twice a year, 'national authorities responsible for financial stability in significant international financial centres, international financial institutions, sector-specific international groupings of regulators and supervisors, and committees of central bank experts' (see the FSF website: *www.fsforum.org*).

The members of the FSF are national authorities from individual nations (one each from the finance ministry, central bank and main supervisory agency in the largest nations); representatives from the IMF, the World Bank, the BIS and the OECD; representatives of the primary international regulatory and supervisory groupings, namely the BCBS, IOSCO and IAIS; and representatives from two committees of central bank experts, the Committee on the Global Financial System and the CPSS. The national authorities represented at the first meeting of the FSF were restricted to the G-7 nations. In June 1999, the membership was broadened to include significant financial centres, interpreted as Hong Kong, Singapore, Australia and the Netherlands. The FSF has a small secretariat based at the BIS. The first chairman of the FSF, for a term of three years beginning in 1999, is Andrew Crockett, who is also general manager of the BIS.

One of the first initiatives of the FSF was to produce a *Compendium of Standards*, a common reference for the various economic and financial standards that are internationally accepted as relevant to sound, stable and well-functioning financial systems. This compendium goes well beyond bank supervision, though the BCBS has been closely involved in compiling it. The standard-setting bodies whose work is collected in the compendium include the IMF, the BCBS, IOSCO, IAIS, the CPSS and the OECD. The intent is to review and update the compendium regularly.

Another initiative was to establish three working groups: on the activities of highly leveraged institutions in financial markets, on the uses and activities of offshore financial centres and on the evaluation of policy measures that might be taken in borrower and creditor nations to reduce the volatility of capital flows and to improve the assessment and management of the risks of excessive short-term external indebtedness. These working groups met several times in 1999 and, after further work, are expected to report to the full FSF by its third meeting in April 2000.

The FSF has also emphasized the training of financial supervisors. The World Bank, the IMF and BIS, acting under the auspices of the FSF, have jointly produced a draft *Financial Supervision Training Directory*. Later on, the directory is to be expanded to include training programmes for securities and insurance supervisors. The stated objective of the *Directory* is to 'contribute to raising the technical capacity and quality of management in supervisory authorities' by 'improving awareness of the broad range of training programmes available in financial supervision and regulation'.

The BIS Committee on the Global Financial System

During the 1960s, staff representatives of the central banks of the G-10 nations met informally at the BIS in a Eurocurrency Standing Committee. The G-10 central bank governors gave this committee a formal mandate in 1971, and made the mandate public in 1980, to monitor international banking markets more closely. The Eurocurrency Standing Committee focused initially on euro-currency markets but subsequently discussed a wide range of financial stability issues. A number of reports were published under the committee's sponsorship. The committee also had responsibility for developing and overseeing the various sets of BIS statistics on international banking, financial derivatives and foreign exchange market activity.

The G-10 central bank governors decided in February 1999 to clarify the mandate of this committee and to rename it the Committee on the Global Financial System (CGFS). The CGFS is to act as a central bank forum for the monitoring and examination of broad issues relating to financial markets and systems with a view to elaborating appropriate policy recommendations to support the central banks in the fulfilment of their responsibilities for monetary and financial stability. The tasks of the CGFS fall into three categories: system-atic short-term monitoring of global financial system conditions; in-depth longer-term analysis of the functioning of financial markets; and the articulation of policy recommendations aimed at improving market functioning and pro-moting stability.

A working group of the CGFS, formed in December 1997 (prior to its name change), issued a report in May 1999 – *Market Liquidity: Research Findings and Selected Policy Implications*. A second working group, formed in March 1999, released a detailed analysis in October 1999 of the turbulent market events of autumn 1998 (see BIS, CGFS (1999a, 1999b)).

Corporate governance standards

The OECD and the World Bank have taken the lead in promoting inter-national discussions in this area. The OECD council, meeting at ministerial level in April 1998, asked the OECD to develop an internationally applicable set of standards and guidelines for corporate governance. The resulting *OECD Principles of Corporate Governance* were endorsed at the May 1999 ministerial meeting. These principles are described as non-binding; they do not aim at detailed prescriptions for national legislation. Their purpose is to serve as a reference point (for a full text of the OECD principles see the OECD website: *www.oecd.org/daf/governance*).

The World Bank has supported reform of corporate governance in developing nations through some of its lending operations. It had already undertaken several corporate governance assessments by September 1999 and was planning a further 12 such efforts in the following 6 months (information about the World Bank's activities in corporate governance is available at a World Bank web site: *www.worldbank.org/html/fpd/privatesector/cg/index.htm*).

The OECD and World Bank recently decided to establish a Global Forum on Corporate Governance. This forum was launched in September 1999 at the IMF–World Bank annual meetings in Washington, DC.

The Joint Forum on Financial Conglomerates has focused attention on corporate governance issues for financial-sector institutions. As noted above, the BCBS issued a paper in September 1999 on guidance for corporate governance in banks.

Core principles for fiscal policies and monetary financial policies

Although standards and guidelines for general macroeconomic policies fall outside the scope of this paper they are potentially very important, and issues about their design and future monitoring are similar to the issues discussed here. These standards are identified as part of this summary overview.

A *Code of Good Practices on Fiscal Transparency – Declaration on Principles* was adopted by the IMF's Interim Committee at its April 1998 meeting. A supporting IMF document, the *Manual on Fiscal Transparency*, provides guidelines on implementation of the standards.

A corresponding set of principles for monetary and financial policies was under development at the IMF during 1999 (prepared in collaboration with the BIS and national central banks and supervisory authorities). The resulting draft, a *Code of Good Practices on Transparency in Monetary and Financial Policies: Declaration of Principles*, was adopted by the Interim Committee at its meeting in September 1999. The IMF staff is now drafting a supporting manual to guide national authorities in implementing the principles (the texts of the fiscal and monetary financial principles, and background information, can be found in the standards and codes section of the IMF web site: *www.imf.org/external/standards/index.htm*).

These two initiatives for international standards are labelled as codes. In practice, the two codes are essentially core principles rather than detailed prescriptions in the sense in which I contrasted core principles with detailed codes above. The fiscal *Manual*, however, does become more detailed in its guidance about implementation. It will be interesting to observe how detailed the monetary financial manual will be when completed and whether detailed manuals will be perceived as helpful and acceptable to national governments.

10.7 THE ALLOCATION OF RESPONSIBILITIES AMONG INTERNATIONAL INSTITUTIONS

As I have mentioned, within individual nations it is controversial whether to have prudential oversight for financial activities concentrated at a single government institution or dispersed across multiple government agencies. The analogous question for the world as a whole is whether to lodge supranational oversight in a single international institution or in several such institutions, and in particular which institution(s).

The Joint Forum on Financial Conglomerates can probably satisfy some of the more straightforward coordination needs among the BCBS, IOSCO and IAIS. It is too early to judge whether the joint forum can be sufficiently effective in tackling the most difficult coordination issues where the supervision of banks, securities firms and insurance companies overlaps. Similarly, the FSF may be able to address the easier of the broader coordination issues where still more international financial institutions are involved. The BIS's CGFS can continue to play a helpful coordinating role among central banks. The most difficult, and the most important, issues about the allocation of responsibilities among the international financial institutions, however, remain.

In recent intergovernmental discussions and papers, a distinction has emerged between an international institution's core areas and those areas which are non-core. The IMF, in particular, has begun to use this terminology. The IMF describes its core areas as those 'central to its [the IMF's] direct operational focus' and delimits these as 'data dissemination, transparency in fiscal policy, monetary and financial policy transparency and banking supervision'. Non-core areas are described as 'areas which, although critical for the effective operation of economic and financial systems, lie outside the fund's direct operational focus'. Examples for the non-core areas of the IMF are given as securities and insurance regulation, corporate governance and accounting and auditing (see IMF (1999b) particularly paras 3, 13–20, 57–70).

The presumption at the IMF appears to be that the World Bank, and other international financial institutions, should delimit their own respective domains of core responsibilities. The distinction between core and non-core areas, however, is far from clear cut for the IMF or any other of the international organizations. The mandates and functional responsibilities of the institutions are not always well differentiated and, in any case, are partly overlapping in certain key functional areas.

The difficulties are well illustrated by the area of bank supervision and regulation. The IMF assigns banking supervision to itself as a core IMF area. The major initiatives in international cooperation in banking supervision, however, have taken place through the BIS, particularly the BCBS. The IMF and World Bank have become more closely involved in the last decade and a half. But certainly on the basis of past history, and even judging by the current intensity of activity, the area of banking supervision is more a core area for the BIS than for the IMF. Collection and dissemination of aggregated financial data on a regional and world scale is another vital area where both the IMF and the BIS have major and partly overlapping responsibility.

In recent decades, the BIS has been run primarily for, and controlled by, the world's major central banks. The BIS serves as the primary locus of their consultation and cooperation. The central banks perceive the BCBS as the forum through which their representatives discuss prudential oversight for banks.[16] Within some individual nations, as we have seen, one or more non-central-bank institutions have always been closely involved in bank supervision.[17] Several nations, including the UK and Japan, have recently separated a major part of the prudential oversight function from their central banks (and in Japan, also from the Ministry of Finance). But even for those nations with multiple government agencies, the BCBS has served as the primary forum for consultations and cooperation.

Beginning with the IMF's 1982–6 lending to nations caught up in debt-servicing crises, the IMF staff began to be pulled into international discussions about bank supervision. This involvement intensified after the Tequila crisis of 1995 and the Asian crises of 1997–8. For example, bank and finance-company restructuring was a dominant feature of the IMF's crisis stabilization packages for Thailand, Korea and Indonesia.

In the future, should the IMF increasingly assume a dominant role in the global aspects of standard setting, data dissemination and prudential oversight for banking, with the BIS playing just a supporting role? This question cannot be addressed as merely a standards and oversight issue. The respective future roles of the IMF and BIS depend at least as much on the global aspects of

---

[16] At its inception, the BCBS involved only the G-10 nations. Subsequently, the committee reached out to non-G-10 nations. The BCBS first invited supervisory authorities from offshore financial centres and some other developing nations to a meeting in 1979. Further meetings and consultations occurred periodically in the 1980s, with still more intensive and systematic inclusion of non-G-10 nations in the 1990s. Notwithstanding the outreach, the BCBS is still dominated by the central banks of the G-7 and a few other European nations.
[17] For example, banking supervision in the United States is shared among the Federal Reserve, the Comptroller of the Currency, the Federal Deposit Insurance Corporation and numerous state authorities. Germany for a long time has had a bank supervisory agency institutionally separate from the Bundesbank.

general monetary and lender-of-last-resort policies, which in turn raise all the delicate issues of political independence for central banks. Today's central banks prize the BIS as their institution, and have not welcomed treasuries and finance ministries inserting themselves into BIS activities. The IMF, on the other hand, is often perceived as more beholden to treasuries and finance ministries in national governments than to national central banks. Which institution, the IMF or the BIS, is the nascent core of a central financial institution for collective global governance – an eventual global central bank for national central banks, even over a very long run a world central bank with its own instruments of global monetary policy? If one presumes that the IMF is that nascent core, will it have to become more politically independent of national governments? Alternatively, is it imaginable that the IMF and the BIS will both eventually survive as powerful global financial institutions and, if so, how will functions be divided or shared among them?

In the short term, the FSF will serve as the main institutional mechanism for keeping both institutions cooperating. The mandate of the FSF is, among other things, 'to give impetus to work on issues that cut across the mandates and expertise of forum members' and 'to coordinate work among forum members, drawing on their comparative advantages'. Eventually, however, the world community – and in particular the central banks of the major nations – will have to decide what roles they wish the BIS to play. Presumably a day will eventually come when, *de facto* if not openly and transparently, difficult decisions about the allocations of functions between the BIS and the IMF will need to be made.

The long-term allocation of functions between the IMF and the World Bank is also difficult and tendentious. Some superficial commentary has noted that the World Bank has gradually assumed functions traditionally associated with the IMF and the IMF has gradually been pulled into functions traditionally associated with the World Bank, and has then suggested that the two be merged into a single institution. The appropriate overall division of labour between the IMF and the World Bank is an important question, but not one that can be discussed here. I mention it because there exists a need for better coordination between the IMF and the World Bank even on issues of prudential oversight for banking and because some observers believe that the IMF should not become deeply involved in prudential oversight.[18]

[18] 'More effective collaboration' on prudential oversight issues between the IMF and the World Bank is reported to be taking place recently through a new Bank-Fund Financial Sector Liaison Committee, which has launched a collaborative Financial Sector Assessment Program. See IMF (1999c), para. 20–4 and Box 3. For two sets of views that the IMF should more narrowly focus its activities, including general surveillance, on macroeconomic and exchange-regime issues rather than becoming deeply involved in microeconomic issues (such as banking supervision and standards monitoring), see the recent reports by an external evaluation team on IMF surveillance and by the Council on Foreign Relations Task Force on architectural reform: IMF (1999a); Council on Foreign Relations (1999).

Monitoring and enforcement of global standards and prudential oversight will receive greater emphasis over time, as I have suggested. In particular, the IMF's process of surveillance through Article IV consultations and surveillance of exchange regimes will assume greater salience. Some reformers want the IMF to be the dominant institution in surveillance of individual nations and the global system, and even recommend that the IMF itself prepare and publish comprehensive transparency reports known as ROSCs (Reports on the Observance of Standards and Codes) for individual nations (see IMF (1999b)). This evolution is bound to result in heightened tension about the allocation of responsibilities among the international financial institutions because the IMF will inevitably make specific judgments about the implementation of standards in areas where other international institutions have the primary, or at least equal, responsibility. If the IMF prepares surveillance assessments of the whole range of global standards, could these assessments be accepted as the product of the international collective governance community broadly defined, or might they be viewed merely as the judgment of the IMF itself? A genuine dilemma exists here, which could become sharper over time.

Where over the longer run does the OECD fit into the collection of international economic and financial institutions? Among the largest international organizations, the OECD's mandate and functional responsibilities are least clearly defined. The longer-run future of the OECD is another sensitive issue not faced at the moment.

Achieving a clearer allocation of responsibilities among the existing international financial institutions will be difficult. But those difficulties are probably surmountable in the medium or long term. Sweeping institutionalist reform – for example, completely redesigning the existing institutions, or setting up entirely new overarching institutions – is impossible, at the least in the short term and probably even further into the future. Henry Kaufman (1998) has suggested a new overarching international institution for prudential oversight, a single super-regulator with responsibilities over a comprehensive range of financial institutions and financial markets. George Soros (1998) has suggested a new international debt insurance agency. I agree with Barry Eichengreen's judgment (1999) that sweeping reform ideas such as these are politically infeasible. Initiatives like the FSF are the most that can be envisaged for the short term.

The most ambitious of the ideas for international cooperation for insolvency and bankruptcy are also non-starters.[19] A world bankruptcy court endowed with genuine political muscle seems an appealing idea in principle, but its political, legal and administrative aspects would be extremely difficult to

---

[19] Proponents of these sweeping institutional reforms include Raffer (1990), Miller and Zhang (1997), and Radelet-Sachs (1998). Eichengreen (1999) discusses these ideas and argues against them on grounds of political unfeasibility.

implement. For the foreseeable future, national governments and judiciaries seem unlikely to yield formally that degree of authority to a supranational institution.

10.8 SOME FURTHER CONTROVERSIAL ISSUES

The areas of standards and prudential oversight usually have low visibility in public discussion and debate. Most parts of the public have little knowledge about them. Usually even the experts do not perceive particular issues to be of overriding importance. Though controversies are as common as in any other areas of professional activity, they seldom become heated enough to attract widespread outside attention. In this section of the paper, I identify three such controversial issues. Although you will never read about these on the front page of your newspaper, their resolution may have significant implications for the global financial system.

Adoption by individual nations of international accounting standards

The various accounting and auditing standards of IASC and IFAC are not legally binding on nations' firms or financial institutions. Each nation's government and the nation's private associations will have to encourage their acceptance and use within the nation's borders. If significant disagreements exist among IASC members, however, implementation of world standards becomes highly problematic.

The tensions are well illustrated by the current situation in the United States. One might think that the United States would be taking the lead in encouraging adoption of the IASC core standards. But many Americans, probably including influential officials in the Securities and Exchange Commission and elsewhere in the US government, are dragging their feet instead of taking the lead.[20] The dilemma confronting thoughtful Americans stems from contentions that the proposed IASC world standards are weaker (less stringent) in some respects than the generally accepted accounting principles (GAAP) that prevail in the United States (see for example, Ignatius (1999)). (However, it is also said that some of the proposed IASC standards, such as rules for mergers, are preferable to GAAP standards.) If US supervisors and accounting firms accept the IASC rules as a substitute for GAAP, the safety and soundness of the US financial system could be undermined to the extent that GAAP rules really are superior to IASC rules. If the United States refuses to adopt the IASC world standards, on the other hand, the largest and wealthiest economy in the world

---

[20] Canadians and the Canadian government may also be in this position.

could impede a global initiative thought to be beneficial for all nations, including the United States itself.

The controversy over IASC standards has apparently spilled over into a tussle between North America and Europe over the governance structure of the IASC itself. European participants have been described as backing a blueprint for structural reform originating with IASC itself while the United States is characterized as leading a breakaway group sympathetic to GAAP rules.[21]

This example is a particular instance of a very general problem, in which the representatives of an individual nation may be under pressure to accept a proposed compromise consensus developed in international meetings when the proposed compromise generates gross costs for the individual nation. If the proposed international consensus generates costs that exceed benefits for the nation – that is, fails to promise net benefits – its representatives should presumably reject the compromise. If the compromise promises significant net benefits for the nation's interests broadly defined, however, the representatives of the nation cannot sensibly be paralysed by the existence of some less broadly defined respects in which the nation will be disadvantaged.

For any international consensus to emerge in the first place, the largest, most influential nations typically have to exert leadership. The United States has at least as much interest as smaller nations in forging agreed minimum world standards for accounting and auditing. The nascent efforts of the IASC and IFAC, and the related International Forum on Accountancy Development, are important for the future stability of both the global and the US financial systems. Americans should try to improve the proposed IASC core standards in areas where they may be less stringent or less effective than GAAP rules. But Americans should also vigorously encourage the widespread adoption of the IASC international core standards and hence endorse the standards for the United States – even if some of the standards can be still further improved. Reluctance to apply the IASC standards in the United States will surely have unfavourable repercussions on the postures of many developing nations as those nations decide how to respond to the pressure for raising accounting and auditing standards in their economies.[22]

---

[21] A newspaper story in the *Financial Times* of 10 May 1999 – 'Accountancy: Battle for World Control' – developed this theme.

[22] I do not have detailed enough information about the differences between IASC and GAAP rules to carry the discussion further. But I conjecture that scope may exist for the United States to strongly endorse the IASC proposals as minimum standards and then to continue to apply GAAP standards in those areas where it can be convincingly demonstrated that the GAAP standards are more stringent. The process of mutual recognition might then eventually force up the IASC standards to the more stringent GAAP level.

Collective-action clauses in bond contracts

Numerous official statements about improving the international financial architecture have suggested that the prevention and resolution of financial crises could be modestly facilitated by introducing more orderly ways of restructuring problem debts. The modest steps suggested have included majority-voting, sharing and collective-representation clauses in new bond contracts and clauses that would require a minimum percentage of bondholders to agree before legal action could be taken. The goal is to prevent a few creditors from instigating legal actions or other means of obstructing compromise restructurings when such restructurings are in the interests of the debtor and the great majority of creditors (Eichengreen (1999, especially pp. 65–78) has a thoughtful evaluation of these proposals).

These modest proposals turn out to be controversial, somewhat understandably from the perspective of private bondholders and prospective borrowers in emerging-market nations, but less understandably from the perspective of the G-7 nations' governments. The issues are not really a topic in prudential oversight or financial standards *per se*. I raise them here because of their similarity to the accounting-standards issue just discussed.

The governments of the largest nations – especially the G-7 team – are strong advocates of encouraging the governments of emerging-market nations to incorporate these changes into their debt contracts for new borrowing. Yet the G-7 governments, and most especially the US Treasury, seem unwilling to introduce administrative or legislative changes that would permit the incorporation of such collective action clauses in their own new borrowing instruments.

I have not yet heard a persuasive explanation of why the United States and the other G-7 nations cannot show leadership in this area by changing their own contracts. The details in each major creditor nation's situation are different. The US government borrows in its own currency. It may not be administratively straightforward in the United States to introduce such changes; perhaps the Congress might have to be consulted or asked to act. Some voices argue that the borrowing rate for the US government might rise by a basis point or two if such changes were made, and that no risk whatsoever of this sort should be allowed.

Yet just as in the case of the proposed IASC world accounting standards, emerging-market or developing nations will watch more closely what the largest nations do than listen to what they say. Adverse selection difficulties will inhibit, for example, Venezuela or South Africa or India from introducing such collective-action clauses into their bond contracts unless the G-7 nations set a good example and do so themselves.

Such modest changes in bond covenants might yield significant, albeit modest, gains for financial stability in the world as a whole. As the quarterback of the varsity first team, the US Treasury should either put its money where its mouth is on this point, or else provide a clear explanation of why it believes that such changes to debt instruments would be adverse if adopted by the United States but would be beneficial if adopted by the junior-varsity and the sandlot teams.

The evolution of capital adequacy requirements for banks

The BCBS believes that the Basle Capital Accord has played a useful role in raising the capital and reducing the riskiness of internationally active banks. A working group of the BCBS submitted a report in April 1999 evaluating the impacts of the capital requirements on bank behaviour (BIS, BCBS, 1999b). The working group concluded that the introduction of formal minimum capital requirements in G-10 nations induced relatively weakly capitalized banks to maintain higher capital ratios than would otherwise have been held.

But the working group also acknowledged that large banks have learned how to exploit the limited relationship between actual risk and the regulatory minimum requirements for capital. These banks have been able to reduce their required capital by reshaping their balance sheets. The banks have often securitized a package of already arranged loans, removing those assets from the balance sheet and accordingly reducing their required capital. Some arrangements for securitization, however, entail the banks retaining some of the credit risk even after the assets are formally off their own balance sheets.

The accord has been criticized on several other grounds as well, and the BCBS itself has acknowledged the criticisms as serious. (Crockett (1997) and Calomiris-Litan (1999) summarize the criticisms of the BIS-sponsored risk-weighted capital standards.) One widely recognized problem is that the classification of banks' assets into a limited number of categories for the purposes of the capital requirements is artificial and masks significant differences among assets within individual classes. For example, whether large or small, whether low-risk or high-risk, claims on corporate entities are lumped together, not distinguishing between their differing credit quality. Mortgage claims are, arbitrarily from the critics' perspective, given a lower risk weight (50 per cent) than claims on corporate entities (100 per cent). A further example: different risk weights are applied to claims on sovereigns (governments) depending on whether the claim is on the government of a member or a non-member of the OECD; claims on an OECD member government bear a risk weight of zero.

Most problematic of all in the current accord, a bank's claims of all maturities on other banks incorporated within OECD nations and its short-term (up to 1 year) claims on banks in non-OECD nations are given a risk weight of only 20 per cent – in contrast to, for example, a risk weight of 100 per cent on claims on non-OECD banks with a maturity of more than 1 year. The lower risk weighting is given to short-term interbank claims even when the claims are denominated in currencies other than the currency of the nation where the borrowing bank office is located. The outside critics of the Capital Accord and the BCBS itself both believe that the lower risk weighting associated with interbank lending was an unfortunate incentive that encouraged excessive interbank lending at short maturities to Asian and other emerging market nations in the 1990s.

The original Capital Accord focused only on credit risk. Although the accord was modified to take market risk into account in 1996, the current requirements are still not shaped by interest rate risk.

The proposed new version of the accord in the 1999 consultative paper is described as resting on three pillars: a revised version of the standardized rules for minimum capital requirements, proposals for supervisory review of institutions' capital adequacy and their internal assessment processes, and 'effective use of market discipline' (see BIS, BCBS (1999a). The proposed revisions are addressed to the identified problems in the old accord. For example, instead of the crude distinction between OECD and non-OECD countries, the new methodology would permit the risk weights applied to claims on sovereigns to be benchmarked to the assessments of those nations' governments by eligible external assessment institutions (e.g. credit rating agencies such as Moody's or Standard & Poor's). Interbank claims might be given risk weights based on the weighting applied to claims on the sovereign in which the bank is incorporated; a second option would use ratings assigned directly to banks by an external credit assessment institution. Most interbank claims would receive at least a 50 per cent risk weighting, and claims on a bank could receive a risk weighting of less than 100 per cent only if the banking supervisory authorities in that nation 'has implemented, or has endorsed and is in the process of implementing, the 25 core principles [of the BCBS] for effective banking supervision'.

The third pillar of the proposed revisions, more effective market discipline, is least well specified. Although the committee rhetorically asserts that it wants to place more emphasis on market-based incentives and fuller disclosure, its consultative paper is short on concrete suggestions for doing so. The committee indicates that it is conducting interviews on the possibilities and 'proposes to develop more comprehensive guidance on public disclosure designed to strengthen the third pillar of the capital framework' (see BIS, BCBS (1999a)).

Harsh critics of the accord are not satisfied with the proposed revisions. Calomiris and Litan (1999), for example, believe that 'the proposed changes, however well intentioned, either are insufficient or conceivably may worsen the preexisting problems'. They believe the modified risk weighting scheme would still fail to reflect the true risks to a bank from its overall portfolio of assets and off-balance-sheet instruments. They argue that it would be a mistake to place great reliance on the credit-rating agencies. Calomiris and Litan propose instead that the BCBS should not merely allow (as at present) but mandate that large banks above a certain size threshold back a certain portion of their assets by long-term uninsured subordinated debt. The debt would be traded in a secondary market; the holders of a bank's debt would not be protected in the event of the bank's failure; movements in the market price of a bank's subordinated debt would serve both a signalling and disciplinary function. Thus a mandatory subordinated debt requirement, they contend, would simplify the setting of capital requirements and facilitate the enforcement of the requirements through the use of market-based signals (see Calomiris and Litan (1999, pp. 28–34 in draft) and Calomiris (1997) for details of the subordinated debt proposal and supporting argument).

The market-based, incentive-based features of the Calomiris–Litan proposal are promising, at least in principle. Administrative and political details would have to be worked out, country by country. But if the BCBS and national supervisory authorities were to incorporate some variant of this suggestion as part of their revisions of the accord, they would have given strong substance to their third pillar of more effective market discipline. If the subordinated debt feature proved successful, moreover, this dimension of the accord could become relatively more important over time, with the committee gradually raising the proportion of required capital to be held in the form of subordinated debt.

10.9 CONCLUSIONS

This chapter focuses on the evolution of international collective governance in the areas of standards and prudential oversight for financial activity. It provides analytical background, summarizes the nascent progress in international cooperation and identifies several of the controversial issues that remain to be resolved.

Most of the wider public perceives this subject as unsexy, if indeed the subject has swum into their consciousness at all. But in reality it is very important. Much more than is commonly appreciated, the vigour and stability of financial and economic activity critically depend on sound standards and effective prudential oversight. I hope the overview given here is a useful reminder of why standards and oversight are an essential part of the foundation for a healthy economy and financial system.

Though I have emphasized the importance of standards and prudential oversight, I do not want to leave the misleading impression that they are somehow magic bullets that can slay all financial difficulties. Even if international cooperation leads to sizeable further improvements in standards and oversight, which I hope it will, financial problems will still abound.

The financial system – within individual nations, and not least the conglomeration of all national financial systems – is inherently fragile, inherently vulnerable to instability. No nirvana exists, not even in theory, in which financial activity can be risk-free and problem-free. Quite the contrary. Deep-seated, innate features of financial activity expose financial activity to episodes of stormy weather, even to an occasional hurricane-level crisis. This potential for instability in the global financial system cannot be attributed exclusively to cross-border features of financial activity. The causes are deeply rooted in informational asymmetries, expectational and informational cascades, and adverse selection and moral hazard problems that pervade all aspects of financial behaviour, domestic as well as cross-border. But there is no question that the cross-border features magnify and aggravate the potential instability.

A balanced view of standards and prudential oversight should appreciate their fundamental importance, yet should not allow them to get out of perspective. Several other dimensions of the evolution of international collective governance, not discussed in this paper, are equally important. In short, sound standards and effective prudential oversight in an integrating world financial system are necessary – but not sufficient – conditions for healthy and reasonably stable financial activity.

Substantial and valuable progress has been made in recent years in international cooperation to strengthen standards and oversight. That observation is probably the main conclusion to take away from this essay. But another observation is a complement to that conclusion: if the governments of the largest nations had been still more far-sighted, progress could have been still more substantial.

Prior to the mid-1990s, consultations among the major governments about international financial reforms ('architecture' was not yet the catchword) proceeded sluggishly. The Tequila crisis of 1995 caught the governments' attention and brought more focus on financial stability issues. But then concern and cooperation subsided somewhat in 1996 and the first half of 1997. The Asian financial crises and the credit-spread turbulence that followed the Russian devaluation in 1998 created a sense of urgency and galvanized much of the recent progress.

With the world economy looking more robust at the turn of the century and the world financial system showing fewer manifestations of fragility, there may be some risk of the major governments slowing the pace once again. That would be unfortunate. Pragmatic incrementalism is the preferred approach to international architectural reform. But the increments should keep accumulating, even without the stimulus of further turbulence. Preferably, major governments should move forward at a brisk pace rather than on tiptoe.

References

Avery, Christopher, and Zemsky, Peter (1998), 'Multidimensional Uncertainty and Herd Behavior in Financial Markets', *American Economic Review*, 88, September, pp. 724–48.

Banerjee, Abhijit (1992), 'A Simple Model of Herd Behaviour', *Quarterly Journal of Economics*, 107, pp. 797–817.

Bank for International Settlements, Basle Committee on Banking Supervision (1997a), *Core Principles for Effective Banking Supervision* (Basle: Bank for International Settlements), September.

Bank for International Settlements, Basle Committee on Banking Supervision (1997b), *International Convergence of Capital Measurement and Capital Standards ('Basle Capital Accord', July 1988, updated to April 1997)* (Basle: Bank for International Settlements).

Bank for International Settlements, Basle Committee on Banking Supervision (1999a), *A New Capital Adequacy Framework: Consultative Paper* (Basle: Bank for International Settlements).

Bank for International Settlements, Basle Committee on Banking Supervision (1999b), *Capital Requirements and Bank Behaviour: The Impact of the Basle Accord*. Report prepared by a working group led by Patricia Jackson. BCBS Working Papers No. 1 (Basle: Bank for International Settlements), April.

Bank for International Settlements, Committee on the Global Financial System (1999a), *Market Liquidity: Research Results and Selected Policy Implications*. Report of a Working Group chaired by Masaaki Shirakawa (Basle: Bank for International Settlements), May.

Bank for International Settlements, Committee on the Global Financial System (1999b), *A Review of Financial Market Events in Autumn 1998*. Report of a Working Group chaired by Karen Johnson (Basle: Bank for International Settlements), October.

Benston, George J., and George G. Kaufman (1997), 'FDICIA After Five Years', *Journal of Economic Perspectives*, 11 (Summer).

Bernard, Henri, and Joseph Bisignano (1999), *Information, Liquidity and Risk in the International Interbank Market: Implicit Guarantees and Private Credit Market Failure*. Draft manuscript, Bank for International Settlements, Monetary and Economic Department, September.

Bikhchandani, Sushil, David Hirshleifer, and Ivo Welch (1992), 'A Theory of Fads, Fashion, Custom, and Cultural Change as Informational Cascades', *Journal of Political Economy*, 100 (October), pp. 992–1026.

Bordo, Michael D., Barry Eichengreen, and Douglas A. Irwin (1999), 'Is Globalization Today Really Different than Globalization a Hundred Years Ago?'. paper prepared for the Brookings Policy Trade Forum, Washington DC, 15–16 April 1999.

Bryant, Ralph C. (2001), *Turbulent Waters: Cross-Border Finance and International Governance* (Washington, DC: Brookings Institution, forthcoming).

Cairns, David (1998), 'IASC – 25 Years of Evolution, Teamwork, and Improvement', *Insight* (quarterly newsletter of the International Accounting Standards Committee), June.

Calomiris, Charles W. (1997), *The Postmodern Bank Safety Net: Lessons from Developed and Developing Economies* (Washington, DC: AEI Press).

Calomiris, Charles W., and Litan, Robert E. (1999), 'Prudential Financial Regulation in a Global Marketplace', in Robert E. Litan and Anthony M. Santomero (eds), *Brookings-Wharton Papers on Financial Services* (Washington, DC: Brookings Institution, forthcoming 2000).

Clark, Robert Charles (1976), 'The Soundness of Financial Intermediaries', *The Yale Law Journal*, Vol. 86, No. 1 (November), pp. 3–102.

Council on Foreign Relations Independent Task Force; Carla A. Hills and Peter G. Peterson, Co-Chairs; Morris Goldstein, Project Director (1999), *Safeguarding Prosperity in a Global Financial System: The Future International Financial Architecture* (Washington, DC: Institute for International Economics for the Council on Foreign Relations), September.

Crockett, Andrew (1997), 'The Theory and Practice of Financial Stability', *Essays in International Finance,* No. 203, International Finance Section, Department of Economics, Princeton University, April.

Dahl, Drew, and Spivey, Michael F. (1995), 'Prompt Corrective Action and Bank Efforts to Recover from Undercapitalization' *Journal of Banking and Finance*, 19 (1995), pp. 225–43.

Diamond, Douglas W., and Dybvig, Philip H. (1983), 'Bank Runs, Deposit Insurance, and Liquidity', *Journal of Political Economy*, Vol. 91, No. 3 (June). pp. 401–19.

Edwards, Franklin R. (1999), 'Hedge Funds and the Collapse of Long Term Capital Management', *Journal of Economic Perspectives*, 13 (Spring), pp. 189–210.

Eichengreen, Barry (1999), *Toward a New International Financial Architecture: A Practical Post-Asia Agenda* (Washington, DC: Institute for International Economics, 1999).

Friedman, Thomas L. (1999), *The Lexus and the Olive Tree* (New York: Farrar, Straus & Giroux).

Garcia, Gillian (1995), 'Implementing FDICIA's Mandatory Closure Rule', *Journal of Banking and Finance*, 19, pp. 723–32.

Gold, Joseph (1984), *Legal and Institutional Aspects of the International Monetary System: Selected Essays,* two volumes (Washington, DC: International Monetary Fund).

Gold, Joseph (1990), *Legal Effects of Fluctuating Exchange Rates* (Washington, DC: International Monetary Fund).

Goodhart, Charles A.E., and Dirk Schoenmaker (1993), 'Institutional Separation between Supervisory and Monetary Agencies' in F. Bruni (ed.), *Prudential Regulation, Supervision and Monetary Policy* (Centro di Economia Monetaria e Finanziaria 'Paolo Baffi'. Universita Commerciale Luigi Bocconi). Reprinted as chapter 16 in Goodhart, *The Central Bank and the Financial System* (Cambridge, MA: MIT Press, 1995).

Goodhart, Charles A.E., and Dirk Schoenmaker (1995), 'Should the Functions of Monetary Policy and Bank Supervision Be Separated?', *Oxford Economic Papers*, 47, pp. 539–60.

Gray, John (1999), *False Dawn: The Delusions of Global Capitalism* (New York: The New York Press).

Greider, William (1997), *One World, Ready or Not: The Manic Logic of Global Capitalism* (New York: Simon & Schuster).

Group of Thirty (1998), *International Insolvencies in the Financial Sector: A Study Group Report* (Washington, DC: Group of Thirty).

Group of Twenty-Two (Willard Group) (1998a), *Report of the Working Group on Strengthening Financial Systems*. Released in Washington, DC, October. (Available on internet web sites for IMF, BIS and US Treasury.)

Group of Twenty-Two (Willard Group) (1998b), *Report of the Working Group on Transparency and Accountability*. Released in Washington, DC, October. (Available on internet web sites for IMF, BIS and US Treasury.)

Helliwell, John F. (1998), *How Much Do National Borders Matter?* Integrating National Economies series (Washington, DC: Brookings Institution).

Ignatius, David (1999), 'Crunching the Numbers the American Way' *The Washington Post*, 31 March.

International Accounting Standards Committee (IASC) (1999), 'IASC Publishes a Comprehensive Standard on Financial Instruments, 5 March 1999'. News release, available at web site of IASC: *www.IASC.org.uk/news*.

International Monetary Fund (1999a), *External Evaluation of IMF Surveillance*. Report of a Group of Independent Experts (Chairman, John Crow) (Washington, DC: International Monetary Fund), September.

International Monetary Fund (1999b), *International Standards and Fund Surveillance – Progress and Issues*, prepared by IMF Staff (Washington, DC: International Monetary Fund), 16 August.

International Monetary Fund (1999c), *Report of the Managing Director on Progress in Strengthening the Architecture of the International Monetary System* (Washington, DC: International Monetary Fund), April.

International Monetary Fund (1999d), *Report of the Managing Director to the Interim Committee on Progress in Strengthening the Architecture of the International Financial System* (Washington, DC: International Monetary Fund), 24 September.

Jackson, John H. (1998), 'Global Economics and International Economic Law', *Journal of International Economic Law*, 1, March.

Kaufman, Henry (1998), 'Preventing the Next Global Financial Crisis', *The Washington Post*, January 28, p. A17.

King, Mervyn (1999), 'Reforming the International Financial System: The Middle Way', speech delivered at Federal Reserve Bank of New York, 9 September.

Lane, Philip, and Gian Maria Milesi-Ferretti (1999), 'The External Wealth of Nations: Measures of Foreign Assets and Liabilities for Industrial and Developing Countries', *CEPR Discussion Paper Series*, No. 2231, International Macroeconomics (London: Centre for Economic Research), September.

Masson, Paul R. (1998), 'Contagion: Monsoonal Effects, Spillovers, and Jumps Between Multiple Equilibria', IMF Working Paper WP/98/142 (Washington, DC: International Monetary Fund, September).

Masson, Paul R. (1999a), 'Contagion: Macroeconomic Models with Multiple Equilibria', *Journal of International Money and Finance*, 18, pp. 587–602.

Masson, Paul R. (1999b), 'Multiple Equilibria, Contagion, and the Asian Crisis', paper prepared for January 1999 meeting of the Society for Financial Economics (Washington, DC: International Monetary Fund), January.

Miller, Marcus H. and Lei Zhang (1997), 'A "Bankruptcy" Procedure for Sovereign States', ESRC Global Economic Institutions Working Paper No. 34 (London: Economic and Social Research Council).

Ostry, Sylvia (1999), 'Future of the WTO', paper presented at the Brookings Trade Policy Forum, Washington, DC, 15–16 April.

Petersmann, Ernst-Ulrich (1998), 'From the Hobbesian International Law of Coexistence to Modern Integration Law: The WTO Dispute Settlement System', *Journal of International Economic Law*, 1, June.

Radelet, Steven, and Jeffrey D. Sachs (1998), 'The East Asian Financial Crisis: Diagnosis, Remedies, Prospects', *Brookings Papers on Economic Activity*, 1, pp. 1-90.

Raffer, Kunibert (1990), 'Applying Chapter 9 Insolvency to International Debts: An Economically Efficient Solution with a Human Face', *World Development*, 18, pp. 301–11.

Rodrik, Dani (1999), 'Governing the Global Economy: Does One Architectural Style Fit All?', paper presented at the Brookings Trade Policy Forum, Washington, DC, 15–16 April.

Soros, George (1998), *The Crisis of Global Capitalism: Open Soceity Endangered* (New York: BBS Public Affairs).

Stiglitz, Joseph E. (1994), 'The Role of the State in Financial Markets', in Michael Bruno and Boris Pleskovic (eds), *Proceedings of the Annual World Bank Conference on Development Economics 1993* (Washington, DC: World Bank).

Tietmeyer, Hans (1999), 'International Cooperation and Coordination in the Area of Financial Market Supervision and Surveillance' (Frankfurt: Deutsche Bundesbank), February [available from the web site of Financial Stability Forum, *www.fsforum.org*].